T0247955

REPAIRING THE WORLD

SHEILA KUSSNER AND THE POWER OF EMPATHY

REPAIRING THE WORLD

SHEILA KUSSNER AND
THE POWER OF EMPATHY

DOUGLAS HUNTER

BARLOW
BOOKS

Library and Archives Canada Cataloguing in Publication data available
upon request.

978-1-988025-95-7 (hardcover)

Printed in Canada

Publisher: Sarah Scott
Book producer: Tracy Bordian/At Large Editorial Services
Cover design: Paul Hodgson
Interior design and layout: Ruth Dwight
Copy editing: Eleanor Gasparik

For more information, visit **www.barlowbooks.com**

Barlow Book Publishing Inc.
96 Elm Avenue, Toronto, ON
M4W 1P2 Canada

For Sheila

Contents

With Love to Sheila

On a sunny Friday morning, my wife, Diane, and I were leaving for a weekend getaway, with the kids excited to be left on their own. We departed even though, earlier that day, Diane felt something abnormal on her breast, a lump. Although we had a wonderful weekend, upon our return to Montreal a whole new episode in our lives began to unfold.

Straight to surgery, to chemo, and the constant fear with which we would now be living. Trying to cope was brutal, and our every day was difficult.

Then, a whole new world opened up. Something happened in our lives ... We started on a journey of hope. We felt a force within our hearts, an inner strength and light, likely inspired by our experience.

But it goes beyond that ...

As you live your life
You can free yourself
Just watch for what's real
And you will come to give.
Those in need will be
Your reason for living
An inspiration for others,
Those who will follow.

With love to our teacher
Our exemplar
Our dear friend – Sheila

Salvatore, Diane,
Jonathan, and Vanessa Guerrera

Foreword

When I was a teenager almost seventy years ago, our home received the monthly issue of *Reader's Digest*, whose Canadian publisher was located right here in Montreal. The part I searched for first and read quickly was the column "The Most Unforgettable Character I Have Ever Met." Sheila would have fit that description then, but today I would suggest a replacement column: "The Most Important Character I've Ever Met." Sheila would feature as the first in the series because her unforgettable characteristic is a relentless empathy, as she unceasingly works to improve the lives of others. What a too-often chaotic, cruel world most needs today is empathy.

Sympathy is not empathy. Sympathy says, "I feel sorry for your pain and your situation." Empathy says, "I understand your difficulty. I am going to learn more about it and about you, and together we are going to do something about it."

This book is the story of Sheila, who as a young woman lost a leg to cancer, looked that loss in the face, and vowed that this would not stop her. Instead, she became determined to take her experience and help others deal head on with cancer. She has spent the rest of her life demonstrating the resilience of dealing with cancer, and above all founding that remarkable institution of support, Hope & Cope. *Empathy* should really be a verb that means "roll up your sleeves and lend a hand to someone in greater need."

During Sheila's volunteer lifetime we have seen such significant meaning given to the words *hope* and *cope*, as our scientific advancements in diagnosing and treating cancer and developing a much greater sophistication in its prevention have grown dramatically. And this has given great substance to hope.

Our late Queen Elizabeth emphasized in her Christmas messages the importance of caring for one another and demonstrating empathy in action. She referred to each act of kindness as a pebble dropped into a still pond that created ripples one after another, covering the entire surface of the water. With Sheila, those ripples have often turned into tsunamis.

If you, like me, are inspired by the stories of empathy in action, read on. You will discover a veritable gold mine because you will see dozens of nuggets that Sheila dropped into the pond of life.

The Right Honourable David Johnston

CHAPTER ONE

Night Ride (I)

On a Thursday evening in October 2021, a Lexus sedan departs a driveway in greater Montreal's town of Mont-Royal with a petite, feisty, elegantly coiffed eighty-nine-year-old woman at the wheel. The driver has one leg, but as it is her right leg, she manages the brake and accelerator fine. She heads east, toward Avenue du Parc and the neighbourhood of Mile End. In large part due to COVID-19, Sheila Kussner has not been out for dinner in almost two years. But with COVID wave number-whatever having given way to an easing of lockdown measures, the city is moving closer (at that moment, anyway) to its normal cosmopolitan exuberance.

Sheila considered eating in but has seized the opportunity to break the bonds of so many months of restrictions. She is bound for her long-favourite dinner destination in Montreal, Milos. Other diners, including her fellow table guests that night, arrive out front and turn their car over to a valet before heading in the front door and up the steps to the multi-level dining area. Not Sheila. She pulls the Lexus around back. The staff greet her, help her with a folding wheelchair that she has relied on for getting around in recent years, and accompany her into the restaurant, through the rear door and the kitchen. She tips, not only for her own table service (and the kitchen staff) but also to cover the valets who will take the cars of her dinner guests. Leaving the kitchen, she bears left and takes her favourite seat at her favourite table. As a long-standing friend, Myer Bick, will explain, the table is reserved for only three well-known people in the city. Sheila is one of them, and she has secured on about an hour's notice a six-thirty seating in one of Montreal's most popular restaurants. How popular? Tables can roll through three seatings on a weeknight. Guests recount tennis star Rafael Nadal appearing with an entourage of nine for a nine-thirty seating.

The proprietor of Milos, Costas Spiliadis, is not on hand tonight, but he and Sheila Kussner have been close for years. They are both iconoclastic originals with forthright opinions, trail-blazing accomplishments, a relentless attention to detail, and an insistence on the proper way of doing things. Sheila is renowned locally as a fundraiser extraordinaire who has transformed cancer research, education, and care, and above all as the founder and driving force behind Hope & Cope, a global pioneer in providing support services for cancer patients and their loved ones that is affiliated with Montreal's Jewish General Hospital. Spiliadis opened Milos in 1979, just as Sheila was fomenting her plans for Hope & Cope. Mile End was the neighbourhood that novelist Mordecai Richler brought to life in *The Apprenticeship of Duddy Kravitz* in 1959, when it was the latest in a chain of Montreal neighbourhoods that Ashkenazi Jewish immigrants from eastern Europe, Sheila Kussner's ancestors among them, had called home. When Milos opened, it was still a community of immigrants, but of Greeks and Italians mainly, along with a large community of Hasidic Jews who had begun arriving in Montreal in the 1920s.

When Milos opened, the restaurant was half of its current size. In that modest space, with fishing nets strung on the walls and forty chairs, Spiliadis redefined Greek cuisine with his simple approach to fresh ingredients from the sea and the farm. In 1997, Spiliadis began branching out from Montreal, with his first of two restaurants in New York City. Friends of Sheila jibe that her spending habits at Milos (which include gift certificates she dispenses) fuelled the international expansion. Spiliadis now operates Milos *estiatorios* (Greek for a restaurant a cut above a *taverna*) in Athens, Las Vegas, Miami, London, and Los Cabos, with Toronto in the planning stage, but the Montreal restaurant remains the flagship. Renovated and expanded in 2015, Milos at 5357 Avenue du Parc offers superb dining in an open concept of white and blue, with white curtains providing sheer spatial dividers.

Sheila and her guests arrive an hour into the restaurant's dinner schedule. Milos is alive with chatter and laughter. The tiered open floor plan contributes to its noise level, and diners find themselves competing to be heard, even across their own table, but there is something essentially celebratory about a crowd at Milos that fuels the volume. It's a space and atmosphere to which Sheila rises, because the public Sheila is boisterous, amusing, and amused. It is a role only she can play, which is not to say that she is artificial, only that when she is out and about, Sheila meets the challenge of being the Sheila that Montreal society has long known and loved, regardless of what pains or discomforts her state of health might involve at that moment. Sheila is at Milos to have a good time, but mainly to ensure that her guests have one, too.

With her back to the wall, Sheila enjoys a commanding, elevated view of the entire restaurant space. She signals her waiter, Camille, who has been with the restaurant more than twenty years and knows her well. She waves him closer. "Who is here tonight?" she asks, and then, with a vaudevillian's polished timing, adds, "Who has money?"

Marvin Rosenbloom, an old friend and associate in the charitable world (including Hope & Cope), will laugh when this moment is related to him. She was being funny, he agrees, but she was also completely serious. "She inventories the name, and waits for the opportunity, or tries to create the opportunity. She's very skilled, very gifted, and we're all blessed that her energies are focussed in the direction of the welfare of the human being."

"Sheila strategizes," says Rubin Becker, a long-standing friend and physician to Sheila and her late husband, Marvyn, who is also an associate professor of medicine at McGill University and associate director of general internal medicine at the Jewish General Hospital. "She knows about a lot of things going on, and about a lot of people. She'll call me and say, 'Where is so-and-so?' She'll *track* them. Sometimes she'll call me and say, 'I know that right now you're doing a house call at so-and-so's.' And, well, how would she know that?"

Sheila would have made a good private detective or skip tracer. "She could work for the CIA or Mossad," Suzanne O'Brien quips. O'Brien has been a friend since joining the staff of Hope & Cope in 1997 and has experienced first-hand Sheila's dogged ability to track down people. A few years after beginning her work at Hope & Cope, O'Brien returned to her native Australia to visit family. The phone rang in her father's house, and he turned to her and said, "A woman from Canada wants to speak with you." Sheila had somehow figured out Suzanne's maiden name and reached her father in Melbourne, O'Brien suspects by calling every single Littleton in the directory until she hit on the right one. "Sheila can find *anyone*," she says. "On the beach, in Monaco..." Her Contacts list bulges with the private cell-phone numbers of some of the most influential people in the country.

"Sheila knows her people," O'Brien explains, "and that's what makes her a good fundraiser. She follows the news and knows if someone's business is doing well." Or not. "She knows people's interests, and their capacity. She'll never ask too much from a donor." Sheila has also been known to direct people to causes beyond her own if what she is seeking support for is not the perfect fit for their philanthropy. There are institutions in Montreal that are deeply indebted to her for steering donors their way.

Alison Silcoff, who has been a friend of Sheila for at least thirty years, stresses Sheila's business acumen. "She had a husband who was a very successful businessman, and she herself has been immersed in the business world." A professional fundraiser, Silcoff worked with Sheila on some of her campaigns, but for twenty-seven years Silcoff was also a rival in mounting the annual Daffodil Ball for the Canadian Cancer Society. Sheila, friends say (and Silcoff seconds the motion), is competitive: whenever she was raising money, she kept an eye on how well Silcoff was doing in her annual Daffodil Ball drive.

Unlike many fundraisers, herself included, Silcoff notes that Sheila is incredibly well informed about cancer care and research. "She can really go the extra mile and persuade people to contribute more than they ever planned to do. She's highly intelligent and irresistibly charming, as well as persuasive. It's a fantastic combination. You cannot say 'no' to her. She's unstoppable." Silcoff says there is no point in asking Sheila how she succeeds at fundraising, "because her recipe can't be copied by other people." Some elements can be mimicked, but there is no way to clone the entire package of who Sheila is and how she goes about doing what she does.

Sheila has no intention of waylaying someone at their table in a bustling Milos on this night to make a fundraising pitch—wrong place, wrong time, wrong atmosphere—but she is alert to any sign that someone with the necessary wherewithal is in the city and within personal reach. Because Sheila is on the hunt, deep into one of her most daunting fundraising missions.

At an age long past the point that most people have retired or sold a business and decamped to Florida for half of the year or sailed away on cruises, Sheila Kussner maintains a pace and a complex agenda that would defeat the better part of the city. She would turn ninety in August 2022, and as she headed to Milos for dinner in October 2021, she had set herself the goal of securing at least twenty million dollars for an endowment that would ensure Hope & Cope can carry on for decades without financial concerns. She has a list of "champions," six-figure donors whose promises have been secured. Having her fundraising goal within sight buoys her spirits. Conversation turns to the honour awaiting her next June, when her name will be affixed to an exterior wall of the Jewish General Hospital, in recognition of her transformative efforts in fundraising, in advancing the quality and span of care at the hospital, and in the creation of Hope & Cope. It's such an unusual if deserved honour, because names on buildings normally are reserved for people who write large cheques, not for people who persuade other people to write them, or who devote a lifetime to volunteer community service.

Costas Spiliadis will be on hand for the June 2022 ceremony at which Sheila's name is prominently affixed to the hospital. Asked then how he feels about her, he will say, "I am humbled," shortly before becoming a donor to Sheila's legacy fund for Hope & Cope. Back at Milos in October 2021, Sheila reiterates that the forthcoming honour is not something she sought out for herself, which is true. "I am very humble," she intones at Milos, in her distinctive, gravelly voice, but the restaurant's din means she is almost shouting to make herself heard. The natural comedian in her recognizes the absurdity as well as the opportunity, like a power hitter spotting a slow fastball pitched right over the plate. Her eyes sparkle at the opportunity. She waves Camille over again. "Am I not humble? *Tell him* I am humble." She turns to her dinner guest and theatrically shouts, "I AM HUMBLE!" Her guest promises to buy her a lapel button for the pink jacket she is wearing, that operates on batteries and flashes the word "HUMBLE." It will have to be carefully placed, so as not to obscure her jacket's discreet pins: one is l'Ordre de Montréal, another is l'Ordre National du Québec, and still another is the Order of Canada.

Cities find their heroes in many forms: star athletes, crusading politicians, musicians with a mic, a guitar, and a cause du jour. They have publicists, and they generate headlines and draw large crowds. Not everyone whose actions can be called heroic—achievements beyond the expectations, inclinations, and seeming capabilities of mortals—is so public, or so performative, let alone paid for what they do. Some heroes have a public-facing facet, but they otherwise negotiate our world in a kind of silence of notoriety. People may know them, or know of them. People also may think they know what it is they do, but they don't, not really. Only a handful of people may truly understand the essence of who they are.

The writer of a 2019 *New York Times* profile of Costas Spiliadis was given Sheila Kussner as a source on what makes Milos special. The article referred to Sheila as a "Montreal philanthropist," which was a brave stab at defining her.[1] A philanthropist is someone who promotes the welfare of others, but we have come to equate the term almost exclusively with someone who finances noble causes. If we were to add up all the money that Sheila (and her late husband, Marvyn) has spent in the course of her activities, she would be deserving of the narrower financial definition, but Sheila's philanthropy has been multi-dimensional. She is a philanthropist in its most fundamental definition: someone dedicated to improving the quality of life of others.

If you want to understand Sheila's engagement with the world, you need to break it down into discrete pieces. Peer support is the original one, arising from her childhood experiences as a cancer patient and an amputee. Another is fundraising for various causes. There is also her advocacy for assorted causes, which have ranged from organizing support for the "no" vote in the 1995 Quebec referendum to helping draw attention in the 1980s to the plight of *refuseniks*, Jewish cancer patients in the former Soviet Union. Foremost, there is her institution-building. She spearheaded the creation of McGill University's oncology department, raising the tens of millions of dollars necessary, and (as an alumnus) served on McGill's board of governors. More than any other achievement, she is known for founding Hope & Cope for cancer patients in association with the

Jewish General Hospital, serving as Hope & Cope's board chair for most of its history. It's impossible to quantify the number of people who have benefited directly from Hope & Cope's services over the past forty-plus years, but a number in the tens of thousands would not be a wild guess.

Sheila is also renowned as someone with an incredible gift for getting other people to make gifts, mainly in the area of cancer research and care. She is hands-down the most accomplished fundraiser for any cause in the annals of philanthropy in Montreal. She could give anyone in North America a run for their money.

"Prospective donor" is a descriptive that has rarely survived Sheila's initial overtures. Silcoff is not the only friend who insists that you cannot say "no" to Sheila, as they recount an array of requests for support, for favours large and small. With Sheila, "support" is not always or even usually about money. It's about doing what you can. But when it *is* about money, Sheila Kussner is relentlessly effective.

Myer Bick came to know Sheila well during his term as president and CEO of the Jewish General Hospital (JGH) Foundation from 2001 until his retirement in 2019. He remembers first meeting Sheila in the 1980s, when she was beginning her fundraising to create McGill's oncology department and endow its various chairs. Bick was in his late thirties, a graduate lawyer who was just beginning his real estate career, as vice-president of David Azrieli's Canadian company Canpro Investments; he also helped set up in 1989 the family's Azrieli Foundation, the largest such private charity in Canada, and served as a director until his mandatory retirement in 2021. Canpro's offices at Sherbrooke and Stanley were one block from the Ritz-Carlton Hotel. Bick and Azrieli often visited the hotel's bar lounge for lunch, which happened to be a prime vantage point for noting the comings and goings at one of the city's prime landmarks. Among the figures they routinely saw was Sheila Kussner.

Elegantly dressed in a pantsuit that concealed her prosthetic leg, Sheila moved through the hotel with confident, energized grace. She was on her way to or from the hotel's famed garden restaurant, where the hotel staff would release ducklings in the fountain in the spring. In tow with Sheila, Bick recalls with a laugh, would be "some sorry duck," usually a man, who was the object of Sheila's champagned-and-dined fundraising.

Sheila has long had a discernible effect on men, a beauty with an effervescent personality and a flirtatious demeanour, qualities that are paired with a quick wit, a broad grasp of current affairs ranging from the local to the international, a formidable mind, and a penchant for speaking that mind. It surprises not at all those who know her well that she and Pierre Trudeau became good friends. (Friends say that Sheila appreciates style and beauty in a woman, as well as brains, but if she must choose, she will always go for brains.) Whenever Myer Bick spied her in motion from his perch in the bar lounge, the odds were fairly good that Sheila had gotten (or was about to get) what she wanted from this lunch date: the promise of a substantial donation.

Phil Gold first met Sheila in the early 1980s, when he was the head of medicine at Montreal General Hospital and was also running the McGill Cancer Centre. "Someone said to me, 'I knew that if you went to lunch with Sheila, you were in for at least a half a million or more.' That was the word on the street. But people did give."

The garden restaurant of the Ritz-Carlton, Myer Bick explains, was one of two nodes of downtown Montreal that Sheila moved between in those years. The other was the high-end department store Holt Renfrew, a block away. "Sheila *owned* Holt Renfrew," Bick says. The staff took her car when she arrived, and she spent and tipped generously, just as she did at the Ritz-Carlton. Into the car would go gifts she would deliver to her sorry ducks, who in truth have never been sorry for their largesse, as tokens of her personal thanks. There were also gifts she lavished on people she knew, simply because she wanted to.

And so it went, when Sheila was at the height of her—*notoriety* is not the right word, more like her *presence*—as a philanthropic force. It would be wrong to suggest that there was some kind of apex from which she then steadily if gracefully declined. Because at eighty-nine, Sheila was still setting a phenomenal standard for charitable fundraising, as she bent her will to raising the endowment that would sustain Hope & Cope for decades to come. Sheila has always been its most important fundraiser. "She was a one-man show," Lillian Vineberg, who has served as chair of the board of Hope & Cope, says of Sheila's many years of efforts. "All the ladies who volunteered to help her fundraise, they were doing the little stuff, getting friends to give maybe fifty, seventy-five, one hundred dollars. She was going for the twenty-five-thousand-, the fifty-thousand-, the hundred-thousand-dollar donations. All by herself, with literally nobody helping her."

The idea that Hope & Cope will have to carry on without her someday has weighed heavily on her. She wants its financial affairs firmly in order. "Once I'm done fundraising," she says in the spring of 2022, "we're going to have enough for another forty years. They can hold a bridge night or a movie night, raise fifty grand, one hundred grand. But anything big—half a million, two million—no. They won't have to."

Sheila's reputation for fundraising, which was well established in Montreal by the 1970s, is a source of two mistaken impressions about her. One is that fundraising defines her. To be sure, as a fundraiser she has been outstanding, not only in the amounts she has raised but also in the way she has gone about raising it: with her trademark style, grace, and impeccable attention to details. Her galas have been spectacles and must-be-seen moments in the city's social calendar, and her one-on-one pitches are carefully orchestrated. At Milos, for example, she has made the corner table very much *her* table, providing her own flowers and candles, and signature matches. Suzanne O'Brien explains that for Hope & Cope staff parties (for which Costas Spiliadis provides a good deal), Sheila brings her own platters and dishes from home, her own mints and nuts. "Who else brings their own food to a restaurant? When she didn't like a restaurant's dessert, she brought in an ice cream cake. They just let her get away with it. Sheila creates a table as if she's entertaining you at her own home. She wants you to feel special, and donors love it. Donors can go to a restaurant any time. Dining with Sheila is not just a meal at a restaurant. It's an experience."

Still, that ability to persuade others to support important causes, and her unique modus operandi, tends to overshadow how critical her vision, strategic acumen, and commitment have been to those causes. Sheila has fundraised because she has concrete plans for the money. Gerald Batist, director of the Jewish General Hospital's Segal Cancer Centre, points to the creation of McGill's oncology department as a prime example of Sheila's contribution not being fully grasped. Batist says many people who were involved in and benefited from the department's creation viewed it as a matter of fundraising, with Sheila in the lead. Her performance truly was a tour de force of style, networking, and (this may not always be thought possible in such a high-stakes undertaking) *fun*, "but it was much more than that. I think it was an example of the money following the vision. People bought into it and wanted to believe in it. She was able to raise money because of the power of her spirit and her vision." If you ask people who have contributed to Sheila's various causes how they got involved, he says, you will find that it wasn't that they were looking for a place to park their money and Sheila happened to come along. "She inspires people. And it's not too often you see people that are like that, and who can be as flexible and forward thinking as she is."

The other mistaken impression is that, as someone celebrated for an impeccable personal style, and for the champagning-and-dining approach to fundraising (and for the many gifts she dispenses), she must be a high-society patroness with bottomless personal resources and a knack for coaxing dollars out of fellow elites. Alison Silcoff, for her part, objects to the idea that Sheila is not of high society, if you define it by measures other than net worth or income. "Sheila can walk into anywhere and mix with anybody as an equal." Still, Sheila does not come from great wealth, nor does she have a lifestyle that matches that of people she persuades to support her causes. She lives in the same Mont-Royal bungalow she and Marvyn moved into not long after they were married in 1953. Sheila and Marvyn raised their two daughters, Janice and Joanne, as Marvyn built up a cardboard-box business he took over from his father.

Sheila has raised many, many millions of dollars over the years, without ever taking a commission or demanding that her considerable expenses be reimbursed. When Marvyn was still alive, his support sustained her generosity, but sometimes bills would come to the Kussner home and even Marvyn (who believed unequivocally in

Sheila's work) would have to say, "Sheila…" Today, she oversees several important accounts (as we will see) for a packaging company that bought Marvyn's business, and the monthly income helps to keep her living securely but hardly extravagantly while providing the funds she continues to spend in support of her activities. The fact that she has refused compensation for any of her activities that support Hope & Cope astounded Marvin Corber, a leading Montreal accountant and fellow governor of McGill (both now serve as governors emeriti) with a considerable track record in philanthropic campaigns. Asked by Sheila to help structure the financials of Hope & Cope about twenty years ago, he could not understand why she wasn't having her expenses reimbursed. It is impossible to think of another fundraiser who has operated at such a level of style and expense and yet has been so efficient at putting donation dollars to work because she has personally shouldered the fundraising costs.

"Sheila has said to me a few times, 'I'm not that wealthy,'" says Alison Silcoff. "I keep saying to her, 'Sheila, you would be, if you weren't giving people five-hundred-dollar gift certificates for Milos or taking them to the Ritz-Carlton a few days a week.' She's incredibly generous. She takes people to the Ritz or Milos and *then* she gives them the talk, after they've had lobster and caviar and goodness knows what else."

The true scope of Sheila Kussner's philanthropy also will elude you, if all you know of Sheila Kussner is the Sheila Kussner of galas and large cheques and fundraising pitches at the Ritz-Carlton and shopping excursions to Holt Renfrew for gifts. Even knowing about Hope & Cope or the oncology department at McGill doesn't get you close to the essence of what Sheila does—day in, day out, and for most of her waking hours.

CHAPTER TWO

Night Ride (II)

On another night—which is most any night—the same Lexus sedan pulls out of the same Mont-Royal driveway. Sheila Kussner is again at the wheel. Sharing the car's interior is an assistant (one lives with her during the week, another on the weekend) and an assortment of items to deliver. They are beginning a night ride through Montreal and its suburban environs. The delivery items vary from one night to another: a prepared meal, baked goods, a thank-you note, a gift of some sort. Although Sheila never puts it that way, she is being true to the Jewish tradition of *matan b'seter*, giving in secret.

Sheila's night rides involve two broad categories of recipients: people she supports and people whose support requires appreciation. You hear about "Sheila's patients." These invariably (but not exclusively) are individuals undergoing cancer treatment. She may know them well, or hardly at all. What matters is that she has heard about their circumstances, knows they need support, and has made up her mind to provide some. The other recipients of her night runs are the people who have done her favours, which usually means they have done something for someone she is looking out for. She also makes a Sunday-night run, a literal bread run, of loaves from a kosher bakery to various households. One of her regular recipients is Jeannette Valmont, one of the earliest volunteers at Hope & Cope who went on to serve as its volunteer coordinator and for a time as co-president. Her husband, René, Valmont explains, likes a certain type of Jewish bread. Sheila visits the bakery and only accepts the bread if it has just left the oven; it arrives in their condominium lobby at ten o'clock on Sunday night, still warm. "Sheila is extraordinarily bright," says Valmont, and also "kooky"—or as René says, "crazy, in a good way."

Sheila has her cellphone with her—an old flip phone; she has no time for more advanced technology, including email—but she also has a landline at home, plugged into an answering machine. She only takes a call on that one if she can see that the caller is someone she must speak to, right away. The cellphone, in the meantime, is almost always busy. Her calls can go late into the night, which is to say into the early morning, if there is another night owl to confer with, advise, or console. Her friend and physician, Rubin Becker, notes that he goes to bed early, but "if she knows my wife is out of town, she says, 'Oh, you can stay up later. I'm going to call you tonight.'" Becker otherwise rises early, which means he can expect regular calls from her at five-thirty in the morning, just to catch up, when his new day is beginning but her old day is not yet over. Sheila is routinely awake until eight-thirty in the morning. After three or four hours of sleep, a new day, with a new set of tasks, begins for her in the early afternoon.

Just off Sheila's kitchen is a space that in any other household would be the sunroom but in Sheila's house is the office. It might better be described as the war room. Along the window-lined wall facing the yard is a long work surface with a telephone, a computer, and the printer she uses to make personalized notes and cards. The short wall to the left features an array of photos and framed items of recognition, including her Officier de l'Ordre National du Québec, Commandeure de l'Ordre de Montréal, Member and Officer of the Order of Canada, and her honorary doctorate of law degrees from McGill University and the Université de Montreal. Somewhere in the midst of all this (or tucked discreetly away) are her Robert Fisher Fellowship Award from Memorial Sloan Kettering Cancer Center, the Jewish General Hospital Distinguished Service Award, President of the State of Israel Award, Canadian Cancer Society Medal of Courage, Government of Quebec Volunteer Award for the Montreal Region, Samuel Bronfman Medal, Queen's Diamond Jubilee Award, Outstanding Volunteer of the Year Award (Association of Fundraising Professionals–Quebec), the Eleanor Roosevelt Humanitarian Award, and the Canada Volunteer Award. The long wall opposite the windows consists of shelving units topped by an enormous tackboard. The shelves are crammed with papers and her supplies of gift cards; the tackboard is covered in the minutiae of contacts and activities.

This is the inner sanctum of Sheila's philanthropy, the complex enterprise that juggles innumerable initiatives. A typical afternoon will find her on the telephone. When she is not fundraising or dealing with Hope & Cope matters, she is working connections in health care, pressing specialists to see a patient or get back to one waiting for a test result, or taking a conference call with a patient and their specialist to review the treatment options available.

"She finds answers," is how Charlotte Colson explains her childhood friend's assistance. "Whenever I have needed anything, I've called Sheila, and gotten an immediate answer. It's not, 'I'm sorry, I'm busy, call me back in a week.' *Immediately*. When you're not feeling well, you want to have the answer. You don't want to wait."

Sheila responds to people's plights precisely because they don't want to wait, and that in turn places pressure on her not to leave people waiting. She gets back to them as soon as she can, and she then finds answers, or the people who have those answers, as soon as she can.

Ninety-nine per cent of Rubin Becker's interactions as a physician with Sheila, he says, are for someone else's benefit, not hers. "She'll call me, almost in a panic. 'You've got to do me a favour.' I always think that it's for her, but it's never for her. She cares about every single person, and because she goes out of her way to help people, people seek her to help them. So she gets calls from all over, from people she has never heard of."

"There are a wealth of directions and things to describe, in terms of her impact," says Jean Remmer, a social worker who served more than a decade as Hope & Cope's coordinator and has remained close to Sheila. "The community, her immediate circle, the outer circle, and her family—they're all the same. She gives equally to everybody. She responds to you. It could be somebody walking down the street. That incredible ability to focus on the person in front of her is her way of pushing forward her goals and aspirations."

Sheila does her homework. When people send her articles and papers, she reads them. "Her due diligence for her responsibilities is exceptional," says Suzanne O'Brien. "She'll read board documents and underline portions. Not too much gets by her." As a governor emeritus of McGill University, she still receives the current board's minutes in advance of twice-yearly meetings, and dutifully peruses them. "She stays up to date on things that really matter to her." In some areas of medicine, she seems to know more than some doctors do.

With cancer, she knows the major treatment centres internationally, not just locally, and who the leading figures are. She hears about clinical trials and puts candidate patients in touch with them. A recent case (the details have been simplified for privacy): A man she knows passingly has a late-stage cancer. A suburban Montreal hospital has told him there is nothing more they can do for him. He is recently married, with an infant son. The news is devastating. Sheila hears of it and gets on the phone. She lassoes specialists at another hospital, and they agree to provide another round of treatment. He enjoys a private room for the duration of his stay. His long-term prognosis may not be much improved, but he goes home to his wife and child, delighted to have been given another chance, a little more time.

Alison Silcoff says her first direct interaction with Sheila came about thirty years ago, when she approached her for help with a friend who had been diagnosed with pancreatic cancer. Sheila gave her three names of the top people at different hospitals in the United States, including a surgeon at the Mayo Clinic who was performing a variation on the Whipple procedure that was available nowhere in Canada. Silcoff's friend lived another seventeen years, an outstanding result for this type of cancer. Only recently, Silcoff shares, her son was diagnosed with cancer. "Sheila knew so much about the type of cancer he had. It was incredible. He was told he wouldn't get his biopsy results for two weeks. Sheila said, 'Rubbish, they'll know a lot within two or three days.' I pulled some strings and, sure enough, we had the results in three days."

"She's a fount of knowledge," says Silcoff. "Doctors respect her and talk with her. She's so interesting to talk to, because everyone is interested in health and the latest in what's going on in the medical world, and she's up on it all, and not just in Canada. I don't know any fundraisers in any field who have the depth of knowledge in what they're fundraising for that Sheila does."

"She's the best resource in the cancer world," says Lillian Vineberg, the former chair of the board of Hope & Cope. "Which doctor to see. Which hospital or clinic to check into for advice on the best treatment. There literally isn't an area of cancer she doesn't know about, and if there's a new one, she'll investigate it to the hilt, and find out who the leader is in the world. And if you can't afford to go there, she'll find funding to help you. She has worked at bonding with every one of these specialists." Vineberg reels off a sampling of leading cancer centres in the United States where Sheila has forged personal connections: the Dana-Farber Cancer Institute at Harvard Medical School, the Mayo Clinic Comprehensive Cancer Center (which has three locales), the MD Anderson Cancer Center at the University of Texas, and Memorial Sloan Kettering Cancer Center in New York. And then there are the resources in Israel. "She's the go-to person. I've experienced that because my late husband had cancer for fourteen years. Sheila adored him, and he adored her, and there was no stone she would leave unturned in finding out what was the best treatment for chronic lymphocytic leukemia. Which was the best hospital? Who were the leading minds?"

When Jeannette Valmont, her friend and long-standing associate in Hope & Cope, developed thyroid cancer later in life, Sheila's response was typical. She advised Valmont knowledgeably on the promising prognosis, and then objected when she learned Valmont's surgery wasn't scheduled for three months. In no time, Valmont was receiving a call from her surgeon. They had an opening: could she come in next Friday? There was no doubt what force of nature had caused the change in the schedule.

Valmont acknowledges that some of what Sheila does on behalf of others can sound like queue-jumping in Canada's public health system, but she notes that Sheila advocates for everyone and anyone for the best possible care. Most anyone who deals with a parking valet, Valmont notes, will limit their interactions to relinquishing the car, getting it back again, and giving a tip. Not Sheila. "By the time she has her car back, she has gotten a whole story from the valet. She'll know they have a son who is not well, that the valet is struggling financially. She will tip him a little more." She will look into the treatment or care the son needs and check back with the valet every week on how he is doing. "The number of doctors that she has found for the gardener, the cleaning lady, the carpenter ... You cannot put into words what she has done."

Although she is known foremost for her advocacy and support in cancer care, there is no diagnostic limit to where she will get involved in someone's circumstances. When Jeannette Valmont developed serious lower-back problems that required surgery, Sheila found her the best available expert. When she heard about a woman in Montreal suffering at home from COVID, she started calling a restaurant and sending over meals—at her own expense, naturally. "The other day," says Rubin Becker in the spring of 2022, "a cardiologist called me and said, 'I got a call from Sheila. She's at the Royal Victoria Hospital. She's going to be calling me tonight, and I just want some medical background on her.'" Becker wondered what Sheila was doing in the Royal Victoria, and what could be wrong with her heart. He couldn't reach her on her cellphone, but he was able to track down Sheila's daughter Joanne, who was away in Arizona. It turned out that Sheila actually wanted to speak to the cardiologist about someone else's care.

Sometimes, Sheila's determination to help others goes well beyond the bounds of medical care. Gerald Batist, director of the Jewish General Hospital's Segal Cancer Centre, learned about Sheila through his mother, Gertrude, a breast cancer survivor who was one of Hope & Cope's early volunteers. After graduating in medicine from McGill, he pursued post-doctoral training in New York, Boston, and Washington. When he returned to Montreal in 1986, "I started getting phone calls from strange young Jewish women. They'd cold-call me and say, 'Sheila Kussner told me you're a really nice guy and not attached.' I actually went on a couple of those dates. They were all pretty disastrous. You don't just connect workwise with Sheila. You connect all the way. She was in my life, whether I invited her in or not, and of course I did."

"Sheila's first response to anything is from the heart," says Suzanne O'Brien. "Ninety per cent of the time, it's the right response. But if it isn't the right one, she'll quickly come to see what is." Sheila is a realist. She knows what is possible, and what is not. She has experienced too many losses in her own life to think some medical miracle is waiting for everyone, if only the right treatment and the right specialist can be found. But she will not accept the impossible without putting up a hell of a fight. And so her car moves into the Montreal night, with personal thank-you cards and tokens of appreciation to deliver to the homes of the specialists who agreed that one man whose cause she rallied to deserved another round of care.

Sheila's ability to stay up to speed on things is far from limited to medical care. In the fall of 2021, a visitor to Sheila's house asked her if she knew Lawrence Stroll, the Montreal billionaire who made his fortune in the fashion world and co-owned the Aston Martin F1 auto racing team. Stroll had become a larger-than-life character in the hit Netflix series *Drive to Survive*. Sheila absolutely knows him. She recounts how she once approached him for a donation, and he promptly sent a car and driver around to her house to hand over a six-figure cheque. She then segues into comments on the driving career of Red Bull's Max Verstappen. When her guest raises his eyebrows at her detailed knowledge of F1 racing, Sheila makes it clear that, if you are asking Lawrence Stroll for support, you are going to make a point of knowing whatever you can about F1.

But Sheila's broader curiosity is not exclusively driven by fundraising. "If you sit with Sheila for any amount of time," says Rubin Becker, "there's no shortage of conversation. She's passionate about everything that's going on in the world. She cares as much about things that are remote as she does about things that are next to her."

When Marvyn was alive, friends tell you, Sheila's life (and the family's life) may have been dominated by her philanthropic works, but there were still dinners at favourite restaurants like Milos, visits to the cinema, and other social outings. Since Marvyn's death in 2013, and with her more limited mobility (she was compelled to rely on a wheelchair around that time), her daily routine has been even more dedicated to philanthropy. Jeannette and René Valmont would rent DVDs for Sheila and Marvyn, and Suzanne O'Brien would feed Sheila's appetite for crime procedural dramas, but she no longer watches television. "I don't have time," she simply explains.

Being Sheila Kussner is more than a full-time job. It would defeat most anyone half her age, but approaching ninety, she is tack-sharp, driven, and organized. If you happen to get a call from Sheila one evening—checking in, making sure your drive home was safe, asking about your spouse's health—you cannot help but sense that yours is one in a long list of calls she has lined up to complete before turning in, and you would not be wrong.

There is very much a Sheila way, and it involves several essential gestures. There are the personally composed notes and letters (always on paper stock; *never* emails; and if printed on a computer, signed by her hand). There are tips—generous tips—for the hired help wherever she goes. And there are gifts of all sorts, always thoughtful, always chosen by her.

Her tipping habits approach the legendary. Rubin Becker has two favourite stories to that end. One involves a hospitalization of Sheila. Every time he came round to see her, a member of the cleaning staff seemed to be in the room. Becker discovered that Sheila had a stash of five-dollar bills in a drawer for tipping staff; whenever this man found some excuse to drag a mop through the room, she automatically handed him a bill.

The other story involves a time when Sheila suffered a pelvic fracture. She was in bed at home with the fracture and tried to transfer herself to a wheelchair beside the bed. With the fracture and the pain, she misjudged the gap and fell between the bed and the wheelchair. Marvyn could not move her, and so, at five in the morning, Becker got a call at home.

He rushed over with painkillers, but he also called an ambulance. As the paramedics tried to extricate her from the spot in which she had become wedged, Sheila was calling out to Marvyn to fetch her purse, because she *had* to tip the ambulance driver. When it turned out she didn't have any change, she turned to Becker. All he had in his wallet was a fifty-dollar bill, which he dutifully gave to the driver.

Tipping the driver, Becker says, "was her first thought. And she was in so much pain that I had to give her a shot of morphine. It gives you an idea of where her focus always is. She needs to take care of others. She's dealt with a lot, in terms of illness and tragedy in her life, but with her demeanour, she's always flipped it around. She's always really caring for the other person. It reduces her degree of suffering and lets her focus on issues important to her. It's very hard to be a doctor looking after Sheila, because she just wants to look after you."

The story of the ambulance driver, as Becker relates it, is hilarious, and Sheila finds it just as funny. Becker stresses it's important to appreciate Sheila's sense of humour, especially about herself, and her own appreciation of humour. "I'll try to leave her smiling," he says of his visits with her, "because it's more important to her than sympathy, without question."

Sheila has been making her personal gestures of gifts, phone calls, notes, and tips for as long as anyone has known her. It's how she has nurtured a remarkable network of personal relationships that is much more meaningful than a rolodex of contacts. Lillian Vineberg, who spelled off Sheila as chair of Hope & Cope when Marvyn was in his final days, recalls meeting Sheila when Vineberg was a kid growing up in Ottawa and her parents sent her to Camp Hiawatha in the Laurentians north of Montreal, to get her out of the city during a wave of polio. Sheila had begun working at Camp Hiawatha as a counsellor when she was seventeen, three years after cancer had claimed her left leg. "Sheila even then was a powerhouse. She was just friendly, warm. She was always a networker. She mastered this from childhood. The things that have made her a success, from my point of view, are her friend-making and net-working skills."

Her gift-giving occasionally goes off the rails. She likes to give books, and in 2011 she checked the bestseller lists so she could send the most popular novel to key patrons and supporters. It turned out to be *Fifty Shades of Gray*, E.L. James's erotic romance of sadomas-ochistic sex. Sheila had no idea what it was about but, after sending out the copies, gave one to Suzanne O'Brien to read over a week-end. When O'Brien explained to her the novel's subject, Sheila quickly recovered in an inimitable Sheila way, by sending hand-written notes to her giftees, asking them if the novel worked better than Viagra.

"Have you celebrated a birthday since you've known her?" her dinner guest at Milos in October 2021 will be asked by Gerald Batist. Sheila is famous for not forgetting birthdays and other key events. As time has passed, the sheer number of events has increased as her world of contacts has grown ever wider and deeper into successive generations. Birthdays and wedding anniversaries of friends are com-pounded by birthdays of their children, then wedding anniversaries of their children, then the birthdays of their grandchildren. "When my daughter was young," says Jean Remmer, the former coordina-tor for Hope & Cope, "Sheila would always send something for her birthday—a clown, balloons—or come to drop off an envelope. My daughter always said it was like getting a visit from the Queen, and whenever she tastes a moment with Sheila today, she'll still say that, and she's forty-one." Everyone assumes Sheila manages a database of some kind (how could she not?), but her unerring ability to mark special occasions in the lives of so many people still astounds recip-ients of the cards, the telephone calls, the gifts that appear at their door. "You can count on her for every birthday, every anniversary," says Remmer. "The birthday of my husband, of his children, of my daughter. She's going to remember everybody."

"Most people remember things like birthdays because they're on Facebook," Becker notes. "Sheila is not on Facebook. She has her own system. And it's not like she wakes up and says, 'Oh, it's so-and-so's birthday. I should call them.' She has thought about it for, like, three days beforehand. She plans."

Myer Bick says when his first child was born, "my wife called me and said, 'Who are Sheila and Marvyn Kussner? I've just had a package delivered by a gentleman, and I think it was Mr. Kussner.' And it was the most beautiful baby dress from Holt Renfrew. I called Sheila, and said, 'Sheila, what are you *doing*?' She was almost angry with me. She said, 'I never forget a friend. So use it for your beautiful daughter.'"

Alison Silcoff has long been baking scones and giving them to Sheila, and has been both touched and exasperated by the response. "Every time I take her some, I get a poem written about scones. It's remarkable that someone as busy as her can sit down and write a ten-line poem, 'Ode to a Scone,' after receiving a couple dozen scones. And there will be an incredibly generous gift. I've threatened never to bake them again unless she promises to stop giving me gifts. Then the doorbell rings and there's someone with an orchid … There's no point in arguing. I think she's a wonder."

In her fundraising, Phil Gold says, "she never did anything for herself. It was always for someone else, to the point that I once said to her, 'You gotta see a shrink. No rational human being does what you do.'"

"I don't think anybody could do more for Sheila than she does for them," says Becker. "If you want to do something for her, it's impossible, because then she has to return the favour, and do more for you." Her own birthday is almost a burden, he says. "First, she has to figure out who she's going to give away her presents to. Second, all the cards and gifts mean she now has to write all those thank-you cards." (On her ninetieth birthday, Sheila will write more than two hundred such cards.) "She spends hours and hours each day, thanking other people in writing, when it should be the reverse." Jeannette Valmont notes that Sheila might receive about one hundred sixty cards or notes at Rosh Hashanah, the Jewish New Year, and she answers every one of them. She also makes a point of personalizing her thank-yous. "She will let you know in the note that she remembers the cake you gave her had four raisins. And she will thank the cleaning lady that made her a honey cake with the same enthusiasm as the Westmount lady that sent her a triple orchid."

"She is super, super genuine," says Marc Weinstein, who first met Sheila in 1995, when he was executive director of the JGH Foundation; he moved to McGill in 2005, where he is vice-principal, university advancement. "She's not doing something because she's trying to get a favour, or to make you feel good. She's a humanitarian at the core. She goes way above the call of duty. If someone calls her about something, she's diving deep into it. She's solution oriented, and she wants to understand how she can help."

The experience of the Sheila way began for her Milos dinner guest in October 2021 before he had even met her. He had been in his hotel room in downtown Montreal no more than two hours when there was a knock at the door. A member of the staff was holding a gift basket brimming with grapes, strawberries, crackers, and an excellent brie. The wicker basket was wrapped in cellophane, and there was a card, in an envelope. On the face of the card was printed *Sheila Kussner* in italic script. The card read:

WELCOME TO MONTREAL!!!
The Keys to the City are yours…
Looking forward to seeing you on Thursday at 3 pm
Warmly,
Sheila

The recipient thought: Sheila must have ordered a gift basket somewhere, and had a card printed and attached. But no. It transpires that Sheila had driven to Marché Jean-Talon, one of the oldest markets on the continent, with Nida Viray, the young woman assisting her on weekdays. They selected the fruit, the cheese, and the crackers, and then assembled and wrapped the gift basket. Sheila composed the card's message, printed it on her office computer, and signed it. Then the pair set out in Sheila's car—with Sheila of course again at the wheel—for the hotel. They pulled up out front and flagged down a staff member. Sheila tipped him and asked him to deliver it to her dinner guest's room. Then Sheila and Nida watched him enter the elevator and waited to see him return to the lobby and then curbside, to confirm the gift got there.

Before their dinner at Milos on that Thursday night in October 2021, as they become acquainted at her kitchen table, Sheila learned that her guest has an adult son with high-needs autism. He lives at home, in Ontario. His parents know they won't live forever, and the options for their son's care and supervision are murky. Sheila questions her guest methodically about his son. When was he first diagnosed? What is the nature of his disability? What sort of treatment and support does he receive now? What are the respite options for his parents? Sheila has a well-honed ability to drill down through the strata of someone's circumstances, irrespective of the specific illness or disability.

At Milos, she interrupts the night's celebratory flow by focussing her gaze across the table on her guest and declaring, "I am very concerned about your son." There is no quid pro quo with Sheila. She does not say things like this because she is trying to impress you with her caring, or because she expects something in return. Sheila is simply stating the fact that, having learned of a total stranger's circumstances, this young disabled man's future is now gnawing at her conscience. She needs to do something about it. Her dinner guest says he appreciates her concern, but that he doesn't expect Sheila, in Montreal, to do anything about a complex problem with someone's long-term care a seven-hour drive away in Ontario.

She leaves the subject alone, for now, but that weekend, her guest receives a telephone call at home from Sheila. She has someone for him to contact. This person is in Montreal, and is not directly involved with autism, but does have some connections and perspective, and would be worth speaking with. She provides the number. Her guest dutifully dials it and connects with a woman with considerable experience in charitable health care in Quebec, who also knows someone in Toronto involved in advocacy for people with autism. They speak for about an hour about his son's circumstances, and she follows up by sending some links to resources and news about plans for one long-term-care facility. Nothing is resolved; nothing moves concretely forward. But the conversation and emails are welcomed.

The next time Sheila's dinner guest sees her, she wants to know if he spoke to the person. "Was she helpful?" she wants to know. Yes, she was. A note, some token of thanks, is almost certainly on the way to the woman.

Sheila has not solved anything, but she has responded to a dilemma, as best she could. Not doing *something* was beyond consideration. And until you have been fully immersed in Sheila's concern and have had Sheila react to your circumstances with her particular resolve—without even having been asked for help—it may be impossible to truly appreciate her instinctual response to the world. That response may be the dictionary definition of the Jewish principle of *tikkun olam*—to perfect or repair the world. It's a response for which she is almost apologetic. "It's a calling," she offers, on a night she is waiting for callbacks from two different doctors for two different patients. "It gives me joy to be able to do something. People can't get their doctors on the phone, but I can. I'm lucky I have the clout. I'm Don Corleone," she jibes, as she wonders aloud if people return her calls because they are afraid of what might happen if they don't.

People who do not live up to Sheila's expectations can hear about it, regardless of their station in life. Of Suzanne O'Brien, her friend and de facto partner in overseeing Hope & Cope, Sheila offers: "She's social. I'm political." Sheila's idea of being politic is to not mince words. She has known Justin Trudeau since he was a child— he was at Sheila's house to give his respects after Marvyn died—and the fact that he is prime minister does not shield him from Sheila calling him (which she can do) and giving him a piece of her mind on some matter of public policy, as she used to do with his father, Pierre. A long-standing friend, Salvatore (Sal) Guerrera, recalls Sheila calling to let him know a friend of his had deeply disappointed her, and that she was writing this friend to tell him that he was not the same quality of human being as Guerrera was. And Guerrera thought, *Dear God, what am I about to get into.* But that is part of the bargain, of being enfolded in Sheila's caring.

And if Sheila welcomes you to Montreal, she is in truth welcoming you to Sheila's world, which is something that geography does not adequately describe. Sheila's world is a network, a living force, and a presence of caring.

CHAPTER THREE

The Scale of Empathy

Sheila's world is an ever-expanding network that requires incredible energy to maintain. Ask people who think they know Sheila well, what they would really like to know about Sheila, and you will get a fairly uniform response: they wonder where that energy comes from, which is partly physical, at her age. But the question of how she does what she does clearly goes deeper than that. People are curious about the *why* behind the *how*.

"A lot of what you see," one old friend says of Sheila's effervescent performance at Milos in October 2021, "is Sheila being Sheila. It's Sheila the persona. We're not Shakespearean, but we all play different roles, and she was playing a particular role at dinner, which was Sheila. And as you say, no one can play it like she can. She's very self-aware that way. What's interesting, what I want to know, is: What drives it originally? What are the wellsprings of that personality? What made her that combo of tough and maternal? And when she finally gets home, and sits down in her little office, and starts to work the phone until two in the morning, what is she worried about? Where is the drive? Where do the ideas come from?"

People wonder about that drive because it fascinates them, but also because we all wish that the lightning spark could be bottled somehow and shared by others. Sheila is a one-of-a-kind, but it would be wonderful if there could somehow be other people, now and in the future, to whom could be imparted some of the magic of Sheila. Her methods are not enough. You could write thank-you notes until the cows come home and would still not have what Sheila has. And without that spark, there is no repairing the world in the way that she strives to do.

The elusive quality we seek in Sheila Kussner springs from one essential element of the human psyche: empathy. Sheila, says David Johnston, "symbolizes and epitomizes empathy in the very best sense of the word. Empathy is not sympathy. Sympathy is, 'I see your situation, and I feel sorry for you. Isn't that sad, and you have my condolences.' Empathy is, 'I see your situation, and I come and walk in your shoes, and we're going to do something about it together.'" Johnston, the twenty-eighth governor general of Canada who was principal of McGill when he met and worked with Sheila to create the university's oncology department, coincidentally was writing his book *Empathy: Turning Compassion into Action* when he spoke about her in November 2021. He marvels at "how well she has perfected and persisted in that empathy, in all sorts of adversity and challenges over the decades."

"If I were interviewing Sheila," Johnston says, "I would be trying to get at the depths of that caring. Where did that spring from, within her DNA? What was her environmental background that caused that to blossom?"

The moral roots of empathy are deep in religion and philosophy. The novelist Barbara Kingsolver made the oft-quoted observation: "Empathy is really the opposite of spiritual meanness. It's the capacity to understand that every war is both won and lost. And that someone else's pain is as meaningful as your own."

Professions in which empathy is (or ought to be) valued have measured levels of empathy as a screening tool during hiring or have made it a focus for improvement during training. Empathy is also critical in the sort of volunteer counselling pioneered by Hope & Cope. It is a capacity to listen, and to understand someone else's circumstances, so that you can respond to their needs appropriately.

In 2015, the American writer Leslie Jamison published a remarkable essay, "The Empathy Exams," that addressed "the labor, the motions, the dance of getting inside another person's state of heart or mind."[2] Empathy, she noted, comes from the Greek word *empatheia*, "*em* (into) and *pathos* (feeling)—a penetration, a kind of travel. It suggests you enter another person's pain as you'd enter another country, through immigration and customs, border crossing by way of query: *What grows where you are? What are the laws? What animals graze there?*"[3] She recounted her experiences in training medical students, as an actor playing the role of various patients, carefully scripted as to their symptoms and behaviour. The students' abilities to interact with the "patient" and diagnose their condition (at times both physical and psychiatric), relied substantially on empathy—on how well they could move inside the other person's existence and tap its secrets.

We may think of empathy as a spontaneous emotional response, a routine automatically executed deep in our mental software, but Jamison viewed it as a skill that requires deliberation and commitment. Empathy, she advised, "isn't just something that happens to us—a meteor shower of synapses firing across the brain—it's also a choice we make to pay attention, to extend ourselves. It's made of exertion, that dowdier cousin of impulse. Sometimes we care for another because we know we should, or because it's asked for, but this doesn't make our caring hollow. The act of choosing simply means we've committed ourselves to a set of behaviours greater than the sum of our individual inclinations. *I will listen to his sadness, even when I'm deep in my own.*"[4]

Researchers have striven to quantify empathy for decades, as it is so fundamental to understanding a person's socialization. What they have found helps us to better appreciate the nature of empathy, and especially of empathetic people. The social psychologist Robert Hogan, in constructing an "empathy scale" in 1969, argued that empathy can be seen as "an everyday manifestation of the disposition to adopt a broad moral perspective, to take 'the moral point of view.'" In taking a moral point of view, "a person is said to consider the consequences of his actions for the welfare of others … A willingness or tendency to put oneself in another person's place and to modify one's behaviour as a result, is clearly an important aspect of moral growth."[5]

Psychiatric researchers interested in empathy dispense with the moral component that Hogan used in social psychology and instead describe empathy as "the ability to identify other people's thoughts, intentions, desires, and feelings, and to respond to others' mental states with an appropriate emotion."[6] But there is much value in retaining Hogan's approach, with its moral component.

Empathy involves two distinct actions or processes. The first is the capacity to mentally step into someone else's shoes, and sense what they are experiencing and feeling. The second, to modify one's own behaviour accordingly, arguably is where Hogan's moral component comes in. A clever psychopath knows how to behave in an empathetic manner, without actually harbouring a shred of empathetic impulse. We're all aware of less extreme cases. Salespeople can be finely attuned to empathy and employ it to their own advantage. But with true empathy, a person is capable of assessing someone else's condition or state of mind, and then asking themselves what the morally appropriate action should be. *What should I do that responds to or respects the needs of the other?*

One might think that identifying highly empathetic people like Sheila would be a matter of tallying up empathetic responses or acts, like a cribbage score. But things get pretty interesting in empathy studies when researchers have searched instead for a constellation of telltale personality traits. Don't look for empathetic people solely through selfless gestures, their findings tell us. Look instead for an assortment of traits—even if those traits don't appear to have anything to do with empathy per se.

Hogan's empathy scale was based on sixty-four self-reported measures. Traits associated with high degrees of empathy included low anxiety, self-acceptance, lack of authoritarian tendencies, and extroversion.[7] In a 1973 study with Esther Grief, Hogan found that the three most significant factors in empathy were even-tempered disposition, social ascendancy, and humanistic socio-political attitudes.[8] The authors of a landmark 1983 paper similarly identified four psychologically distinct components: social self-confidence, even temperedness, sensitivity, and nonconformity.[9]

The inclination to nonconformity is particularly intriguing. A high scorer in nonconformity "is someone who is unconventional, innovative, and politically liberal and who prefers unstructured, ambiguous, and novel situations."[10] Adjectives with a high correlation with empathy included "not shy," "assertive," "outgoing," "cheerful," "good-natured," "caring," "emotional," "rebellious," and "experimenting." A strong negative correlation was found with shyness, personal distress, self-control, rule attunement, and agreeableness. We can interpret agreeableness in this context as being a tag-along, a get-along, someone who doesn't rock the boat, who defers to the opinions of others.

People who rate high in empathy thus have a fascinating, even contradictory, mixture of traits: individualistic, outgoing, and nonconformist, and yet they are attuned to the experiences, perspectives, and needs of others. They are highly self-confident, very much their own person, and uninterested in aligning themselves with crowds or the status quo. That quality on its own could make for an overbearing and insensitive person, but people with strong empathy ratings are able to divine what others feel, internalize those feelings as if they are their own, and, most important, act upon them appropriately. We seem to be in the presence of individuals with a heightened perception of other individuals, and while we can imagine them working in collectives, their strengths are at the level of the one-to-one: of grasping what it means to be another human being. As self-confident individualists, they're not antisocial: on the contrary, the ability to understand and treat others as if they were themselves is a powerful binding agent for society.

By now, anyone who knows Sheila Kussner has begun to nod at the many boxes she checks in the structure of empathy. Confident?

Check. Independent and strong-minded? Check, check. Cheerful, good-natured, and caring? Check, check, check. Rebellious? A big check. If Sheila ever shied from challenging the status quo, nothing she has accomplished would have come to pass.

The question posed by many who know Sheila, as we have seen, is how this remarkable personality came to be. (Although not everyone is curious. As one friend says, laughing, "I just remember what a rabbi said about miracles. You don't question them. You just go with them.") The presumption is that Sheila could not have been born that way: some thing, or things, in the course of her life must have nudged, guided, or even jolted her onto a trajectory of responding so determinedly to the needs of others.

The nature-versus-nurture question surrounding empathy is crucial to anyone who hopes that we can nurture a new generation of Sheilas, rather than sit back with fingers crossed and wait for even one new Sheila to be born. In 2018, a team of psychiatric researchers, employing genetic data gathered by the company 23andMe, proposed that two genes do play some hereditary role in low "Empathy Quotient" (EQ) scores for several psychiatric conditions, and that genetics could account for about eleven per cent of variation in EQ results in the 23andMe data.[11] They also confirmed what other studies had determined: that women tend to be more empathetic than men, and that the female advantage increases with age. But genetics could not explain those gender differences, and the researchers thought that education and socialization, or "postnatal learning," could be in part at play.[12] Which takes us to Robert Hogan's ideas in

1969 about empathy and moral development. He was confident that even someone with a deprived upbringing could avoid delinquency by learning to recognize the existence of the rights of others and adopting the moral point of view.

We can be fairly confident that empathy is taught, nurtured, and consciously employed, as part of the basic tool kit of a social being. Individuals can get by with a bare minimum of empathy, but societies rely on most of us having some empathy and a few among us having a surfeit of it. And those with a surfeit of it are a powerful force for increasing empathy in society. "I tell people I went to Sheila University," says Jeannette Valmont. People volunteer that being around Sheila makes them want to be a better person. They consciously model their own behaviour on hers, even if it is something as basic as responding to favours and kindness with personal notes. Her actions delineate a much broader landscape of possibilities of individual action than people might have recognized. Individuals who already might consider themselves empathetic and responsive will say to themselves, "I can go further." Sheila's empathy is also inspiring in that it defies the self-defeating containment of "Well, what can you do?" When she senses someone's need, she does not accept institutional or social barriers. She finds ways through or around them.

When we come upon someone like Sheila with a supercharged state of empathy and wonder, "How did they get this way?" we suspect that their upbringing moulded them, and that formative experiences into adulthood shaped their personalities. We can tease the answer out of the long arc of someone's life experiences, but we also need to account for the experiences of their family and community, because those spaces are where the socializing does (or does not) happen. In some ways, we become who we are before we are even on this earth, because of what our families and mentors first go through and bring to the process of shaping us. The nurturing roots that help make us can go deeper than we might even be aware, and for Sheila Kussner, the verifiable foundation of who she is lies in a surprising place and time.

CHAPTER FOUR

Golden Opportunities

In the winter of 1895–96, two Jewish peddlers, recent immigrants from Eastern Europe, could be seen on the snow-strewn streets of Charlottetown, Prince Edward Island. The older man was manoeuvring a pushcart through the ice and slush, while the younger man had command of a horse and wagon. We don't know precisely when they arrived in Canada, nor can we say with absolute certainty where they came from, but we do know their names and ages, and that they were father and son. Managing the cart was Abraham Golden, who was fifty-two. Urging the horse and wagon through the provincial capital's messy streets was his twenty-year-old son, Myer (Meyer; Mier). They were, respectively, Sheila Kussner's paternal great-grandfather and grandfather. They had secured peddlers' licences—ten dollars for Abraham, on foot; twenty for Myer, with the horse and cart—from Prince Edward Island in August 1895.[13]

The fact that Jews of any name or profession were active in Prince Edward Island in the late nineteenth and early twentieth centuries was all but unknown until Joseph B. Glass showed a professional interest. A geographer and former professor at the Hebrew University of Jerusalem, Glass emigrated to Canada and taught at Centennial College in Toronto from 2009 to 2016. After moving to Prince Edward Island, he began delving into the unexplored history of Jews in the province. "I found that nothing had been written about them," he told CBC in 2018. "All together there was about two paragraphs."[14] Thanks to Glass's interest, and much additional sleuthing in census and other genealogical records, we now know something that comes as complete news to Sheila Kussner: that her paternal grandfather and great-grandfather had been peddlers in the island province, and that her father had spent some of his earliest years there.

Abraham and Myer Golden were part of a mass migration of Jews out of Eastern Europe that began in earnest in the late nineteenth century. Between 1881 and 1914, some two million left the Pale of Settlement, the western frontier of the Tsarist Russian Empire that stretched from the Black Sea north to the Baltic Sea and incorporated in whole or in part nations that we know today as Ukraine, Poland, Lithuania, and Belarus. Jews were only allowed to live in the Pale under various strictures that limited education, movement, and profession, and that in most cases barred them from larger cities and some agricultural areas. They became people of small towns or villages, *shtetls*, with little economic opportunity.

From 1881 to 1884, Jews in the Pale suffered the first widespread antisemitic attacks on people and property called pogroms, which set off the exodus. While most of the Jews who left the Pale headed for the United States, many opted for Canada; they came as well from other Eastern European regions outside the Pale, including the Austro-Hungarian Empire and Romania. In Canada, Montreal became the main destination, and the city's Jewish population began to soar, doubling to 814 people between 1871 and 1881, then tripling, to about 2,500, by 1891.

As Pierre Anctil has explained, Eastern European Jews who emigrated to Montreal "had a very particular socio-economic profile which distinguished them from other immigrants in the city. They mainly came from small towns in the Russian Empire where Jews had traditionally been intermediaries between the rural population and the dominant classes. They were principally city dwellers who had for several centuries occupied a special position within the overall economy of Tsarist Russia. In the shtetl, Jews were tradesmen and artisans; they brought goods from the surrounding farms, sold manufactured goods in distant industrial centres, and sometimes administered large farms on behalf of absent landowners." They also had "a literacy rate that was considerably above average and they spoke several languages fluently. These very deeply entrenched markers of cultural identity were to become the defining characteristics of the future Canadian Jewish population."[15]

The documentary record for Eastern European Jews in Canada in the late nineteenth and early twentieth centuries is spotty and often contradictory. Spellings of names vary, as do birth years, places of birth, and years of emigration, especially in census records. Individuals also wander in and out of city directories, but just because a directory fails to record them in a particular year does not mean that they were not in fact there. For Abraham and

Myer Golden, various census records give stated years of emigration ranging from 1891 to an impossible 1903, while their nationality or country of origin ranges literally all over the map of eastern Europe. Sometimes they are Austrian (a probable reference to the Austro-Hungarian Empire), and at other times they are German. But there are consistent mentions of Romania, including the peddlers' licences of 1895—Romania, in fact, is given not only as their origin, but as their present address. And while some census records indicate they arrived in Canada as early as 1891, it seems possible that Abraham, his wife Kanne, and at least one offspring, Myer, arrived not long before the peddler's licences were secured, and headed directly for Prince Edward Island.[16]

Why they did so could be explained by the presence of another Romanian Jewish immigrant—Albert (Alter) "Goldin," who appears in the 1901 census as a Jewish merchant on lot 58 in East Queen's County, east of Charlottetown, with a wife, Rebeka, and four children. Born in 1866, Albert could have been a younger brother or a cousin of Abraham. Census records tell us he arrived in Canada in 1886 or 1887, and that his future wife, Rebeka, followed a few years later from Romania. They probably married around 1890, when Rebeka was nineteen and Albert was twenty. Their first two children were born in Ontario, in 1892, and in Quebec, in 1893. A third child arrived in P.E.I., in 1895, placing Albert and Rebeka in the province at precisely the time Abraham and his son Myer secured their first peddler's licences there.

Jewish peddlers begin to appear in Prince Edward Island licence records in the mid-1870s, but their most active period was from the 1890s, when the Goldens arrived, until 1914.[17] Joseph B. Glass has noted that almost all the fifty-five licenced Jewish peddlers he has identified were men. Their ages ranged from seventeen to six-ty-six; some were single, others married with children, and almost all were born outside Canada. Some lived on the island; others made repeated visits for several years. Some travelled in pairs or groups, using a town as their base and dividing the territory between them-selves. For a few years in the 1890s, Abraham and Myer Golden fit the pattern of men working together in a particular territory, and only living on the island for part of the year. We don't know what they dealt in—we have no idea for any of the Jewish peddlers on the island—but Myer's horse and wagon suggests he would have been able to transport more goods than his father, and venture further afield. We can imagine him engaging in the sort of two-way trade other Jewish peddlers in North America were known to pursue, car-rying odds-and-ends goods into the countryside and returning with produce from farmers to sell in town. Perhaps there was a connec-tion to exploit with Albert Golden, the merchant in neighbouring East Queens. As Glass notes, "Jewish peddlers were often connected through familial relations and business networks."[18]

Something else is important to remember: a peddler, however humble, was a public-facing trade. It required someone who could make deals, buy and sell, and in the process engage with others, very often strangers, and hope to make repeat customers of them. A peddler had to build and manage relationships in which people saw value, in selling to as well as buying from him.

Being an Eastern European Jew with a pushcart or wagon of goods in late nineteenth-century Prince Edward Island could not have been easy work. Clearly, it was not always profitable. As Glass has shown, licence records are full of individuals who tried for a season or two and then moved on. He notes that Jews endured slurs about being filthy and carrying lice, and they were generally accused of dishonesty; some P.E.I. merchants placed newspaper advertisements alleging Jews traded in fake or inferior goods. Even P.E.I. novelist Lucy Maude Montgomery piled on. In *Anne of Green Gables* (1908), a peddler, a German Jew, calls at Green Gables, and as Anne confesses to Aunt Marilla, he had

> a big box full of very interesting things and he told me he was working hard to make enough money to bring his wife and children out from Germany. He spoke so feelingly about them that it touched my heart. I wanted to buy something from him to help him in such a worthy object. Then all at once I saw the bottle of hair dye. The peddler said it was warranted to dye any hair a beautiful raven black and wouldn't wash off. In a trice I saw myself with beautiful raven-black hair and the temptation was irresistible. But the price of the bottle was seventy-five cents and I had only fifty cents left out of my chicken money. I think the peddler had a very kind heart, for he said that, seeing it was me, he'd sell it for fifty cents and that was just giving it away. So I bought it, and as soon as he had gone I came up here and applied it with an old hairbrush as the directions said. I used up the whole bottle, and oh, Marilla, when I saw the dreadful color it turned my hair I repented of being wicked, I can tell you. And I've been repenting ever since.[19]

Thanks to the deceit of a stereotypical Jewish peddler, Anne's red hair was now a hideous green.

Abraham and Myer Golden both secured fresh peddler's licences in Prince Edward Island, good for one year, in June 1896. Myer identified himself as living in Charlottetown. While Abraham's residence was again given as Romania, he had established a second base of operations. In 1897, he appeared for the first time in the Montreal directory as a peddler at 1 Theatre Lane.

Ashkenazic Jews had already been in Montreal and thriving for decades by the time Abraham Golden arrived in Montreal. They had a sometimes-uneasy relationship with Montreal's much smaller, established Jewish community, whose members tended to be wealthier; more Anglicized, with ties to England; and more religious. As Anctil has noted, "Jews of British origin and outlook found their world overrun by the large number of newcomers to Montreal."[20] Culturally, many of the established community members were "Spanish Jews," Sephardim from Atlantic Europe, and they adhered to the Orthodox tradition. The Ashkenazic newcomers spoke Yiddish and were a diasporic population of the Middle Ages in Germany and France that had migrated to Eastern Europe, and now to North America.

The first Ashkenazic synagogue in British North America, Shaar Hashomayim, was founded in Montreal by English, German, and Polish Jews in 1846. Known as the German Synagogue, it was located on Cadieux Street (formerly St. Constant, now de Bullion), near Vitré, east of St. Lawrence Boulevard. As the congregation's members prospered, they built a new *shul* farther north, toward Mount Royal, on prosperous McGill College Avenue, in 1886, a move that reflected geographically their upward mobility. The Ashkenazic Jews driven from the Pale by the pogroms of 1881–84 acquired the old shul and established B'Nai Jacob, which was known as the Russian Synagogue.[21]

Theatre Lane, where Abraham Golden first appears in a city directory, was in the original Ashkenazi neighbourhood, between Craig and Dorchester and close by the port. The streets that the Goldens walked and the buildings in which they lived, worshipped, and were educated have vanished. The neighbourhood is now buried beneath the Ville-Marie Expressway and the Palais des congrès, but in the 1890s, Theatre Lane was at the heart of the growing immigrant Jewish community. Just north of Theatre Lane, on St. Urbain near La Gauchetière, the Hebrew religious school, United Talmud Torahs, was established in 1896. The park called Dufferin Square, on the northeast corner of Dorchester Street and Chénéville Street, was where the community gathered, to "hear the latest news, look for work, and read the newspapers."[22] On the east side of the square was Dufferin School, where their children were educated. The Romanian Synagogue, Beth David, was on Chénéville, near the square.

Across St. Lawrence Boulevard, on St. Elizabeth Street, a few doors north of Craig, was the Baron de Hirsch Institute. Jews of all denominations in the city had long recognized the need for charitable support of newcomers from Eastern Europe and had founded the local Hebrew Philanthropic Society in 1847 and formally established the Young Men's Hebrew Benevolent Society (YMHBA) in 1870. In 1891, the YMHBA secured a gift from the Paris-based, Bavarian-born Baron de Hirsch through his Jewish Colonization Association, which aimed to aid Russian Jews in establishing themselves, both in the city and as agricultural settlers in western Canada. As a result, when Abraham Golden arrived in Montreal, the YMBHA building on St. Elizabeth Street was now known as the Baron de Hirsch Institute and was providing free language lessons to newcomers of all ages, including, perhaps, Abraham and his family.

Other members of the Golden family may have been on hand at the turn of the century. In 1903, Morris and Moses Goldman appear in the city directory as tailors on lower Chénéville. Moses at least is captured in the 1901 census living in the neighbourhood; he gives his age as twenty-one, his place of origin as Romania, and his year of immigration as 1894, when he would have been fourteen, which suggests he arrived with older relatives. And so it is very possible that Moses (and Morris) were additional sons of Abraham, or nephews, especially as we find Myer Golden living next door to Morris on Chénéville in 1904.

The Jewish community's growth continued at an exponential rate. Its population of some 2,500 in 1891 (already up from about 800 in 1881) reached 7,000 by 1901. Before the century had turned, the community was expanding north, at first to "Uptown" and later Mile End, following northward a corridor of streets around St. Urbain. "Uptown" (distinct from "Uptowners," the name given to wealthier, established Jews who had moved into the prosperous neighbourhoods of Montreal's Anglo-Scot elites) lay between Dorchester and Ontario streets (the Baron de Hirsch Institute relocated there to a new building, on Bleury Street north of Ontario, in 1901). In 1898, we find Abraham listed as a peddler on Leduc Lane, which ran east off St. Dominique Street, south of Ontario, a location that has long since been consumed by a large block of lowrise apartments.[23] Some Jewish peddlers in Montreal were *klappers*, door-to-door salesmen. Others were custom peddlers, who repped a particular merchant, and Abraham may have been doing so for a local grocer, J.W. Bloom.[24]

In 1898, we also find Abraham's son Myer in Montreal; his second P.E.I. peddler's licence, like that of his father, had expired in June 1897. On March 20, 1898, Myer, who would turn twenty-one that October, married at the Russian Synagogue, B'nai Jacob, nineteen-year-old Leah (Leia, Lilly) Schwartz, who was almost certainly a neighbour on Leduc Lane. The daughter of Judah Schwartz and Chaick (Chaie) Berman, she had arrived from Galicia, in the Austro-Hungarian Empire on the frontier of the Russian Pale, in 1896.[25] On October 26, 1899, Myer and Leah Golden celebrated the arrival of their first of five children. Jacob, better known as Jack or Jake, was Sheila Kussner's father.

The young family was living at 375 Cadieux, up the street from B'Nai Jacob, but they did not remain in Montreal for long. The couple returned with their infant son to Charlottetown, where Myer made a step up from peddling to junk dealing. (He may already have been using his horse and cart in his earlier years in Charlottetown to pursue the junk trade.) His father, Abraham, also made a return to P.E.I., securing another peddler's licence for June 1899 through January 1900 while giving his place of residence as Montreal. What happened to Abraham Golden after that is unclear,[26] but Myer and Leah were captured in the 1901 census in Charlottetown with a growing family: there was now an infant daughter, five-month-old Ida, born in P.E.I.

Life in Charlottetown must have been extremely isolating for recent Jewish immigrants from Romania, especially after the bustle of Montreal's rapidly growing community. There was no Jewish community to speak of in Prince Edward Island, let alone a synagogue. How long Myer and Leah stayed in Charlottetown is unknown. Another son, Moses, arrived in 1903, and he may have been born in Montreal, as we find Myer next door to the tailor Morris Golden in the 1904 city directory in the old neighbourhood, on Chénéville near Craig. Two more children, Abraham (1906) and Gurtie (1909) followed.[27]

The family returned to a Jewish community in Montreal that experienced astonishing growth, fuelled in large part by the failed Russian Revolution of 1905 and the oppression of Jews that immediately followed in the Pale. By 1911, the city's Jewish population reached 28,000. The community had not been uniform before; however, thanks to the exodus from Tsarist Russia, in addition to the community's cultural and religious diversity it was now teeming with an array of political voices: socialists, anarchists, Zionists, anti-Zionists, and atheists, to name but a few. But as fractious as it could be, an effectively new community arose, and the Goldens were on hand to witness it, and help shape it.

CHAPTER FIVE

Building a New Society

As Pierre Anctil has written, "it was as if the 1905 revolution in Imperial Russia had given birth to the Eastern European Jewish community in Montreal. It was in the context of the intense battle to liberate the masses of Jews in Eastern Europe that the first attempts were made to establish an organizational network among Montreal Yiddish speakers." Before this influx from Eastern Europe, Anctil notes, there had been synagogues and genuine charitable organizations in the city, but they had operated "very discreetly, in the manner of British Jewry. With the arrival of immigrants from the Russian Empire, a new spirit of ideological and cultural affirmation spilled over into the public sphere thereby affecting other segments of society." A "revolutionary fervour and assiduous desire to improve the society in which they had chosen to live," Anctil has observed, distinguished Montreal Jews from other immigrant groups that arrived in Canada at the same time.[28]

"Across the country," Allan Levine has written, "Jewish communities—large, medium, and small—quickly learned that no one was responsible for the welfare of their members except the communities themselves."[29] There was no social safety net, but for the one that they could weave. The Montreal community's activities went far beyond the simple charity of haves providing for the have-nots. Its members found collective solutions, and often extended the benefits beyond the community.

One motivating factor, Anctil notes, arose from religion, in the concept of *tikkun olam*, to perfect or repair the world. And already, the Jewish community of Montreal that predated the late-nineteenth-century surge from Eastern Europe had been motivated in founding philanthropic organizations by the obligation of Jews to share their wealth (*tsedaka*) and perform good deeds (*mitsvot*). Another factor was secular and political. As Simon Belkin has argued, Canadian Jewry "became fertile ground for the boundless activism of the working class and socialist and Zionist sympathizers. Passionate and enthusiastic, the Jewish people never hesitated to respond to a call to action at any time, in order to build a new society and to transform Canadian Jewish society, Canada in general, and the entire planet, too."[30]

Myer and Leah Golden were back from Prince Edward Island and living in Montreal's old neighbourhood of Jewish immigrant arrivals by 1904, at the lower end of Chénéville, a few doors from the Montreal Street Railway stables. Next door was a tailor, Morris Golden, who was probably Myer's brother or cousin.[31] For more than a decade, the couple and their children roamed through various Montreal addresses, when they didn't disappear altogether from the city directory. Unless Myer left the city for spells, the family must have made a common roof with relatives.[32] We do find "Mayer" Golden in 1906, living at 340 Cadieux, north of Duluth Avenue East, and employed as an "operator," which probably meant a job at a machine in one of the garment factories where about thirty-five per cent of Montreal's Jews found work.

Myer must have done what he could to support his family, enduring the severe recession of 1907–08, when Canada's gross domestic product fell almost eight per cent, and the downturn that followed in 1912. He was a common labourer for at least two years, in 1910 and 1911, probably performing such menial work as digging building foundations or toiling in the nearby port area.[33] The circumstances would have been discouraging for a man in his mid-thirties who was married with five children and had been in the country for perhaps fifteen years. As Israel Medres would recount, the goal of Montreal's recent Jewish immigrants was to move up and out of (if not avoid entirely) the ranks of tailors and other garment workers. A peddler in the city could aspire to open their own store or even become a wholesaler. Alternatively, a peddler could take to the countryside, and after working there for only a few months, could "settle down in a small town, open a store, buy a house, and earn a comfortable living. On Rosh Hashana and Yom Kippur, he could come to the city, buy a seat in a synagogue, and be 'all right!'"[34] But things had not turned out "all right" for Myer Golden. There had been no progress from peddler to home-owning storekeeper, only a short stint as a junk dealer in Prince Edward Island. He was, yet again, starting fresh in Montreal, only now he was competing for employment amidst a fresh wave of immigrants (and not only within the greatly expanding Jewish community) in grim economic years.

Newcomers like Myer by and large were filling the rolls of low-wage labourers, and Montreal's large underclass faced an array of challenges exacerbated by their living and working conditions and limited financial resources. It was hard for any low-wage worker to secure a loan, but for members of the Jewish community, anti-semitism was undoubtedly a factor in denying them services from established commercial sources. In response, two Jewish co-operative loan societies were formed in 1911, led by the Hebrew Free Loan Association; another eight followed in 1912, and fourteen more in 1913. By 1929, on the eve of the Depression, at least fifty-nine Jewish co-operatives were active in Montreal.[35]

Health too was a major focal point of community self-help. In 1900, the Baron de Hirsch Institute began expanding its relief activities under a new charter, and opened a medical department that employed doctors who could, if necessary, visit poor Jewish patients in their homes. In 1912, the institute opened a proper clinic, the Herzl Hospital and Dispensary (later simply the Herzl Dispensary), the first step toward a hospital supported by and serving (although not exclusively) the Jewish community.[36] As well, in the first decade of the century, the community began to create sick benefit societies, which would provide a doctor's care, weekly benefits if a member or "brother" was too ill to work, and, if things went very badly, arrange a funeral.[37] A dozen such co-operatives existed by 1911; the oldest, Hebrew Sick Benefit Society (HSBS), was organized in 1882 by Yiddish printer A.L. Kaplansky (who also worked for the Baron de Hirsch Institute). For six dollars a year, HSBS members were eligible for sick benefits of five dollars a week, and a death benefit of two hundred twenty-five dollars (one hundred twenty-five dollars in the event of their wife's death).[38] Other medical initiatives of the Jewish community included the Mount Sinai Sanatorium for tuberculosis patients, established in the Laurentian community of Sainte-Agathe-des-Monts, and the Hebrew Maternity Hospital.

The maternity hospital's formation was a harbinger of Sheila Kussner's efforts in creating Hope & Cope and the McGill department of oncology, in that it owed its existence to the indefatigable efforts of one community member, Taube Kaplan. Precious little is known about her, but the 1911 census tells us that in 1906, Taube had arrived at the age of fifty-one from Vilnius in what is now Lithuania with her sixty-one-year-old husband Jacob (Yaakov) as part of the fresh wave of Jewish emigrants after the failed Russian Revolution of 1905. Taube left behind three adult children in Vilnius, and this may have been a subsequent marriage. Jacob Kaplan was a rabbi in the literal sense of being a teacher rather than a congregational leader, although he was affiliated at some point with Chevra Shaas (Spanish and Portuguese Synagogue).[39] Jacob struggled to provide for the couple: in 1911, he reported working at home forty hours a week, fifty-two weeks of the year, and making four hundred and sixteen dollars, which was less than the average labourer's wage. *Rebbetzin* (a rabbi's wife) Kaplan helped make ends meet by teaching Hebrew and religion for a few hours a week.

One reason we know so little about women like Taube Kaplan is that wives of "downtowner" rabbis who served the Eastern European and Russian immigrant communities were rarely mentioned in either English or Yiddish newspapers.[40] But for the most part, Taube Kaplan remains elusive because she consistently turned down honours and other official positions, preferring to work in the Jewish tradition of *matan b'seter*, giving in secret. She went about her works quietly and diligently, choosing "for her life's mission the creation and extension of facilities for Montreal Jewry and probably contributed more than any other individual, at least in terms of effort, to the fulfillment of that dream."[41] She began her charitable work as a fundraiser and a member of the coalition that founded the Herzl Hospital and Dispensary. She then mounted an ambitious plan of her own to create a maternity hospital for the community. Infant mortality rates in Montreal were appalling—in 1900, one in four babies died before reaching their first birthday, a rate thought to be exceeded only by Kolkata, India—and prenatal care for poor Jewish mothers was almost non-existent.

The Kaplans always lived in the heart of the old immigrant Jewish neighbourhood, in flats on Sanguinet, de Montigny, St. Elizabeth, and Cadieux, and Taube went door to door among people no better off than she was, "collecting pennies, nickels, dimes, and quarters from anyone who had anything to spare."[42] With the aid of several other fundraisers, and the support of some influential figures, including James Goodall, who had been named professor of obstetrics and gynecology at McGill in 1912, she was able to collect seven thousand dollars, enough for the down payment on a house at 892 Cadieux Street.[43] There, the Hebrew Maternity Hospital of Montreal opened in November 1916.

Taube Kaplan was an archetype of pragmatic activism in Montreal's Jewish community, as well as a pioneer in civic action by women in its Orthodox community. The history of the Jewish General Hospital says that she was largely unaware of all that would be required to found a maternity hospital when she started her campaign, but we know so little about her life that her grasp of logistics should not be dismissed entirely. It should be noteworthy that she succeeded in creating the maternity hospital when an initiative mounted by two young doctors to raise funds for a general hospital had failed in 1907.[44] There is also a distinct echo of this assessment of Rebbetzin Kaplan in attitudes Sheila Kussner would face in founding Hope & Cope: while Taube Kaplan might have known what she wanted to accomplish, she might not have understood the nitty-gritty realities of the solution. Nevertheless, while poor, Taube Kaplan plainly was educated, singularly determined, and undaunted by the fact that her fundraising was trying to amass thousands of dollars through donations of pocket change. Having recognized a need, Rebbetzin Kaplan managed to network among elites and find influential supporters, including experts like Dr. Goodman, while at the same time convincing community members no better off than she was to contribute to the cause. In fleeing Vilnius, she had come to a better world, but in some ways, it was a shockingly broken world, and she did what she could to repair it. She would not be the last.

By 1910, Myer Golden had at least been able to follow the steady northerly migration of the city's immigrant Jews and reached 1260 Cadieux in St-Jean-Baptiste Ward, east of Mount Royal and north of Duluth Avenue. Myer Golden may have re-established himself as a peddler in 1912, but for the next four years, he disappeared from the city directory for all but one year, surfacing briefly as a tailor in a home on nearby Rivard, south of Duluth, in 1915. The short stretch of Rivard between Roy and Duluth became the Goldens' home, as Myer found regular work, first as a tailor in 1915, then once more as peddler in 1917, then, finally, as a steadily employed operator in 1919.[45] Although living further north than the Kaplans, Myer Golden and his family doubtless would have known Rebbetzin Kaplan, and perhaps they contributed what nickels or dimes they could spare to her community medical causes.[46]

It was about the time of Myer Golden's struggles to support his family during the First World War that his eldest son, Jack, began to make his own way in the world. At sixteen, around 1915, Jack secured a clerk's position at the Imperial Life Assurance Company of Canada in the Liverpool and London and Globe Building on the Place d'Armes.

Israel Medres would describe how insurance became part of the life of new immigrants. Sick-benefit society meetings were a way for a newcomer to meet more established members of the community, to hear about (and be urged into) more profitable lines of work. "It was always fascinating to hear how the brothers earned a living as they were engaged in a variety of occupations. One was a sack salesman; a second peddled bananas and vegetables; a third travelled to the countryside to purchase animal hides, chickens, and eggs; a fourth was a sewing machine salesman; a fifth ran a junk shop in Point St. Charles or a second-hand shop on Craig Street or St. Antoine Street; a sixth was a grocer."[47]

As Medres explained, a newcomer to the country would meet at the society "one brother who appeared more intelligent, aristocratic, educated, and Canadianized than the rest." He was an insurance agent. "He made clear to the immigrant that a brother in the society [who is] provided with sick benefits and cemetery plots, is nonetheless alone and vulnerable without an insurance policy." The agent would explain the necessity of life insurance, which was a completely alien concept (as so many things were) to someone newly arrived

from Eastern Europe or the Pale. "It was difficult for the immigrant
to refuse the insurance agent who had spoken with such friendliness
and persistence ... After having obtained the insurance policy, he felt
more at ease, secure, protected, and connected to the new life in the
new world."[48]

Medres might as well have been describing a young Jack Golden.
Moving into sales, he became Imperial Life's most productive agent.
In addition to winning every top award that Imperial Life could
bestow (including its National Quality Award, twenty-three times),
he was the company's leading agent in every year but three between
1932 and 1961. During his hottest streak, he sold more than $25,000
worth of insurance every month, for thirty consecutive months, a
performance the company said was a world record.[49] The family of
Romanian Jews who had arrived in Canada in the 1890s had at last
made their great leap forward in its third generation, in Jack Golden.
Sheila Kussner remembers little about her grandfather, Myer, only
that he was something of a loner and lived on his own in an apartment in Mile End, on Avenue du Parc. She does recall her father's
generosity in supporting other members of his family.

In December 1924, just as he was starting out as an insurance
salesman, Jack Golden married Sophia (Sophie) Saxe at B'nai
Jacob (which had relocated to Mile End). In 1908, around the age
of eleven, Sophia had emigrated from Lutsk, now in northwestern
Ukraine, as part of the great Jewish out-migration from the turbu-
lent Russian Empire. Records for the rest of her family are elusive;
her mother, Sheive Schwartz, had died by the time of her marriage;
her father, Nathan, was a printer with the *Montreal Star*, and Sheila
well remembers visiting him often. "He was adorable. I was close
to him." One senses an essential independence and capability in

what little evidence remains from Sophia's early days in Canada.[50] A border-crossing document at Vermont in 1918 finds her heading to New York to work as a clerk for six months.

Jack and Sophia had two sons, Clifford and Ronald, followed by Sheila in August 1932. As Jack prospered, the family moved out of Mile End to a large semi-detached home on Beloeil Avenue, in nearby Outremont. It was a testament to the opportunities Canada afforded that a man who had spent his infancy in Prince Edward Island while his Romanian Jewish father tried to make a go as a junk dealer was now raising a family in one of Canada's better residential neighbourhoods and building a career as the greatest insurance salesman in his company's history.

But perhaps the most remarkable member of that couple was Sophia Saxe. "Her mother was incredible," says Sheila's long-standing friend, Charlotte Colson (née Stilman), who has known Sheila since she was twelve. "I loved her mother, very dearly. She was very healthy, and I don't mean just physically. She was healthy in everything she did. A very fine, very strong woman, who ran a beautiful home. There was no nonsense with Sophie. It used to be very good, going there. And her father was a dynamic insurance salesman. You couldn't beat Jack Golden in anything."

Sheila loved her father, but she was much closer to her mother. Jack Golden was a peculiar combination of gregarious salesman and self-contained, private individual. "He worked hard," says Sheila. "He was eccentric, not sociable, but he was smart, and a very good insurance man." He had a strict routine that made him somewhat removed from the family's daily life: up at five, out the door at six, and once home at the end of the working day, in bed around eight. He was busy providing while Sophie was busy nurturing.

Sophie's influence was felt in the closeness that would mark Sheila and Marvyn's household. "Our family was very much immediate family, and some extended family," says Janice, their elder daughter. "Joanne and I came from very much a family-oriented family." Sophie, says their younger daughter, Joanne, "was anchored: very smart, stable, and strong, and regal, like a queen. She was calm, and very quiet, where my grandfather was very talkative, like my mom and like me. My mom has a bit of Grandma, but there's quite a lot of her father in the sense that my mom can be a bit eccentric, sometimes off-kilter a little bit," she says, laughing. "My grandfather was also very generous, and my mother is the same way." Jack and Sophie Golden loved their children fiercely. According to Lillian Vineberg, Sheila's brothers could be a handful, but Sheila was "a perfect child," the delight of her parents.

For the Goldens and other Jewish immigrants that transformed Montreal, getting into the country had been the easy part, as the country threw open its doors to about 150,000 Jews between 1901 and 1927 alone. By 1921, seven per cent of Montreal's population was Jewish, and Yiddish was the city's third most-spoken language. But after 1927, the community's growth through immigration was throttled back, as nativism and antisemitism began to play their hands in federal policy. Restrictive immigration laws ensured that only about 5,000 more Jews arrived in the country between 1933 and 1939. Already, before the First World War, Montreal and McGill University was a global centre for eugenicist thinking, and antisemitism within the city's Anglo-Scots elites was most baldly expressed by quotas on admissions of Jewish students at McGill, including medicine. De facto segregation was most keenly felt throughout the city's medical system. Nursing training for Jewish women was all but non-existent, and some of the city's most prominent hospitals, including the Montreal General and the Royal Victoria, did not allow Jewish doctors (with very few exceptions) to practice there.

The most ambitious project yet undertaken by Montreal's Jewish community was the creation of a general hospital—something capable of serving far more patients in far more ways than the Herzl Dispensary and offering far more career opportunities to Jewish professionals than the establishment medical community was willing to extend. As noted, an early effort to fund and organize a hospital by two doctors had failed in 1907. After the maternity hospital opened, Taube Kaplan began a door-to-door fundraising campaign for an envisioned Neta Israel (The Plant of Israel) Hospital in 1917. At the same time, a hospital plan was being mounted by figures associated with the maternity hospital and the Montreal Clinical Society, a group founded by the city's Jewish physicians in 1923. In 1924, Rebbetzin Kaplan turned over more than seven thousand dollars that she had raised under the Neta Israel name to what became the Jewish General Hospital project and continued to fundraise for it. Her contribution was enormous: members of the Clinical Society in November 1924 pledged four thousand one hundred dollars, and Kaplan's infusion represented more than half of the monies or pledges in hand by December 10, 1924.[51] The momentum the hospital project now enjoyed was due in substantial part to Kaplan's tireless determination.

Still, those fourteen thousand dollars in December 1924 were scarcely a start on a project that would demand funding well into the six figures. An undertaking of such scale and importance would have to unite in a common cause a Jewish community that was fragmented into different synagogues, observances, economic and social classes, and neighbourhoods. A "Provisional Campaign Committee for a Jewish General and Maternity Hospital" was launched mainly by east-end citizens in 1928, with Dr. Max Wiseman its president. To broaden the project's support base, Wiseman's committee called a meeting for May 5, 1929, at the Baron de Hirsch Institute for all interested parties, including representatives of Jewish organizations across Montreal, "most notably synagogues, sick benefit societies, loan syndicates, the Clinical Society, and the Sir Herbert Samuel Society."[52] It was, according to Wiseman, a "fateful day." Allan Bronfman, who opened the meeting with an enthusiastic address, was essential to rallying support for the hospital plan among "Uptowners." A resolution to accept funding offers from loan syndicates, the maternity hospital, the Clinical Society, and the Herbert Samuel Society passed unanimously. Peter Bercovitch, a Jewish lawyer (and McGill graduate) who represented the east-end riding of Montréal-Saint-Louis in the provincial Liberal government of Louis-Alexandre Taschereau, told the crowd that it could probably count on his government to supply at least an initial two hundred thousand dollars. With an estimated total budget of five hundred thousand dollars, one hundred and thirty-five thousand dollars were left to fundraise, and the community was willing to take it on.

As Wiseman would recall: "I shall never forget that scene. Pent-up emotions were let loose. People who never met before shook hands. Women cried. East met West. It seemed that the unnatural demarcation of a barrier separating people into east and west had been completely wiped out."[53]

Defying the Great Depression, by August 1932, when Sheila was born, construction was underway in the city's west end on the Jewish General Hospital. In October 1934, a first-class, five-storey, 226-bed facility opened. For the Jewish community, it was so much more than a medical building. Its creation had given a fragmented community a common cause that would persist for generations. "The Jewish" became a point of convergence for charity and collaboration, not to mention a source of excellent care, for members of the Jewish community and beyond.

The Goldens became great supporters. Jack and Sophie Golden were among the more generous donors in 1944 through the Combined Jewish Appeal as the hospital prepared to expand—their one-hundred-dollar contribution had the purchasing power of about sixteen hundred dollars today. As well, Sophie Golden was a patroness of the Women's Auxiliary's Life Saving Fund, which in 1945 established an annual grant of one thousand dollars to defray costs of penicillin for non-paying ward patients and to subsidize work on the control and prevention of pneumonia. They had risen to the challenge of serving the community through the hospital, but they were soon looking to the hospital to serve them in unimaginable circumstances.

CHAPTER SIX

Making and Facing Choices

On November 9, 1999, Sheila Kussner delivered the keynote address for Choices, the annual women's event of the Federation Combined Jewish Appeal (CJA) at Congregation Shaar Hashomayim in Montreal's Westmount neighbourhood. Central to the Congregation's and the CJA's activities is *tikkun olam*, to perfect or repair the world through human action. It is a call to serve one's community, to act with kindness (*chesed*), to help those in need in the fulfilment of the value of *tsedaka* (justice and charity). For most anyone who had heard of Sheila Kussner—and it was almost impossible not to have heard of her in charitable circles in Montreal, within and beyond the Jewish community—she fulfilled *tikkun olam*, *chesed*, and *tsedaka* through her indefatigable dedication to improving cancer research, treatment, and counselling, foremost through Hope & Cope but also through other initiatives within the hospital, including palliative care. And then there were the many acts of kindness and charity that took up so much of her days in advocating on behalf of people seeking answers from the medical system.

Almost one thousand people were on hand to hear Sheila's address. Sheila had become a very public person, but she had never been at ease in delivering formal public addresses. She prepared the Choices keynote fastidiously, crafting a speech with her long-time collaborator, Hena Kon. Even after the speech was printed and ready for delivery, Sheila worked on it in minute detail, adjusting the wording with a pen, underlining where she needed to deliver emphasis, marking in the phrasing breaks, and repeatedly writing "slow" in the margin, a reminder not to allow her delivery to become a runaway train. By the time she was done preparing, she could deliver the speech by heart.

Kon provided the quote in her opening words, from Robert Frost's "The Road Not Taken": "Two roads diverged in a wood, and I— / I took the one less traveled by, / And that has made all the difference." It was a perfect choice for a speech that was intended to address choices, and it was freighted with multiple layers of meaning.

Sheila's speech was not what that audience was expecting. By 1999 Sheila was renowned as a fundraiser and as the driving force behind Hope & Cope. She had been asked several times to deliver this annual keynote, but had declined, not being especially fond of public speaking. Now that she had finally agreed, the audience was probably expecting an address that recited her achievements, that related the choice she had made to advance cancer research and care through charitable endeavours. Instead, the audience witnessed something so deeply affecting that it would remain with people for decades. Sheila chose to use the speech to address something that she had never done before in public. She chose to tell the substance of her own story, as a cancer survivor.

The essence of Sheila's story was not new. The fact that she was an amputee had been known to anyone who had read about her work in Israel in the 1970s counselling wounded soldiers. And in April 1995, a column in *Montreal Scene* had delivered the gist of Sheila's experience of being diagnosed with cancer as a child and losing her leg as a result. But neither the amputation nor the cancer were things she had ever dwelled on, or made the cornerstone of her public endeavours. It had been possible to read a lengthy profile of Sheila in *Canadian Jewish News* in 1983 that lauded her accomplishments as a fundraiser and with the recently founded Hope & Cope, and come across no mention of the cancer or the amputation. But in 1999, presented with the opportunity to speak before the large audience of Choices, at her own synagogue, Sheila decided that it was time to tell her story, with raw, heartfelt frankness. Sheila did not choose to have cancer; but she had chosen how she would respond to its consequences.

"I was very emotional," Sheila remembers, twenty-two years later, sitting at her kitchen table with Suzanne O'Brien as they examine the annotated draft of the speech. "I had to stop for a minute, then continue. You remember—" She looks at Suzanne, who had been there. Suzanne had only started working with and for Sheila at Hope & Cope two years before the keynote.

"People still reference this speech," says Suzanne. "They remember the emotion of the speech. They may not remember the story. They had never seen you be so personal."

"The first time," Sheila says. "The first and the last time."

"They were expecting a more—" Suzanne searches for the right word.

"Objective speech," Sheila fills in.

"I've talked to many people about it," Suzanne says. "People said, 'I have never heard Sheila talk with emotion.' This was a pivotal, a seminal moment. You had never spoken about your father and your mother in such personal terms."

Sheila agrees. "And never about myself. I've been asked to repeat the story, twice, and I've said no."

"It was a one-off moment," Suzanne says, "that you could not replicate, because you spoke from the heart. People remember that. They had a different take on you."

Sheila's other guest at the kitchen table then asks her to talk about it all over again, more deeply than she had been prepared to share with that large, astonished synagogue audience.

Sheila is fishing in a reservoir of memories some seventy-six years' deep, hoping to hook details that swim elusively through the murkier spaces between recollections that are sharp, bright, and firm. *I was not on the road. I was on the sidewalk, in front of the school.* The next day, she telephones, having gone back to that reservoir for another try. *I was not on the sidewalk. I was in the schoolyard.* She was alone because there was no one to help her.

This is clearly an unrehearsed story, something that has not been smoothed into a pat format through repeated telling. The most surprising part of this story may be the fact that Sheila steadfastly declined to tell it, in much of any detail, until that keynote speech in 1999. In an age of celebrity confessionals, of public figures leveraging details of their struggles to personal benefit, one might have expected that Sheila, in decades of selfless service to advancing cancer treatment and care, would have made her own story of cancer survival into an oft-told address. Instead, she had kept the details out of the limelight. People who had known her for years, even medical professionals, only knew that she had had cancer when she was young—some were not even sure what sort of cancer, or how old she was—and that she was an amputee as a result. Most of it is coming to light now, as she thinks deeply and methodically.

It was 1945, a Friday night, after school. She then reconsiders. It was a Friday, but Guy Drummond Elementary School was out for the summer. She had just finished grade seven. Germany had surrendered in May; Japan would follow, in August. It was a time so pivotal for Canada, the world, and Jewish communities the world over, as the horrors of the Holocaust emerged in full understanding. In late 1945, Montreal's Jewish community sent a delegation to Europe, to confront the scale of Nazi crimes. "Montreal Jews greeted the news of the destruction of their home communities with dismay and disbelief," Pierre Anctil has written. "They discovered that the cities and villages which many of them had left several decades earlier had been obliterated and their populations massacred ... The Holocaust had wiped out the living source of Eastern European Judaism, from which Jewish social and cultural life had modestly sprung at the foot of Mount Royal in the early years of the twentieth century. The branch of the Ashkenzic diaspora that had recently taken root on Canadian soil was stunned by the catastrophe."[54]

Sheila was twelve years old, her bat mitzvah behind her; her thirteenth birthday would be in late August. She was coming of age in a period of terrible losses, but also of hope. After a decade of global depression, a catastrophic world war, and the horror of the Holocaust, there might now be better times. In these times, given the devastating losses of Jewish communities in Europe, "the demographic centre of gravity of Jewry shifted to North America."[55] Montreal became a centre of Jewish life that no longer looked to the (obliterated) communities of the historic Pale for its cultural cues. And as a young girl now becoming a young woman, for Sheila there was all the excitement, the anticipation, of a life unfolding. High school was approaching, and hopefully then university. And there were the socials, dances, and dating; marriage; and motherhood. The changes could come with bewildering speed, but they were thrilling. That was what the troubled and yet hopeful summer of 1945 promised.

She wonders aloud: *Why was I at the school?* She had walked there, almost a kilometre from home, for some reason, that Friday. Was something going on at the school? She simply cannot recall. But she was there, by herself, in the schoolyard, on a summer evening in Outremont. A boy whose name she recalls with absolute certainty— *you don't have to name him, he felt terrible*—was chasing her, on his bicycle. She was running, to get away.

They collided. Sheila's right foot was caught in the spokes of one of the wheels. She went down on the schoolyard's hard asphalt.

From that moment, everything about her life would be different, and not in the way that a summer at the end of a war had promised to a girl about to turn thirteen. She would become different physically, to be sure, but also, to her own mind, in the very person she was. That was due to circumstance, but also to choice.

As a skater, Sheila was used to coming down hard on rinks and getting up again. But on that Friday night in the summer of 1945, after disentangling her foot from the spokes of the boy's bike on the playground of Guy Drummond Elementary School, she could not stand. Word reached Hymie Pascal, a friend of her parents who lived nearby. He tried to reach Sheila's parents, but they were out, visiting someone in hospital. Her brother, Clifford, arrived by bicycle; an ambulance was called, and she was whisked away to the Jewish General.

By the end of the Second World War, the stark, discriminatory divide in medicine that isolated the Jewish community from Montreal's medical establishment had begun to ease as the Jewish General was accepted as a first-class facility. In 1939, it became one of five area hospitals where McGill graduates could intern. The same year, Alton Goldbloom was appointed an assistant professor of pediatrics at McGill, and other Jewish doctors were soon being appointed lecturers. One of the Jewish General's innovations at war's end was its X-ray capabilities. Its X-ray room was thought to be the most sophisticated in Eastern Canada.[56] "The Jewish" boasted a mechanized, adjustable table that meant in fracture cases X-rays could be taken right in the operating room—the first of its kind in Canada—and a portable machine that allowed patients to be X-rayed in their beds.

An X-ray of Sheila's right ankle revealed multiple fractures. The attending physician set it improperly, which meant S.E. (Sal) Goldman, an orthopedic surgeon, was called in to reset it.[57] She remembers being hospitalized for ten days or more, before being allowed to go home. In the fall, she was back at Drummond Elementary, attending grade eight and anticipating the move to Strathcona Academy, the English-language high school a block from the Golden house.

While her right ankle healed without any problems, her left knee began to trouble her. She was developing a lump on its side, at the base of the femur, and a painful limp. While she was having her right ankle treated, no one had thought to check her left knee, because it wasn't giving her any problems. During the winter of 1945–46, her limp became so progressively worse that her mother took her to the family doctor. He thought a specialist should look at it because it wasn't getting any better.

As noted, the Goldens were great supporters of the Jewish General, but when it came to their daughter's health, they were going to seek out the best medical minds, wherever they happened to be. So Sophie took Sheila to Fraser Baillie Gurd, the city's most eminent surgeon, at Montreal General.

The Gurds were one of Montreal's great medical families. David Fraser Gurd graduated in medicine at McGill in 1879 and worked in the city as a family physician and obstetrician. His son, Fraser Baillie, trained at McGill and in Munich and served with Britain's Royal Army Medical Corps in the First World War. On his return to Montreal, Fraser B. Gurd became renowned as a trauma surgeon, specializing in fractures, and as a thoracic surgeon was an expert in chest infections and tuberculosis. He was appointed chair of McGill's department of surgery in 1944. It would have been difficult to think of anyone more authoritative in Montreal when it came to diagnosing Sheila's condition.

Fraser B. Gurd's son, Fraser N., served in Europe as a surgeon with the Canadian Armed Forces in the Second World War. After returning to Montreal in July 1945, Fraser N. found his father "remarkably unchanged." He had been slowed by arthritis in his hip but was performing "a large amount of major surgery and was happy as could be. In his pocket he still carried a large tin of Goldflake cigarettes—each day he smoked a full 'flat fifty'—and every night he took a pumice stone and scrubbed the nicotine stains from his fingers."[58] In June 1946, he would be named to a newly created position, surgeon-in-chief, at Montreal General.

Fraser B. Gurd was about sixty-three years old when Sophie took Sheila to see him. Sheila found him brusque, cold, not particularly concerned with bedside manner. After examining her troublesome knee with his nicotine-stained fingers, he delivered a diagnosis that would remain with her always. "You have a very sick daughter," he declared to her mother, in front of Sheila. "That's cancer."

Sophie Golden's reaction was a not uncommon one to such a devastating prognosis. On the way home in a cab (Sophie did not drive), she declared, "It's not true. That doctor, he doesn't know what he's talking about. It's silly." Mercifully, disbelief did not metastasize into denial. "We're going to get another doctor," Sophie announced.

The Goldens secured an appointment with Alfred Turner (A.T.) Bazin, a surgeon at the Royal Victoria. Bazin was even older than Fraser B. Gurd. He had graduated from McGill in 1894 and became a professor of surgery in 1924; he had taken a turn as chair of McGill's department of surgery in 1937–38. Sheila found him a much kindlier figure than Gurd. "He took a look, and right away, he knew," Sheila recalls. But the aging surgeon tried to be comforting, and at the same time thorough. "It may not be so serious," Bazin said to her mother. "Let's have a biopsy taken and see what it shows. It could be nothing." Those words, *could be nothing*, stayed with Sheila.

She was admitted to hospital for a large biopsy on the growth, and remained for some time—eighteen days, as she recalls. The results were devastating. It was as Gurd had already pronounced. She had a malignant, growing bone tumour at the base of her left femur, which if left untreated would kill her. The only possible treatment was ablation—amputation, above the knee.

Sheila's parents would not accept such a dire prognosis and treatment without exhausting every possible expert opinion. Because Jack Golden was a prominent insurance salesman, in the years before public health care in Canada, he had many connections in the medical world. He sent the biopsy results to several major international centres, Johns Hopkins in Baltimore among them. Six replies came, all by telegram, which underlined the urgency of the messages. The Montreal doctors were right, and the only solution indeed was amputation, which had to be done immediately.

Sheila had been diagnosed with osteogenic sarcoma, now better known as osteosarcoma. It is the most common form of bone cancer, but bone cancers overall are rare. In many ways, she fit the standard profile for this unusual malignancy. In a study of forty-six cases between 1955 and 1973 at UCLA Center for Health Sciences, osteosarcoma overwhelming appeared in patients between ages eleven and twenty, with a median age of sixteen; cases dropped off steeply after age eighteen. Most instances—twenty-eight in that study—involve the femur, with the cancer arising as the body went through a growth spurt during puberty. Sheila was exceptional only in that cases are more commonly seen in boys than in girls.

For some time, doctors suspected that such a tumour was associated with some previous trauma, like a fracture, and this was the case with Sheila: perhaps her tangled spill in the schoolyard of

Drummond Elementary had triggered the runaway growth of bone cells. But researchers would instead conclude that when a trauma like a fracture occurs, its treatment simply leads to the discovery of a pre-existing tumour. In a way, that is what had happened with Sheila. Her accident and fracture of her right ankle had made both Sheila and her family more sensitive to her physical condition, and when she began to limp, they suspected that the bump on her left knee had something to do with the same accident.

Sheila's parents knew that the cancer was serious, and that if left untreated, it would kill her. They were also warned that, even with the amputation, she might not live long enough to reach university. In fact, her chances of survival after amputation were devastatingly low. Early amputation had become the recommended recourse in 1879. As a 2013 paper on the evolution of osteosarcoma's treatment put it, "the outcome was dismal; nonetheless it was accepted as the 'standard' of treatment." Sir Stanford Cade, a British surgeon and radiotherapist who advocated radiation therapy for osteosarcoma in 1931, told a meeting: "Gentlemen, if you operate, they die, if you do not operate they die just the same; this meeting should be concluded with prayers."[59]

When Sheila was diagnosed, no significant treatment progress had been made, despite the experiments in radiation therapy. The survival rate was less than ten per cent. In one group of sixty-two patients managed between 1958 and 1970, who were treated with radiation and/or amputation, the five-year survival rate was no greater than five per cent.[60] Long-term survivors among the forty-six patients seen at UCLA between 1955 and 1973 only numbered eleven. *No one* in that patient group had survived for five years after having only surgery. The tumour registry of the Hospital for Sick Children in

Toronto was no less devastating: there was not a single "five-year survivor," regardless of treatment strategy, among eighteen children diagnosed there between 1928 and 1958.[61]

Outcomes were so discouraging that surgeons came to question whether the "mutilation" of amputation was justified. As an osteosarcoma study published in the *British Journal of Surgery* advised in 1964, "conventional treatment by immediate ablation does not save the majority of patients from early death by lung metastases, so that many limbs are sacrificed in vain."

The greatest danger lay in this cancer's propensity to metastasize and move to the lungs. In at least eighty per cent of osteosarcoma patients around the time of Sheila's case, these fatal pulmonary micrometastases were already present at the time of diagnosis. Not visible through conventional imaging, they tended to kill the patient within one to two years. The 1973 study in Los Angeles found that among patients who developed metastases, eighty-seven per cent had them within fourteen months of the initial diagnoses; the average time for metastases to appear was five and one-half months from the onset of therapy. Only with the arrival of effective chemotherapeutic agents in the 1960s to 1980s did cure rates of sixty to seventy-five per cent become possible, with about eighty per cent of patients also becoming eligible to have their cancerous limb salvaged.

For every week, for every *day*, that the Goldens delayed in having Sheila proceed with the amputation, the odds of the cancer moving to Sheila's lungs and killing her before she finished high school became ever higher. Jack and Sophie accepted the prognosis. Two of Montreal's leading surgeons and telegrams from the world's specialists told them there was no choice but to amputate. But Sheila was adamant about not proceeding.

"I said to my parents, 'I'm sorry. I'm not having my leg amputated. That will be the end of my life.' My mother let me talk, and rant, and rave." Her oldest brother, Clifford, who had started medical school and would become a leading pediatrician and then return to studies to become a psychiatrist, tried to persuade her. Her school friends assured her they would help her learn to walk again. "I continued to be in denial, hoping for a way out of this nightmare," she told the Choices audience in 1999. "I simply could not process the idea of losing a leg. I repeatedly told my parents I was not going to do it, and they repeatedly reaffirmed their love and support for me. 'We'll help you get through it,' they insisted."

On a Saturday in the spring of 1946, the Goldens had a visitor: Charlotte Stilman's father. Like Sophie Golden, he had been born in a corner of the Russian Empire now in Ukraine, in his case Staraya Ushitsa in Khmelnytskyi Oblast. Abraham had fled during the Bolshevik revolution, attending university in Belgium before arriving, alone, in Montreal in 1925, to study medicine at McGill. In 1926, he married Tania Miller.[62] He became secretary of the Jewish Community Council, joined the Jewish General's staff as a physician and surgeon, and by 1945 was one of two associates in its department of urology. He would also publish four novels and a collection of short stories (as Abram Stilman) in Yiddish and receive the Canadian Jewish Congress literary award in 1962.

Abraham Stilman was close to his daughter, Charlotte, and Charlotte was close to Sheila. He knew about the crisis in the Golden household, and as a surgeon at the Jewish General, he probably knew more than a little about the stark reality of the osteosarcoma diagnosis. In the 1930s, the Jewish General had developed a high reputation for cancer treatment. The hospital hired an experienced cancer researcher, pathologist David Seecos, opened a multidisciplinary tumour clinic, and used its X-ray expertise to experiment with radiation treatment. But Sheila's path of diagnosis had led instead to the Montreal General. It made no difference. The prognosis was unequivocal, and Stilman called on the Goldens, in hope of talking sense into a terrified, uncooperative girl.

They took tea together, in the lovely garden at the rear of the Beloeil Avenue home.

"Sheila," Dr. Stilman said, "you're being selfish."

That took her aback. *What did he mean, selfish?*

"You have two brothers, and you're the baby. You're the only daughter your parents have. They're not going to have any more children. And if you don't have that operation, you're not going to be here. That would be a terrible, terrible thing, for your brothers, but particularly for your parents. You can't do that to them. You're taking a very selfish attitude."

"But that's going to be the end of my life," she told him. *"Nobody else has an amputation. None of my friends."*

"You are right," Dr. Stilman said. "It is rare to have an amputation, and the cancer is rare, but it *is* cancer. You saw the telegrams. You have to have it done. You don't want to die at your age. Or *do* you want to die?"

"It's better than becoming an amputee," she remembers replying. "I was very angry that I was going to lose my leg. *Why me?* I took it badly."

"You have a chance to live," Dr. Stilman counselled. "And if you don't have the surgery, you won't live. And your parents will be devastated."

After Dr. Stilman's visit, Sheila's parents took her for a drive—just the three of them. Sheila and her mother were in the back seat, with her father at the wheel of the luxurious sedan made possible by his ability to persuade people to shield themselves and their loved ones against actuarial odds. It could be a challenge to convince people in the prime of life that life insurance was something worth paying for. Now he had a child, facing death from a rare condition, and no policy in the world could avert or mitigate the looming loss.

Sophie Golden reached into her purse and produced the telegrams from six of the leading bone specialists in the world, confirming the biopsy diagnosis.

"You have no alternative," Sophie told Sheila. "Look at the telegrams. Yes, it's going to be difficult. But we are here for you. Your brothers are here for you. Your friends are here for you. There is a lot of life left in you, and a lot that you can do, even with only one leg."

Sheila looked to her father. "Daddy, do you believe this?"

"It's true," he said. "It has to be done." He turned the rear-view mirror around, so that she could not see him sobbing. It was the first and last time Sheila ever saw her father cry.

"I said, 'Mommy, I guess I should have it done.'" Sheila relates this terrible, unavoidable decision more than seventy-five years later, a cancer-free span almost inconceivable for a diagnosis of osteosarcoma in 1946.

CHAPTER SEVEN

Bitter or Better

Sheryl Miller (now Sheryl Miller Adessky) was eighteen, in her second year of CEGEP in Montreal, when she was diagnosed with Hodgkin's lymphoma in 1980, the year before Hope & Cope was founded. Through radiation therapy, Sheryl survived. Her mother became one of Hope & Cope's early volunteers, and Sheryl would pioneer its support services for young adults.

"Yes, Sheila created Hope & Cope, and it's truly phenomenal," Adessky says. "But to me, the unbelievable part of Sheila is that I know how difficult it was to deal with cancer as an eighteen-year-old in 1980. I can't for the life of me begin to imagine how much harder it had to have been for her. If I found it excruciatingly hard, and physically the worst thing that happened was losing my hair. It didn't compare with being diagnosed in 1946 and having your leg amputated when you're thirteen years old." Adessky heard Sheila deliver her "Choices" speech in 1999 and has heard her address the experience at other times, but the account has still left an enormous gap in comprehension. "I sometimes feel like saying, 'Sheila, how did you do it?' *Thirteen years old.* Adults struggle with cancer. It still amazes me that she was able to bounce back from that at thirteen. It's an incredible story."

Sheila Kussner underwent the amputation of her left leg above the knee in the spring of 1946, a few months before her fourteenth birthday. She remained in hospital for several weeks. Her friend, Charlotte Stilman (Colson), was able to visit her regularly. "An amputation is always traumatic," Colson says, "but in those days, it was highly traumatic."

Sheila was stricken by phantom limb pain, a terrible sensation that the missing limb is still there. It was so excruciating that her brothers feared she might die. "I was convinced that I still had my leg," Sheila would tell her Choices audience in 1999. "For weeks after, especially on waking up, I would try to put two feet on the floor. While the physical agony was unbearable, the emotional pain was even worse."

At first, Sheila refused visitors. "I often cried, especially when well-meaning individuals told me to put on a brave face. I was convinced that my life was over, and I was partially right. The life that I had known was over, and a new one was about to begin. But there was no road map."

Sheila remembers leaving hospital with her parents at eleven-twenty on a Thursday morning, wearing a skirt, blouse, and a woollen stump sock, and balancing on her crutches. Jack Golden announced that he was taking his daughter out to lunch. "I was horrified and at first refused to go. Once again, it was my mother who spoke the words that I need to hear. 'You have nothing to be ashamed of. You didn't rob a bank and you didn't murder anyone. This was an act of God. Life dealt you a cruel blow, but you must learn to accept it. If people stare at you, that's their problem. You're going to rise above it.'"

"My grandma was really outstanding as a mother," says Sheila's daughter, Joanne, "and she did things with my mom that were very wise, that helped her cope."

"Grandma Golden was the force of strength, and vision, and support," says Sheila's daughter, Janice. "She said, 'Sheila, you can do anything you want in your life.' She was beyond amazing. She and my mom had a very close relationship." Sheila agrees. "My mother was instrumental, in me pushing ahead."

Sheila's father was a different case. "My grandfather, through his whole life, was angry—not angry at Mom, but kind of angry at what had happened, and he doted over Mom," says Janice. "Whenever there was a snowstorm in Montreal, Grandpa would call, and if I answered, he would say, 'Janny dear, where's your mother?' And I'd have to lie because she was out doing her errands. Grandpa was so protective of Mom, and we had to cover for her. He never really got over it. Grandma Golden dealt with it head-on, in the most wonderful, gentle, pragmatic way. She was a huge reason for how Mom's life unfolded."

Expectations within the Golden family were already high for the children's lives before Sheila's diagnosis. Sophie Golden was not going to accept anything less than success and happiness for her daughter. "My mother said, 'You're the same person you were. And mark my words, you're going to be somebody.'" Sheila, however, was saddled at a formative age by four enormous burdens: the threat of recurring cancer, the stigma of cancer, overcoming her significant physical disability, and overcoming her status as an amputee.

There were difficult moments between Sheila and her mother: Sheila can remember shouting at Sophie that her amputation was all her mother's fault, that she didn't want to be alive, that she should have been put to sleep. But it was overwhelmingly through Sophie's patience and guidance that Sheila came to a core acceptance: she could be bitter, or she could be better. That mantra, "bitter or better," became a key message that Sheila would deliver, over and over. And "better" has more than one meaning. You can be better in the sense of healing, which has psychological as well as physical elements. And you can make the world around you better—*tikkun olam*, repair the world, even as you repair yourself. Both are an ongoing, never-ending process.

But it was an enormous emotional and psychological challenge for Sheila to carry forward without missing a step, as it were—without pausing to acknowledge an irreversible loss. Many years later, after Sheila founded Hope & Cope, Suzanne O'Brien attended a conference at which Edward Kennedy Jr. spoke. When he was twelve, in 1973, he was diagnosed with osteosarcoma in his right leg, and like Sheila underwent an amputation. When O'Brien returned from the conference, she related to Sheila what he had shared. As a Kennedy, he explained, he was expected to suck it up and get on with life. He was not allowed to grieve, he said, which is not to be confused with self-pity. He was not given the opportunity to acknowledge a loss in a healthy, emotional way, and he stressed to the conference audience the importance of grieving in such circumstances. For the first time O'Brien saw Sheila shed tears. "That could have been me," Sheila said. The chance to grieve had not been understood or appreciated when she was a child. Now, we know that the healing, the process of becoming better, does not mean denying the reality of a loss.

"Bitter or better" is not a saccharine, Pollyannaish message, the sort that places even more burden on burdened people to accept that their problems or challenges can be breezily swept aside—and that if they don't or can't, there must be some deficiency in their character. Sheila had no illusions that her disability could be made to disappear, or that she should expect herself to go through life as if it didn't exist. "You never really get used to being an amputee," Sheila told the Choices audience. "You integrate the trauma into your life and it becomes part of you. Its significance resurges and recedes in the course of a lifetime, but you never, ever get over it." As she reviews her Choices speech at her kitchen table, Sheila allows, "It wasn't easy. It's not that I'm better, but I'm not bitter. I was for a while." The message rather was: *This is what life has dealt you. Now do something, whatever you can, with that life.*

A year after the Choices speech, Sheila would be at Notre Dame Basilica, attending the state funeral of Pierre Elliott Trudeau. Theirs had been one of Montreal's more interesting, cosmopolitan friendships; at the funeral, she had been seated in the second row, behind the family.

As the mourners filed out, Sheila hung back for a spell. A senior member of the clergy spotted her. "I know who you are," he said. He also knew what had happened to her, as a child. "God spared you," he assured her, so that she could perform the good deeds she was known for. She still attended synagogue and had faith in a supreme being, but she could not imagine that G-d had contrived a plan for her that involved her enduring a particular trauma and loss, so that she could embark on a path that could help others grapple with similar traumas and losses that might *not* ultimately spare them. She listened politely, she says, but she also says that she didn't believe him.

There may not have been a larger purpose to Sheila losing a leg to cancer, but in surviving the trauma, purpose emerged.

Sheila had missed the balance of grade eight because of the amputation, but Miss Hay, the principal of Strathcona Collegiate, assured her parents that she would be accepted that fall in grade nine regardless. The question was whether she would still be alive to attend.

By September, Sheila was ready to return to school. But as it would take about ten months from the time of her operation to receive a prosthetic limb, she had to get about initially on crutches, on her remaining leg. Strathcona Collegiate was just around the corner from the Golden home, but Beloeil Avenue had enough of an incline that Sheila's father arranged to have her driven to and from school.

Sheila had expected to have Latin as her home-room class, which was considered the place for the highest performing students, but the classroom was on the third floor, and the prospect of negotiating the flights of stairs with one leg, on crutches, was too much, so she switched her home room to biology, on a lower level. Charlotte switched from Latin as well, to be with her, as did another friend, and Sheila would be forever grateful for this gesture of solidarity. She can recall a day when the three of them, almost spontaneously, broke down in tears. The school nurse told them that crying was a good thing, that the grieving allowed them to relieve the stress that had built up around Sheila's condition.

Formal support was otherwise non-existent. There was no phys-
iotherapy to help her maintain strength in the amputated limb, or
to adapt to the prosthetic device when it did arrive. It was cumber-
some, compared to the artificial limbs that later amputees would be
able to employ. Instead of having a modern fixture attached to the
stump with suction, Sheila had to master a heavy device that strapped
around her waist and placed strain on her lower back. Counselling
and peer group support were beyond available. Professional interest
in the psychological aspects of the cancer experience was years in the
future. She does recall being one of seven local bone-cancer patients
to have undergone an amputation and being the only to survive.

As a disease in which the body's cellular mechanism turned into
a runaway, self-replicating machine, cancer was poorly understood.
But at the time of Sheila's diagnosis, there were promises of treatment breakthroughs. Sidney Farber at Boston's Children's Hospital
was conducting controversial experiments in treating anemia that
led him in 1947 to tackle childhood leukemia. As a condition affecting white blood cells, leukemia scarcely seemed to belong to the same
order of disease as other cancers that surgeons addressed with exci-
sion and amputation. In December 1947, Farber treated a boy with
a class of drug called antifolates. He received such dramatic results,
reducing the child's white blood cell count to near-normal levels,
that it seemed as if he had struck upon a cure. Unfortunately, the
boy's stunning progress quickly reversed as the cancer rebounded
aggressively from remission, as it did with other children he treated
at the time. However, Farber had taken a major step in cancer
research and treatment, effectively creating the field of chemotherapy.[63] Medicine now had three tools with which to address cancer:
surgery, radiation, and chemicals. But there was nothing like a cure

for any form of it, beyond bombarding certain tumours with X-rays and otherwise cutting away a portion of the body and hoping the cancer did not reappear, there or elsewhere.

Until the Second World War, tuberculosis had been a far greater health scourge than cancer. Treatment for this bacterial lung infection largely consisted of rest, fresh air, and fresh water, which caused a proliferation of sanitaria in the Adirondacks of New York, the Muskoka Lakes region of Ontario, and the Laurentians of Quebec, where Montreal's Jewish community had opened Mount Sinai Sanatorium.[64] With the advent of penicillin at the outbreak of the Second World War, followed by streptomycin, tuberculosis rates plunged. While Mount Sinai Sanatorium continued to operate (and would eventually relocate to Montreal and become Mount Sinai Hospital), the Hebrew Consumptive Aid Association, which had been focused on tuberculosis, elected to change its mission. In 1942, it opened the fifty-bed Jewish Incurable Hospital in the city's east end, for the chronically ill and disabled.

The name was almost immediately changed to the Jewish Hospital of Hope.[65] But the change could not conceal the institution's essential character. It was, as the dark humour of the local medical community put it, a place of hope for the hopeless. The hospital's administrative office, which it shared with the Hebrew Consumptive Aid Association, was on St. Lawrence Boulevard in Mile End, but the actual hospital was about fifteen kilometres to the east. Abraham Fuks, a long-standing friend of Sheila's who has served as McGill's dean of medicine, remembers how as a young doctor he could only marvel at how far the Hospital of Hope had been placed from the city's heart. It was so far east on Sherbrooke Street that today the former site is beyond Longue-Pointe, on the opposite side of Route 25. "It was situated, just like leprosaria were, far away from the city," Fuks says. "You had to travel several miles on the streetcar to get to your poor relation who might be at Hope with a chronic, unremitting illness, and would die there."

"Hope" at the time of Sheila's diagnosis, then, was an institutional label that all but declared a patient's future to be beyond the intervention of medicine and best left to the realm of prayer. True, the land on which the Hospital of Hope was built would have been affordable, but the remoteness also spoke of aversion and rejection, and a compulsion, widespread in Western society, to isolate people for whom there was no apparent chance of a cure. The mentally ill, the terminally ill, the physically and developmentally disabled, the fearfully contagious, were all too often assigned to or warehoused in large, remote institutions, far from family and community.

Cancer was a stigma and would remain so for decades. Cancer marked you, not only physically, after aggressive surgeries like an amputation or a radical mastectomy, but also morally and psychiatrically. Many people thought that tumours arose through some failing of character.

A new field was emerging in the United States, called psychosomatic medicine. Although "psychosomatic" to most people today probably suggests hypochondria, psychosomatic medicine was interested in the relationship between personality and illness. An influx of psychoanalysts from Europe in the 1930s helped to drive a fascination in American psychiatry with what would become known as the mind-body (or more precisely, the mind-over-body) issue. A journal, *Psychosomatic Medicine*, was founded in 1939 and the formation of the American Psychosomatic Association (which adopted the journal as its official publication) followed in 1942.

With the rise of psychosomatic medicine, the hunt was on for personality types associated with cancer. It didn't take much of an intellectual leap to believe that certain personality types caused cancer. One of the foremost figures in the rise of this new field (and the public's fascination with it) was Wilhelm Reich, an esteemed member of Sigmund Freud's Vienna Psychoanalytic Polyclinic. Reich's professional standing was already slipping when he arrived in the United States in 1939, the year he published *Bion Experiments on the Cancer Problem*, but his work nevertheless found a popular audience. *Charakteranalyse* of 1933 was first published in English as *Character-Analysis* in 1945, in a translation by Theodore P. Wolfe, professor of psychiatry at Columbia University, who had studied under Reich. The respected New York publishing house, Farrar, Straus & Geroux, issued a third, enlarged edition under its Noonday Press imprint in 1949.

In *Character-Analysis*, Reich attributed cancer to societal repression that manifested itself in physical illness.[66] Reich's ideas became increasingly bizarre, but psychosomatic medicine carried on without him, with some researchers continuing to seek evidence that psychiatric conditions or personality types were precursors to cancer. As Susan Sontag would note in her influential *Illness as Metaphor* (1978), Reich was crucial in defining cancer as "a disease following emotional resignation—a bio-energetic shrinking, a giving up of hope."[67]

Even without the burdens of early psychosomatic medicine's worst tendencies, cancer patients have been stigmatized by the logic of medical care. If the doctor's strategies work, the doctor has succeeded. But if the strategies don't work, the patient, as Abraham Fuks has pointed out, can be implicitly to blame. It became routine for physicians to say a patient "failed chemotherapy" rather than a particular treatment strategy failed to bring results. Such words "attribute to the patient the responsibility and blame for the loss ... What should concern us is the inappropriate attribution of blame and responsibility to the innocent patient."[68]

Early psychosomatic medicine, as advocated by Reich and some adherents, doubled down on a patient's responsibility for their condition. Advocates for mental positivity in both the prevention and treatment of cancer walked a fine line between empowering and blaming the patient. In an era of limited treatment options, a diagnosis of cancer was not only a reason to lose hope—losing hope could be cited as the very source of the disease, and the cause of a patient's inability to survive it. After all, if a positive mental outlook could prevent or cure cancer, then one could argue that someone's mental state could have caused it in the first place and prevented them from fighting it off.

Cancer became something shameful, in every possible way. Shame could bring on cancer, and shame was also cancer's consequence.

When Sheila Kussner was diagnosed with osteosarcoma, "cancer" was a word that many people, doctors among them, could scarcely speak out loud, and that reluctance would remain for decades. Abraham Fuks has written that in the middle of the twentieth century, "cancer was a stigmatized illness, with the diagnosis kept secret, sometimes from patients themselves. The word was uttered with trepidation and foreboding. The image of cancer was the crab with its connotations of inexorable spread, destruction, and imperialist takeovers."[69]

"You didn't talk about it," Sheila's friend Charlotte Colson says simply. Cancer so often was a death sentence, and as doctors had no formal training in how to deliver bad news, they often chose not to deliver it at all. With many doctors omitting cancer from diagnoses they delivered, the shame of the disease lay as much in the physician as it did in the patient. It could be difficult for such an elevated, patrician profession to admit that there was an illness for which it could do nothing, and so physicians would simply decline to admit to the patient the illness was even present. A reluctance to acknowledge the limits of care also made it easy to shift blame to the patient for having the disease, or for not responding to treatment.

Although experimental radiation therapy was being applied to some cancers after the Second World War, and the first promises of a chemotherapeutic approach were emerging, treatment otherwise was limited to surgery. With so little knowledge surrounding cancer, which was exacerbated by the taboos within the medical community about even speaking to patients about it, the vacuum created by ignorance naturally was filled with misinformation, and there was room for Reich's blame of patients' psychology to spread.

It may be more than coincidental that in 1946, the same year in which Sheila was diagnosed with osteosarcoma, the Life Saving Fund of the Jewish General Hospital's women's auxiliary sponsored an exceptional education program in co-operation with the hospital's Tumour Clinic. Three leading figures in cancer research and treatment were brought to the hospital, to deliver addresses.[70] Gordon E. Richards, professor of radiology at the University of Toronto, spoke on mouth cancer, and to the women's auxiliary on "Hopeful Aspects of the Fight Against Cancer." George Papanicolaou of Cornell University addressed "a method now widely used for the early diagnosis of certain types of cancer," which was the hospital annual report's discreet way of addressing his discovery of the pap smear, on which he had published in 1943. The third and final speaker, and the most significant one where Sheila was concerned, was Henry L. Jaffe, director of laboratories at the Hospital for Joint Diseases in New York City. A world authority on bone disease, Dr. Jaffe was secured to speak on bone cancer. It is tempting to see Sophie Golden, as a patroness of the Life Saving Fund, playing a lead role in making this series possible. Dr. Jaffe may well have been one of the authorities to whom Sophie and Jack Golden had turned for an additional opinion on the biopsy that A.T. Bazin performed on Sheila.

"All of these lectures have attracted city wide attention and were attended by large audiences including leading physicians from the staffs of the other Hospitals in the City," the hospital's annual report noted. Notwithstanding the fact that the report's authors could not bring themselves to print the words "cervical cancer" where Dr. Papanicolaou's work was concerned, the hospital was striving to better educate not only physicians but also the public about a broad class of disease that was otherwise shrouded in secrecy, dread, and shame.

At age eighty-eight, Charlotte Colson does her best to try to place herself back in her own shoes, as a young teen, as she considers how the world responded to Sheila's cancer diagnosis and the amputation. For their friendship, it made absolutely no difference. "I was a child, but it didn't seem to impact on us that strongly. We had one another. We were all right. In school, she was herself. She was always a charming, vivacious person. Her personality hasn't changed, in all these years. The weight of problems may have changed, but not her personality. We accepted so much in those days, too. 'That's the way you are? Then that's the way you are.' To me, the way she was, was normal, so it must have been normal to the outside world, too." But she also acknowledges that Sheila's condition may have made a difference to others.

"There was nobody else in the whole school that had cancer," Sheila recalls of her days at Strathcona Collegiate. "As they say in Hebrew, *shum d'var*—nothing." Sheila remembers some fellow students in their ignorance refusing to sit next to her at lunch, fearing that her cancer might be contagious. A more complex response came in Sheila's selection as Miss Strathcona, which was essentially an award for the most popular female student, as voted on by the student body. Having been voted Miss Strathcona seems like prima facie evidence of Sheila's acceptance and popularity. And Colson can remember a photo of Sheila, crowned with a feathered hat, smiling for the camera. But Sheila's memory of the award is more nuanced.

When she came home and told her mother that she had been chosen Miss Strathcona, Sophie Golden was delighted. But Sheila was angry and sobbing. Decades later, she strives to articulate exactly what so upset her.

"You felt patronized?" her visitor proposes. Sheila smiles grimly and nods. "So much so. I was like, 'Okay, why are you doing this? Is it because you feel better about yourself when you're doing this?'" Two other girls were nominated, and in her mind, either one of them was more deserving of a popularity award. She felt that the award did not indicate that the student body was blind to her status as an amputee, rather that they had chosen her over the other two *because of* that disability. It came uncomfortably close to her peers awarding a prize to themselves, for being so unjudgmental about her condition, when her condition in fact had been a key factor in their judgment. ·

Marvin Corber, who was a year ahead of Sheila at Strathcona, and was in a class with her brother Ronald, demurs. "She was always a beautiful person. In my opinion, she would have won it anyhow, regardless of her leg."

Notwithstanding her disquiet with her selection as Miss Strathcona, Sheila was popular, in high school and at McGill. She and Charlotte Colson were almost inseparable at McGill, joining the same sorority, Sigma Delta Tau (founded at Cornell University by seventeen Jewish women in 1917), and enrolling in the same bachelor of arts program in 1949. Charlotte thinks the only class they didn't take together in their three years of study was a second-language option, for which she chose French and Sheila chose Spanish. When she graduated in 1953, Sheila's yearbook profile read: "Be always merry as ever you can, / For none delights in a sorrowful man."

Sheila worked diligently on her gait; in slacks, the fact that she was an above-knee amputee was all but undetectable. "I knew what a perfect walker looked like," Janice Kussner recalls of her childhood, "because I had my mother as an example." Her condition was not common knowledge at McGill. About the only thing that could tip a hand to Sheila's physical condition was a set of stairs. She could not bound up or down them, and instead would have to take them one step at a time, getting both feet to one step before moving on to the next. When she and Charlotte graduated, Sheila made sure that Charlotte was in front of her as they ascended the stairs to receive their diplomas, so that Charlotte could walk slowly enough that Sheila's negotiation of the steps would not be so apparent.

Sheila dated regularly: she was smart, funny, effervescent, and pretty. But there were moments of rejection that would stay with her, when the interest of seemingly smitten suitors soured and she went from being Sheila to being something damaged and undesirable. There was a house party she well remembers, where a young man asked if he could take her for a coffee and drive her home at the end. She said yes, but then she heard him talking in a group across the room and him being told, "Don't you know who that is? That's Sheila Golden. She's an amputee." He never came back to treat her to the coffee and the drive home. And there was the McGill football player who took her to the movies. As they ascended a set of stairs, he watched puzzled as she negotiated the steps, and asked if there was something wrong. She realized, *he doesn't know*, and so she told him. He never asked her out again.

But there were others, for whom the amputation did not matter. One was from Ottawa. He was wealthy, drove an impressive sports car, and truly loved her. He had a rival in Montreal, who could check none of the same socio-economic boxes but would prevail in the end.

CHAPTER EIGHT

Marvyn

Simon Kussner, grandfather of Marvyn Kussner, was approaching the age of fifty when he emigrated around 1888 to the United States from Bessarabia (a part of the Russian Empire in what is now Moldova) with his wife, Sarah Goldman, and their two young sons. Edward Jacob (Jack), born in 1882, was Marvyn's father; Abraham was born in 1884. The family settled first in Philadelphia, then relocated to New York City, and the sons followed their father, a tailor, into the garment trade.

While the Kussners were naturalized as American citizens soon after the turn of the century, the family turned to Montreal for fresh opportunities. Abraham, with his wife and three children, moved to the city in July 1913; Abraham's brother, Jack, and their parents followed soon after, if not at the same time. In November 1914, Jack Kussner married Tana Moscovitch, the daughter of Simon and Sarah (née Gersonovitch) Moscovitch. The Moscovitches had emigrated from Russia in 1900, with five children—two more arrived in Montreal—and they formed a busy white-collar household on Sherbrooke Street, just off St. Urbain. Simon was a real estate agent, and in the 1911 census, among the oldest children, Tana and her brother Joseph were bookkeepers, and their sister Esther was a stenographer with the Grand Trunk Railway.

The Kussner brothers became local manufacturers in the Montreal garment trade, with a business called the National Waist Company Ltd. "Waists," or "shirtwaists," were women's blouses, which were all the latest fashion rage. A letters patent issued by the Canadian government on July 2, 1914, indicated the company would "manufacture and deal in ladies' waists, suits, skirts, children's wear, whitewear, costumes, dresses for women and children, both wholesale and retail." Abraham was initially in charge, but in 1920 Jack became the president; by then, Jack and Tana had three daughters, Jean, Mavis, and Gladys, and they moved into a fine, three-storey row house on Dorchester Boulevard, on the south side of Westmount. On February 21, 1930, their only son, Marvyn Sidney Kussner, arrived, by far the youngest child and beloved by everyone in the household.

The Kussner brothers carried on with their garment business, until the Depression began to bite hard. By 1935, National Waist Company Ltd. was failing. Abraham had already begun to run other garment businesses out of his home in Outremont. For most of the next seven years, Jack was affiliated with no business at all in the city directory, other than a two-year stint operating Acme Dress out of the Dorchester Boulevard home.

Suzanne O'Brien can recall driving past the Dorchester Boulevard home with Marvyn and hearing him recall the jarring fall from prosperity his family had experienced, which eventually forced them out of the home. "Marvyn's family saw the wealth, such that it was, evaporate. It was hard to go from one extreme to the other." Sheila would come to know the story of Marvyn's family, and O'Brien sensed that it increased the empathy at the core of their marriage. "There was a strong work ethic in both of them. But they were always aware that, while you can work hard in life, there are no guarantees that you will be hugely successful. They realized there are talented people, good people, who just don't get a chance sometimes, and that was part of them wanting to give others a hand, a step up." Sheila would be unable to understand how those who were fortunate enough to secure great wealth might prefer to hoard it rather do as much good with it as possible.

In 1942, Marvyn's father Jack started a business that was exactly what its name sounded like: the Used Corrugated Box Company. Dealing in second-hand cardboard boxes was not a line of work that someone in his sixtieth year who had spent his working life in the garment trade would have preferred, but it provided for the family. The daughters all married and moved out, leaving the youngest, Marvyn, with his parents. He attended Westmount High School, which was only a few doors from their home, and at fifteen he served as president of the youth division of Montreal's Combined Jewish Appeal. But life remained precarious. The Kussners were unable to remain in their Dorchester Boulevard home until Marvyn had completed high school. In 1946, Jack, Tana, and Marvyn moved to an apartment on Macdonald Avenue in the emerging Jewish neighbourhood of Hampstead on Montreal's west side. After finishing high school at Westmount High, Marvyn entered McGill in the faculty of commerce in 1947. In addition to his studies, he busied himself with basketball, tennis, and badminton, and the B'Nai B'rith's Hillel Foundation.

Marvyn and Sheila would never have met, and may never have married, were it not for Sophie Golden. After Sheila's amputation, Sophie was adamant that Sheila have the same life as any other teen, and that included summer camp. Camp Hiawatha was one of several camps in the Laurentians that catered to anglophone, mainly Jewish clientele, and had been founded by Lithuanian immigrants, Albert and Goldie Wener. After Albert's death in 1940, the Wener family continued to run the camp, and both the camp and the family (prominent in the history of Shaar Hashomayim) were supporters of the Jewish General alongside Sophie Golden. Joseph Wener was a cardiology resident at the time of Sheila's cancer diagnosis. Sheila and her brothers all attended the camp, and Sophie made sure that Sheila returned, over her objections. "I wasn't going back to camp as an amputee. My mother said, 'Sheila, you're *going*,'" and at seventeen she returned as a counsellor trainee.

Sheila worked as a counsellor at Camp Hiawatha into her McGill years. The only exceptions made for her was that she stayed with the couple who managed the camp, rather than the campers and her fellow counsellors, and she didn't take charge of showers for her young charges, boys four to six years old.

The story of how she and Marvyn met plainly delights her. It must have been the summer of 1949. She was with her boys when the son of the camp's co-owners, the Hymans, arrived for a visit. Accompanying him was Marvyn, "who said to him, 'Who is that girl in the white pants and white top?' I had a ponytail with a white bow in the back. 'That's Sheila Golden,' Marvyn was told. 'She's pretty,' Marvyn said. 'Is she seeing anybody?' The other fellow said, 'Marvyn, don't be silly. She's an amputee. What do you want … Are you kidding? Don't get involved.' 'I don't care if she's an amputee,'

Marvyn said. 'She's gorgeous.' Anyway, he came over to talk to me. I didn't know who he was."

Marvyn was about to begin his final year at McGill, serving as treasurer of the United Jewish Student Association, just as Sheila was arriving. "We started to date, and we dated quite a bit." But Sheila continued to see a wealthy Ottawa suitor, and after her graduation, both he and Marvyn wanted to marry her. If money and a life of leisure were the only criteria, it would have been no contest, and Sheila admits that the Ottawa suitor's lifestyle "turned my head a bit." Marvyn, on the other hand, since his own graduation had been toiling as a jobber in his father's used cardboard-box business, making eighty-five dollars a week. Sheila could not make up her mind. It was Sophie Golden who not so much made the decision as helped her daughter see the choice more clearly.

"My mother liked both of them," Sheila says, "but she loved Marvyn." Sophie made her think not in terms of who these two young men were now, but in terms of what either one of them would mean to her, over the long arc of a life together. Is this someone you wanted to grow old with? And there had, admittedly, been one significant wobble with the Ottawa suitor. His mother had doubts about Sheila; either because Sheila was an amputee or because she had survived cancer, the mother had gotten it into her head that Sheila might not be able to have children. Marvyn, meanwhile, became so distraught that he took to bed. His parents summoned a doctor, who could find nothing physically wrong with him. The doctor, with infinite diagnostic wisdom, said, "Marvyn, are you by any chance entertaining thoughts of a young lady?" Yes, he admitted, he was. He was in love, and he was afraid that he was going to lose her.

Sheila graduated from McGill and turned twenty-one on August 24, 1953. She married Marvyn on September 6. Two healthy, happy daughters followed.

When Sheila was at McGill, she wrote an essay for a sociology class, entitled "And Now to Live Again," about her cancer and her recovery. Her professor was so impressed that he thought she should submit it to *Reader's Digest*. She was unsure, but he felt that publishing it could help many people facing the same situation. With Sheila's permission, he spoke to her mother, to secure her approval. "My mother said, 'No, I don't want that published. I don't want her to have that kind of recognition. I know it might be good for others, but it's not good for her.' And we never published it. He felt very badly." She kept the essay. "It's here, somewhere," Sheila says at her kitchen table. "I never threw it out."

It was a telling moment. At a time that cancer was so stigmatized, Sophie Golden did not want her daughter publicly identified as a cancer victim—because people who had cancer then were victims, and there was all the shaming and misunderstandings of the time. But helping other cancer patients, one to one, was another matter. These were private acts of charity, and her mother knew and approved.

Some time after Marvyn and Sheila were married, a member of the McGill faculty who knew of her cancer episode reached out for help. There was a girl, twelve years old, who had the same diagnosis of osteosarcoma. Perhaps Sheila could serve as a mentor. The girl, who we will call Anna, had a single mother, and the mother had been difficult, objecting to the very idea that her daughter must lose her right leg. The mother finally accepted the necessity of the amputation, and Sheila joined her, along with a rabbi, in hospital, as the surgery was performed.

The surgeon entered the waiting room to tell them the amputation was successful, but that it was too late; an X-ray had determined that the cancer had already spread to her lungs. They debated what the mother was going to tell Anna. "You *can't* tell her," Sheila insisted. "And I'm not going to let you tell her." The girl might only have a year or two to live, but she deserved to enjoy some of the time left to her. The rabbi agreed, and the mother listened. They said nothing.

Sheila adored the girl and helped prepare her for her bat mitzvah. Sheila wanted her to have a pair of shoes in the style of ballet slippers and took Anna into a store. The girl was on crutches, missing a leg, still traumatized, as Sheila herself had once been, by the surgery and loss. "We only need one pair," Sheila declared to the salesman. "One slipper for each of us." The salesman was confused—Sheila was walking perfectly, giving no hint that she might only have a right foot to go with Anna's left. Sheila hiked up her pantleg so that he could see her artificial limb. This was Sheila at her wisecracking, mischievous best, but the moment was about the girl, about Sheila making Anna feel that she was not alone, and that there was no need to be ashamed.

The cancer was not long in claiming Anna. "She got sick very quickly," Sheila remembers. When Anna died, Sheila served as a *shomer*, a watcher, with the mother in the house—staying after the rest of the guests had departed, waiting for the girl's body to be removed. The three of them were alone together, in the gathering dark, bearing witness to an unfulfilled life. "I couldn't leave her be," Sheila recalls. "I loved that child. She was lovely, pretty, and bright. She was such a good kid. And she had so much to—" Sheila pauses. "Anyway, she's gone."

Between Sheila's survival and Anna's loss, volumes could be written about the individual experience of illness in prognoses and outcomes. Medicine as a science strives to diagnose and treat, and then to measure the efficacy of clinical responses with hard data. With the direst illnesses, medical science wants to know how many patients survive a particular remedy or recourse, and for how long. What are the five-year survival statistics? What is the rate of recurrence? But something fundamental is missing in these necessary quantifications. There is no way to capture statistically the crucial phenomena of the roles played by Sheila's mother and Anna's mother, for example. Sheila Golden had been stunned by the initial diagnosis from Fraser Baillie Gurd, but she did not close her mind to the danger and had pressed immediately for second opinions, and then urged her daughter to accept the course of action. Anna's mother had simply rejected the idea that the amputation was necessary. Had she waited too long, before at last being persuaded that there was no other choice? Would immediate surgery have made any difference for Anna? It is impossible to know, these many years later. But we know that a patient's support, during diagnosis and treatment, and in the aftermath of whatever course of treatment or intervention is taken, is fundamental not only to survival but also to quality of life, whatever the outcome.

Sheila did everything she could, after the surgery, to give Anna as much of a life as a child could expect. She could not make a difference, after the fact, in how the child arrived at the point of surgery.

Her own survival and the remarkable cancer-free life that followed cannot be attributed solely to the attentiveness of her parents and the counselling of figures like Abraham Stilman, but they cannot be imagined without that circle of informed support.

Marvyn Kussner would have preferred to study law, according to his daughter Janice, but he was loyal to his father, and as he assumed command of the family business, he aimed higher. "My father was a good sport," says his daughter Joanne. "He never wanted to be in corrugated, but once he had to be, because of his father, he decided to make it into something significant. He built a big sheet plant, where he was a manufacturer of corrugated." By 1962, Marvyn was operating as Biltwell Containers (Emballages Biltwell). What started out as a box company would diversify into corrugated signage and display products, through a division run by Joanne. In the early years, after Marvyn's father died, his mother Tana was listed as Biltwell's president, and Sheila as vice-president, while Marvyn served as secretary-treasurer and purchasing agent, but in truth, Biltwell was Marvyn's domain, while Sheila focussed on the domestic front. Biltwell, says Joanne, "was his dream."

The Kussners built a comfortable but not extravagant life at their Mont-Royal bungalow. "Everybody knows what my mother does for other people," says Joanne, "but she was really an exceptional mom. She spread herself very thin. It was tough sharing her with the world."

Janice notes that her grandfather, Jack Kussner, died shortly after her parents wed (and that she was named for him). Her grandmother, Tana Kussner, lived for quite some time. "She got along exceptionally well with the Goldens and was a big part of our life. Dad looked after her, for all those years. We went to see her on a Sunday, the same way we did with Grandma and Grandpa Golden. Dad was her only son, and a superb son, and Grandma Kussner loved Mom, and vice versa. Mom was as attentive to her as she was to her own parents."

Marvyn had a sister in Montreal and another in London, England. They were, as noted, much older than him, but they remained close. "His sisters loved him," says Janice. "Dad was very much an adored child in the family. Growing up with Dad, I could see why. His whole DNA was that of just a hell of a nice guy, genuine and authentic, proud, and values driven. Joanne and I came from a very much family-oriented family, a grounded family."

Janice has warm memories of her parents' support. Her father helped with homework. The family ate dinner together every evening and enjoyed an occasional restaurant meal as a treat. Ruby Foo's was a favourite destination, and later, Milos. Skating, for Janice, was where her parents particularly shone in her life. "I grew up on cheese-cutter skates at Beaver Lake on Mount Royal," she explains, and became a serious competitive figure skater, winning the Eastern Canadian singles title. "I went to Hebrew school three times a week, and the rule of thumb was I could stay on the ice as long as I did well in school. Toller Cranston and I were studying under the same coach in the early years. I was a busy kid, and I had two parents who were completely supportive, both financially and in terms of putting themselves out, schlepping me around, coming to all my competitions. Dad got up with me at five in the morning because I was on the ice at six o'clock. My skating boots were made by Stanzione in New York City, and my blades needed to be sharpened in Toronto, so dad would take my skates to Dorval airport, and send them off."

Ask about domestic life with Sheila Kussner, and you will hear about food. Food has long been central to Sheila: preparing it, sharing it, serving it, delivering it. If you visit Sheila at home, you will, almost inevitably, be fed. There will be tea and coffee, cookies, small cakes, crackers, cheese, assorted fruit. Her day help will be serving while Sheila is the attentive hostess. *Have you tried the cheese? Have a cookie. You haven't had any cake. Do you need another coffee? Is the food hot?* If you need another coffee, your cup will not be refilled. Her day help will come with another serving in a new cup. Sheila was once a guest at Mar-a-Lago, before Donald Trump was president. When Trump came round to her table, asking how everything was, and was probably expecting the usual obsequious praise, Sheila said: "Well, if you want to be a first-class facility, when a guest asks for a second cup of coffee, you shouldn't refill the dirty cup. You should bring another serving in a clean cup." The Donald didn't seem amused, but Sheila was only telling him what she thought he ought to hear. That is the way you do things, if you are Sheila and you know how things are done.

"I was a good baker," Sheila says, seated at her kitchen table. "I was an okay cook." Because of mobility issues, Sheila can no longer work her magic in the kitchen quite the way she used to, but whatever her actual merits were as a cook, she was a fabulous baker. Sheila was famous for an array of offerings, among them her schnecken, those delectable pastries that spiral like snail shells (*schnecke* means snail in German). Nothing she produced in her kitchen was more renowned than her chocolate cake. It was so good that Sheila had discussions with the Sara Lee people about a signature version. The negotiations broke down, she says, when the company could not shoehorn her complex recipe into an industrial process.

Food is sustenance, but it is also comfort, ritual, and hospitality. It is communal. It is a form of sharing, of entertainment, of celebration. Janice remembers, "we ate exceptionally well. Mom very much loved to have people in the house and cook for them, not unlike her mother. Grandma Kussner was a great baker, as was Grandma Golden. As a kid, I was able to walk to school, and very often I came home for lunch. Mom would say to bring a friend, or a couple of kids, and lunch was a whole extravaganza. She would make Jell-O figures, with coconut for the hair and Smarties for the eyes."

It was all done just so. If you served a cold drink, you used a tray. If someone wanted a Coke, the Kussner kids would put a slice of lemon or lime on the rim of the glass, and add a little umbrella, maybe a maraschino cherry. Those standards of serving and entertaining never faded. Suzanne O'Brien recounts how Sheila always says "Coca-Cola," never "Coke," that the drink must be poured into the glass held at a particular angle to control the foaming, and that the umbrella garnish must be placed on the right-hand side as served. Abraham Fuks recalls visiting the Kussners when Marvyn was still alive. "Marvyn says, 'Abe, do you want a drink?' And I said, 'Sure, I'd love a Scotch.' And Sheila says, 'Marvyn, did I not tell you to make fresh ice? You can't use ice two days old.' I cracked up. It was hilarious."

"Special" is the word that most comes to mind when Joanne tries to explain her mother's propensity for making every event at the home meaningful. "We did big, big things, at the house. Our birthdays were always a big deal." Janice adds: "It was all about the house being an experience for people. Halloween, birthdays, whatever the occasion was, it was never vanilla, never average. It was always creative, innovative, welcoming, generous, and thoughtful. That's what Mom created, since we were very young kids, and for as long as she could."

Food can be a measure of prosperity, and of security. If you are not wanting, you can put food on the table. It also can be an act of charity. If others are wanting, you can put food on *their* table. Food can also be a burden. One of the most helpful things you can do for someone undergoing cancer treatment is to ensure they and their loved ones are fed. If you are a single mother with three children, when you leave your latest chemotherapy appointment, preparing a meal (never mind going to the grocery store and sourcing all the ingredients) can be almost more than you can manage. And if you are living alone and ailing, whatever the reason, a prepared meal at your door is a godsend. When Hope & Cope established its Wellness Centre in 2006, the kitchen was a key element of its design. It's where volunteers gather to prepare an arsenal of ready-to-eat meals that are provided to clients with cancer, for themselves and their families. The preparation is therapeutic and communal, and the delivery of it is of enormous relief to recipients.

Long before the Wellness Centre existed, Sheila was preparing meals and baked goods and delivering them on her daily and nightly rounds. As noted, she will call a restaurant and order a meal to be delivered to someone's home, regardless of how well she knows them, if she hears of their circumstances. On a guest's recent visit to her home, Sheila had a legal pad with two pages of densely packed script. She had been composing a letter to a woman undergoing cancer treatment, who she heard about from the woman's mother. Knowing that the woman was living alone, Sheila had ordered up a restaurant meal for her, and was now composing the letter.

Sheila was very close to philanthropist Hyman Polansky, about whom we will hear more where Sheila's campaign for palliative care is concerned. When he was diagnosed with cancer, Sheila was an indefatigable supporter, and that support inevitably included food. After her father died, says his daughter, Eden, "I was going through my father's phone messages. There were a few recordings left, from just before he passed away. One, of course, was from Sheila." Eden recites from memory the sound of that familiar, bubbling, almost frantic voice. "Hi, Hy, you didn't pick up. I missed you, but I know I promised you—I'm making you my lemon chiffon cake." Her father, Eden notes, loved Sheila's lemon chiffon cake. "I feel so badly, I didn't have time. I've had a couple busy days, but I'm promising you, I'm buying the eggs, and I'm going to buy the flour, and I hope you're feeling well and I feel badly you didn't pick up and I didn't speak to you." Sheila was still checking in, still hoping to connect, still promising, still caring, still feeding. "It was just so Sheila," Eden says. "She has a thousand things to do, but my dad loves her chiffon cake, so she's going to make it for him."

Sheila and Marvyn Kussner "were such a good couple," says Joanne. "They had one of those fairy-tale marriages. My father was perfect for my mother, because he allowed her to grow, and she needed that very badly. Not all men are like that." As Janice says, "Dad truly was the wind beneath her wings."

Sheila Kussner's transformation from an attentive mother and housewife in Mont-Royal into an extraordinary fundraiser and advocate for cancer treatment, research, and care, by her own account was a product of suburban stir-craziness. "I concentrated on Marvyn and the children," she would tell the *Canadian Jewish News* in 1983, "and all the kids from the neighbourhood used to come in and out for parties. Then when Janice and Joanne grew up I almost went crazy. What do I do with my time? So I turned to the community." But Sheila was already engaged in volunteerism when the girls were still at home, and they remember the demands on their mother's time and the concessions the family made, which would only accelerate as she began to build Hope & Cope. "My mom sort of drove the bus," is how Janice summarizes the priorities of Sheila's charitable work within the family.

Initially, and for years, Sheila's volunteerism in terms of peer support was focussed on amputees. Sometimes, cancer was involved, but it wasn't the defining criterion for her involvement. The *Montreal Star* in 1975 called her "an encouraging friend in need who helps new amputees come to terms with their loss."[71] After the October 1973 war between Israel and a coalition of Arab states, she visited Israel as part of a mission of the Montreal branch of the Organization for Rehabilitation through Training (ORT), which had been founded by Russian Jews in St. Petersburg in 1880 and grew into a global network dedicated to vocational training. She met with soldiers who had just lost limbs. "When the boys look and see somebody," she explained, "they are not interested in a person with two hands and legs. They like to know they are not alone in their problems and they were shocked when they learned I am an amputee." One soldier was cheered to know that she had married after she had lost her leg, not before.

"I get calls from surgeons, psychiatrists, doctors and patients themselves and I go to visit young women and young girls too," she told the *Star*. The secret, she said, was not to force herself on the patient.

"They have to want to see me, and some aren't ready to see you right away. Everyone reaches a point where they feel very sorry for themselves, and this is not the time. Mostly, I listen so they can get their feelings and fears out. It's something they've never fathomed before and which they have never experienced, and they need somebody who has been there. It's not me, it's the fact that I've been there."

At the time, Sheila's empathy had already pulled her in a new direction, after the twenty-two-year-old son of friends was paralyzed playing university football in 1971. She began counselling patients who had suffered paralysis as well and tried promoting to Montreal hospitals a reading device developed by students at the Syngalowski Centre in Tel Aviv that quadriplegics could manage themselves, rather than relying on someone else to turn pages for them.

Today, Sheila struggles to explain how she transformed into a fundraiser extraordinaire. Her parents gave generously to causes, but her father was never directly engaged in any campaigns. Sophie Kussner was involved in a Hadassah chapter, and Sheila remembers her mother hosting a large meeting at an apartment on Côte-Saint-Luc Road that her parents lived in after the nest at Beloeil emptied. But on a fundamental level, Sheila's success is not difficult to understand. She is her father's daughter—after all, Jack Golden was the greatest insurance salesman in the annals of Imperial Life. He had an unmatchable gift for making clients understand the importance of the policies he sold. Sheila too has that gift. She doesn't just get money out of people: she makes them understand the greater good that a donation will fulfill, or that cannot be fulfilled without it. Janice also believes that Jack Kussner set an example for Sheila in tipping generously, and engaging waiters and the like in conversations about their lives, and giving them money if they were in need. "She watched and learned from her dad."

"I'm like my father," Sheila allowed in 1983, when the *Canadian Jewish News* saluted her as "Montreal's top woman fundraiser"— actually, she was probably the top fundraiser of any gender in the city. "I'm a people person. I genuinely love people and give of myself, like my father. I'm animated, my face and hands are always moving. Strangers can talk to me on the street, in restaurants. There's always a bustle around me."

"When she comes into a room," says her old friend, Jeannette Valmont, "you know she's there. She storms in. She's not a quiet person. And she's usually a little late, so that makes the entrance even better. And she has a phenomenal sense of humour. That's really important with her. She can say things that, if you and I did, would sound disrespectful. She has people in stitches."

Ask her how she became someone who could routinely persuade people to write six-figure cheques, and she must pause and think. Sheila says that, when she was growing up, her family would have been considered wealthy, but it was never wealth of the sort we see today, nor did she and Marvyn live at the level of people in the community who amassed fortunes. But the postwar Jewish community of Montreal was fairly united, a small, intertwined world, especially after the Jewish General Hospital provided a focal point for its many different neighbourhoods, synagogues, and cultural roots to unite in a common cause. The community's volunteer activities and its obligations to serve brought together people from all walks of life, rich and poor.

Sheila recalls getting her start as a local fundraiser for the Combined Jewish Appeal, working within a circle of women volunteers called a *chaverot*, which in Hebrew means "girlfriends." (A group in Hebrew otherwise is a *chavura*, also *chavurah* or *havurah*, an assembly of like-minded people, as in a kibbutz.) She would secure donations from people willing to help in whatever way they could, climbing the multiple flights of Montreal's distinctive exterior staircases in neighbourhoods like Mile End to collect a small monthly donation. She was negotiating the same streets and calling at the same doors that Rebbetzin Kaplan had in funding first the Hebrew Maternity Hospital and later the Jewish General Hospital.

Sheila was collecting ten dollars, twenty dollars, sometimes even one hundred dollars. There was a walkathon for cancer research in which she was thrilled to secure donations in the hundreds of dollars. The cheques kept getting larger, and the causes for which she secured them multiplied. In 1977, her efforts for the Combined Jewish Appeal were such that she became the first woman to receive its President of the State of Israel Award. Sheila Kussner had become the powerhouse of fundraising in Montreal.

"I really care about people," she said in 1983, when asked to explain her fundraising success. "I have empathy and it shows when I speak. I'm overly expressive. It's my nature. And people veer toward me. Maybe it's my sincerity, my credibility. I have to believe in it. I believe what I'm saying. And when I thank a person he believes me. They are giving to me because I worked at it and cared—and that money is needed and important."

Sheila became such a fundraising phenomenon that, as noted, it became possible for her to be the subject of a lengthy profile in the *Canadian Jewish News* in 1983 without her status as an amputee or a cancer survivor even being mentioned. Her success and dedication seemed not to require any backstory or elaboration. Sheila today allows that her status as an amputee and cancer survivor may have helped at times. Certainly, few people can make a more persuasive case for the importance of cancer research and care than a cancer survivor or someone undergoing cancer treatment. But as Marvin Corber advises, "she's a very difficult person to say no to, and I think the reason is not that you feel pity for her, because she has no self-pity whatsoever. It's just that she's made this her life's mission, and you want to help her." And yet there was something fundamental and deeply personal about Sheila's rise that eluded grasping and otherwise went unacknowledged amid the effusive press and accolades. Because by the mid-1970s, Sheila was engaged in a desperate struggle to save Marvyn's life.

CHAPTER NINE

Jim and Jimmie

"Nobody would have been surprised if Sheila had chosen a much different path in her life," says Bram Freedman, president and CEO of the Jewish General Hospital (JGH) Foundation. She could have devoted her energies to something smaller and less all-consuming. Instead, he says, "Sheila went big." Why that happened is a consistent source of wonder.

Advocates and activists do not emerge through some random process of engagement. People do not wake up one day and decide, "I am going to dedicate myself to cause 'X,'" without a personal impetus. They act out of some compelling individual reason, something in their own circumstances—their own health or well-being, or that of a family member or friend.

That motivation may be "selfish," in the sense that the advocacy and volunteerism is driven by concern for improving their own life or that of a loved one. People with a family member or friend in need routinely step into this role. But there is something different about cases like that of Sheila Kussner—and of the people Sheila has inspired to join her. You may have a child with a learning disability, and advocate for their education with a teacher or a principal or a school board, but that seldom translates into a lifelong dedication to improving education for all children with learning disabilities. You may be diagnosed with prostate cancer, and you and your spouse may do everything within your power to ensure you have the best available care, but that seldom translates into a lifelong dedication to improving prostate cancer research and treatment for every man who has prostate cancer or will be diagnosed with it.

One could argue that networking with others in similar circumstances amounts to a pragmatic recognition of strength in numbers in achieving a selfish goal. But something propels certain people beyond the selfish. They stay engaged with an issue, after their own circumstances have been resolved or that issue is otherwise no longer part of their life. Most important, they stay engaged because of their concern for others beyond that selfish circle.

This question of motivation is not an esoteric matter. The world of advocacy and volunteerism thrives on the selfish, but ultimately is sustained by the selfless. When people who know Sheila want to know what propels her forward, they are ultimately wondering what secret psychological elixir, what philosopher's stone, makes someone like her possible. Because without extraordinary people like Sheila, causes collapse. Cancer care alone is replete with examples of volunteer organizations that could not be sustained beyond the energies of their founders. There was no one capable or willing to take up the torch; there was no way to bottle the founder's elixir, preserve it within an organization's constitution, and ensure the perpetuation of one individual's remarkable energy and devotion.

In 1998, a Long Island clinical psychologist, Janice Stefanacci, described for *The New York Times* what she called the Phoenix Factor, "the quality that allows some people to rise above grief and anger in the aftermath of a personal tragedy." As she explained, "their lives are torn to ashes, but they find something inside of them that gives them the strength to contribute and make a difference. They turned meaninglessness into meaning, so that the tragedy of their lives wasn't in vain. Many of the best fighters were just living normal lives when lightning struck."

Several "Phoenix Factor" people in Long Island profiled by *The New York Times* echoed Sheila's experiences and attitude. Mitchel Shapiro became legally blind and severely hearing impaired because of Usher Syndrome, a retinal degenerative disease that also causes hearing loss. Along with the disabilities came a series of personal setbacks: divorce, a family business sold, then a breakup with a girlfriend. "I felt like I had reached rock bottom. Then I came to an awakening. It started with a poster with the message: 'Your greatest weakness is your greatest strength.' That poster nagged at me for two and a half days until I finally got it—my greatest weaknesses, my vision and my hearing, are my greatest strengths. I could either give in and feel sorry for myself, or take control of my life." In other words, *be better, not bitter.* He became a public speaker and advocate for the blind and hearing impaired. Jill and Stuart Gleiber became advocates for people with head injuries and their families after their thirteen-year-old son was hit by a car. They offered that their motivation to become activists was "strictly selfish," being concerned only about their son. "But in our selfishness," Jill said, "we have taken hundreds of other children with us on our path."

Sheila Kussner's status as a cancer survivor and an amputee unquestionably helped to shape her personality, especially her
determination. The loss of a leg was something she was going to
overcome, to the degree that anyone who didn't know better would
not suspect the loss. Acceptance can be a powerful motivator for
achievement. And while it would be wrong to say that empathy was
lacking until she experienced trauma herself, that trauma honed her
appreciation of obstacles faced by others and helped her to see that
merely feeling sorry for someone was not an effective response. Pity
was as good as saying, "your situation is hopeless." She recognized
that people had deep inner resources that could be tapped, if other
people would support and understand them.

The fact that she had beaten the vanishingly small odds of surviving osteosarcoma gave Sheila the experience and nerve to offer
encouragement to anyone with a poor prognosis. If someone says
their particular cancer has a sixteen per cent survival rate, Sheila's
response invariably has been: someone has to form that sixteen per
cent, so why not you? She has never expected people to defeat cancer
on attitude alone, but she wants people to live with hope. Having
hope is a way of coping.

For all that Sheila's personal traumas in childhood influenced her
character, they only partly explain her extraordinary transformation in the 1970s, and the extraordinary transformations in cancer
support and care that she made possible. It was when she was suddenly faced with the prospect of losing her beloved Marvyn that
Sheila's volunteerism went into overdrive. Sheila is a Phoenix that
rose more than once.

At age nineteen, Sheila Golden sailed passed the critical five-year threshold, by which time the vast majority of diagnosed cases of osteosarcoma treated only with amputation had died, and she kept on thriving. But risks remained. Although metastases in the lungs that claimed most patients almost always turned up within about fourteen months of the initial diagnoses, there were cases in which the cancer had bided its time. In the 1973 UCLA study of forty-six patients, one patient was spared the metastases for almost four years; for another, eight years and five months passed.[72]

There was also a heightened risk of experiencing another incident of primary bone cancer. A massive European study of almost seventy thousand survivors of childhood and adolescent cancer in 2018 determined that osteosarcoma patients who survived five years still faced an excess risk of a primary bone cancer seventy-eight times higher than the general population.[73] As well, a study of about twenty-three thousand Canadian children from 1992 to 2014 found that having some form of bone cancer as a first cancer "considerably increased" the risk of developing leukemia and soft-tissue cancers.[74] The risk of developing another primary bone cancer, at least, faded with the years. It may be a truism that the longer an osteosarcoma patient lives, the longer they live.

Some twenty-eight years after osteosarcoma had taken away her leg, cancer finally returned for Sheila Kussner. It did not return *in* her, but it returned nevertheless. At age forty-three, Marvyn Kussner was diagnosed with a malignant form of lymphoma, reticulum-cell sarcoma, also known as non-Hodgkin's lymphoma. As its name suggests, it is a cancer of the lymph system, involving lymphocytes, or white blood cells. It often starts in the lymph nodes but can occur anywhere that lymph tissue is found. While the prospects were not nearly as poor as they had been for Sheila with osteosarcoma, non-Hodgkin's lymphoma remained a "terrible"[75] prognosis into the new millennium.

Sheila would admit to being angered by Marvyn's diagnosis. It was as if cancer was something external to the afflicted body, a malevolent entity that demanded unreasonable offerings. She felt that she had given cancer more than enough through osteosarcoma. It had taken her leg. Why was it now knocking on her door, demanding her husband as well?

If there was anything fortunate about Marvyn's diagnosis, it was that it came around 1973, just as chemotherapy was overcoming a stigma of experimental failure. Had non-Hodgkin's found Marvyn even a few years earlier, it might have proved fatal. Chemotherapy had made so little progress since the 1940s that in the 1960s, there was still no such thing as medical oncology, the discipline dedicated to researching and treating cancer. As Vincent T. DeVita Jr. and Edward Chu have explained, "those who were given the task of administering chemotherapy at most medical centers were regarded as underachievers at best. The main issue of the day was whether cancer drugs caused more harm than good, and talk of curing cancer with drugs was not considered compatible with sanity. The prevailing attitude toward the use of chemotherapy can only be described as hostile … It took plain old courage to be a chemotherapist in the 1960s and certainly the courage of the conviction that cancer would eventually succumb to drugs."[76]

The tide turned with advances in the treatment of acute lymphocytic leukemia in children and Hodgkin's disease. By the end of the 1960s, "it was now clear that anticancer drugs could cure cancer."[77] Seeking a cure for Marvyn's lymphoma would bring Sheila to the door of one of the most renowned cancer researchers in the world, a key figure in discovering a cure for childhood leukemia.

In 1972, the prestigious Albert Lasker Clinical Medical Research Award was given to sixteen international researchers for their breakthrough discoveries in chemotherapy. Among them was James F. Holland of Roswell Park Memorial Institute in Buffalo, New York, honoured for his contributions to combination therapy in treating acute leukemia in children. Holland had already been elected president of the American Association for Cancer Research in 1970. He was just twenty-eight when he became chief of medicine at Roswell Park in the early 1950s and had been striving to cure childhood leukemia since the mid-1950s.

Holland chaired Acute Leukemia Group B, an international collaboration of physicians and scientists researching new chemotherapy regimens. In 1956, the group's one-year survival rate for childhood leukemia was thirty per cent; the five-year rate was a mere four per cent. By 1966, Holland's group had increased the five-year rate to twenty-seven per cent. Then came a startling breakthrough. A new therapy that used combinations of drugs rather than individual drugs saw twenty-nine of thirty-three children treated in 1968 still alive in 1972. With that astonishing leap forward, childhood leukemia became curable for most patients. Researchers working in parallel on Hodgkin's disease achieved a similar, startling breakthrough.

In 1973, the field of medical oncology, which included chemotherapy, was officially established in the United States as a subspecialty of internal medicine. That year, Holland left Roswell Park to establish a department of neoplastic diseases at the Tisch Cancer Institute at the Icahn School of Medicine at Mount Sinai Hospital in New York City, where he oversaw an ever-growing array of clinical trials in chemotherapy for cancers of all kinds, including interleukin-2 in the 1980s. With Emil Frei III, a fellow winner of the Lasker award in 1972 for his achievements in treating childhood leukemia and Hodgkin's disease, Holland would write in 2006 *Cancer Medicine*, the literal textbook on cancer treatment now in its ninth edition.

Back in Montreal, Marvyn Kussner was diagnosed with non-Hodgkin's lymphoma just as oncology was becoming a recognized specialty and drugs were beginning to outright cure some cancers. But he struggled with his treatments. Effective chemotherapy was in its infancy, and there was no such thing as a department of oncology at the Jewish General, or for that matter at McGill University. Sheila remembers Marvyn having an allergic reaction to his treatments. Despairing, she turned to Richard Margolese, a surgeon at the Jewish General who was also participating in an important long-term study of breast cancer treatment, and asked him for the name of the greatest authority in the field, wherever they might be. And Margolese, who had done a one-year fellowship in cancer surgery at Roswell Park in 1966–67, said: "James Holland." Which was all that Sheila needed to hear to send her in the direction of Holland and Mount Sinai.

James Holland was as complex as the diseases he devoted his life to curing. He would recall shifting his interest from cardiology to what became known as oncology as a young doctor when he had an interim job at Columbia University Hospital. There, he met a four-year-old girl, Josephine, with leukemia. Initially, she responded to treatment. "I had come to love this child, and she loved me," he would say. "Her remission was extremely meaningful to me, but by the same token, it was tragic when she relapsed and died." Josephine "was only a child. A crying child."

He seemingly hardened himself against individual suffering as he devoted himself to trials of experimental and at times fatal courses of chemical treatment in search of cures for an array of cancers. "Patients have to be subsidiaries of the trial," he bluntly declared in 1986, by which time he was overseeing fifty clinical trials involving about thirteen hundred patients at Mount Sinai. "I'm not interested in holding patients' hands. I'm interested in curing cancer." Medicine's Hippocratic Oath—"First, do no harm"—had no place in his work. "If you do no harm," he explained, "then you do no harm to the cancer either. I'm interested in the curability of these diseases."[78] His job was not to help cancer patients in his trials "die gracefully." They were data to him, whatever their individual outcomes. He knew that the experimental chemical cocktails could and would kill some of them before their cancer ever did, and that these patients amounted to consenting guinea pigs. "I have a fundamental love of life for others," he asserted, and he was in fact a deeply caring man. But in his clinical research, it was the fates of future generations that concerned him. If he could find a way to cure cancers, by experimenting on willing patients who were otherwise going to die, then whatever harm he did to individual enrollees was justified.

Cancer treatment trials into the 1980s remained controversial. Some doctors were reluctant to refer patients, knowing or fearing the suffering that might lie in wait. Researchers striving to find the right cocktail of drugs and radiation in the 1960s in search of a cure for childhood leukemia had struggled with ethical controversies, or at least found workarounds. Two key chemotherapy experiments for Hodgkin's disease almost didn't proceed because of professional resistance. But a protocol achieved a complete remission in about sixty per cent of patients with advanced Hodgkin's, and by 1975, investigators were able to report the cure of advanced diffuse large B-cell lymphoma.

The ongoing experiments of Holland and his colleagues opened avenues of hope for cancer patients where none had previously existed. The human will to live is fierce, and as Holland's renown spread, so did the demands from patients with nothing left to lose to be included in his trials. Sheila Kussner, seeking a cure for Marvyn, was just one of many people who came calling.

By the mid-1980s (if not sooner), James Holland (who died in 2018) was uncompromising and unsentimental about who he would and would not accept for his clinical trials. He did not care how much money they had, who they knew, or how desperate they might be. Actually, he *did* care about desperation, because their mental state might disqualify them as a reliable trial candidate. As *The New York Times* reported, Holland was "not interested in what patients want or their friends want but rather what best fits his research. For most experiments, patients who have received other therapies such as radiation or drugs, for example, are immediately eliminated as being 'contaminated' for the purposes of his research. So are patients whose disease is so far progressed that they are not given a good chance of tolerating new medications. Still other patients are eliminated because they are assessed to be psychologically unstable and likely to back out in midstream."

To the best of Sheila's recollection, Marvyn was one of the fortunate ones whose case James Holland agreed to take on in a clinical trial. Reticulum cell lymphoma was rare, and Holland was interested in Marvyn and the family history. If the fact that Marvyn might already be "contaminated" by his earlier treatments was an issue, Holland overlooked it. Marvyn did not draw the short straw of becoming a trial participant who served as a control comparison to other patients who received an experimental regimen; nor did he become one of the patients for whom the experimental regimen proved so toxic as to be fatal.

Sheila says when Holland walked into a room and you met him for the first time, he could be loud and gruff, "all doctor, all medicine. He was friendly if you knew him, not so friendly if you didn't. But he was a wonderful person. Very bright, knowledgeable, not condescending."

Marvyn responded well to his treatment. "We were going to New York every three months, then every six months, then twice a year, then once a year," Sheila says. Holland did not cure Marvyn, but he kept him alive, and he lived for another forty years. "He was never completely one hundred per cent," Sheila says. "I was conscious of whether he was going to be okay. But as a husband he was unbelievable." Unfortunately for Marvyn, and for Sheila, Marvyn was never entirely healthy for the last half of his life. Prostate cancer too would come along, and so would heart disease.

Marvyn nevertheless pursued an active, engaged life, with family, friends, and colleagues. He loved classical music, and golf was a great source of friendship and laughter. From spring until early fall, Marvyn generally spent his Saturdays on the links at Elm Ridge Country Club. "It was a wonderful and healthy outlet for him," says Janice. "He loved being with his golf friends, who he adored and they adored him. Dad had a very good sense of humour, as did a few of his golf friends. Laughter is a wonderful thing to be able to participate in, especially when dealing with life's vicissitudes." Before heading to the club, Marvyn's friends would drop by the house for breakfast. "Mom would have baked one of her famous specialties, a coffee cake that was fluffier than fluffy and beyond delicious, to complement freshly squeezed orange juice." James Holland bought Marvyn an enormous amount of time, and he made the most of it.

At first with Marvyn, James Holland maintained a professional, doctor-patient relationship. "They became friendly," Sheila says, and Dr. James became Jim. "Jim liked Marvyn very much." Whenever Sheila and Marvyn were in New York, they would take Jim Holland out to dinner. Marvyn, unsolicited, provided Holland with funds that helped him to attend an important conference in Europe. As the relationship became social, Jim's wife, Jimmie, entered their small circle.

Jimmie was a psychiatrist. Someone in psychiatry could have had a field day with the mentalities of scientists and physicians engaged in the search for cancer cures, as the process was so potentially traumatizing for the professionals involved and had raised at times troubling questions about ethics. But Jimmie Holland was interested in the psychological impact of cancer on patients. Her concern proved life-changing for patients around the world, but especially in Montreal.

In 1927, a half-mile-wide F4 tornado swept through northeast Texas, almost wiping from the map the town of Nevada. About the only thing that put the town of a few hundred souls back on the map was the birth the following year of Jimmie Coker Holland. She was the only child on a cotton farm in what she called the "blackland

Sheila, age sixteen.

Sheila's mother, Sophie
(née Sophia Saxe) Golden.

Sheila's father, Jack Golden.

GOLDEN, SHEILA RUTH
"*Be always merry as ever you can,*
For none delights in a sorrowful man."
Born Aug. 24, 1932, in Montreal. Attended Strathcona Academy. Entered McGill, 1949.

Sheila in the 1953 McGill
University yearbook.

Sheila and Marvyn Kussner on their wedding day, September 6, 1953.

Sheila in Palm Beach, Florida, 1962.

Sheila (back row, second from left) with the original Hope & Cope volunteers and their first coordinator, Megan McLeod (back row, second from right), at their 1982 orientation.

Sheila with Pierre Trudeau and Yitzhak Rabin on the occasion of Sheila receiving the State of Israel Bonds Eleanor Roosevelt Humanities Award, 1983

Marvyn (top left) and Sheila,
with Jim and Jimmie Holland.

Sheila and Marvyn with their daughters Janice Kussner and Joanne Kussner Leopold;
Joanne's husband, John Leopold; and Joanne and John's children, Justin and Carolyn.

Sheila receiving her honorary doctorate of law degree from McGill University, 1990.

Sheila and Justin Trudeau at a Denim and Diamonds fundraiser for Hope & Cope.

Sheila with Joan Unger (left), a founding member of Chaverot (Friends) of Hope
& Cope; long-standing volunteer Deborah Bridgman (right); and Hope & Cope's
Suzanne O'Brien.

Sheila looks on as Montreal mayor Gérard Tremblay releases a butterfly, the symbol of
Hope & Cope, at the opening of the Wellness Centre.

Salvatore Guerrera with Sheila and Marvyn.

Sheila and her friends, family, and colleagues at the formal unveiling of her name on the exterior of Montreal's Jewish General Hospital, June 22, 2022.

Bible-totin'" part of the state, where, as she would quip, girls got boys' names and boys got girls' names.[79] She managed to escape via Baylor University School of Medicine in Houston, where she was one of only three women to graduate in her class.

Jimmie Holland chose to specialize in psychiatry, which she studied in St. Louis. Psychosomatic medicine was in vogue, but Holland never showed any apparent interest in the controversial branch, rooted in psychoanalysis, that sought some precursor in personality for a patient developing cancer. Her interest, instead, was in how the experience of illness was expressed in psychiatric terms by patients. How did the mind of the individual respond to physical illness—the lived reality of having it, being treated for it, and facing the consequences of it?

Jimmie Holland secured a residency and fellowship at Massachusetts General Hospital, where J.E. Finesinger, a Harvard professor and head of the psychiatric division, was publishing groundbreaking studies of psychological mechanisms and feelings of guilt in cancer patients. In 1955, Holland and a hospital staff member, Martin R. Coles, conducted a study of polio patients who were hospitalized during the Boston epidemic that year. (Finesinger later published on psychiatric issues in polio patients.) Their results were presented at the 112th annual meeting of the American Psychiatric Association, in Chicago in the spring of 1956, and published in 1957. Jimmie Holland would not produce another paper for twenty years. The study is absent from biographies of Holland, and she does not include it in her personal backstory in her book, *The Human Side of Cancer*. But the Boston polio study is a remarkable harbinger of her work in psychosocial oncology (also known as psycho-oncology), and of her role in helping Sheila Kussner establish Hope & Cope.

Doctors at Massachusetts General had begun noticing "unusual psychological phenomena" in their acutely ill polio patients and alerted the psychiatric staff.[80] Here was an opportunity to understand the mental dimension of a terrible, recurrent plague that has been called the most feared disease of most of the twentieth century; polio caused more than fifteen thousand cases of paralysis a year in the United States alone in the early 1950s. In the worst cases, patients were unable to breathe on their own and confined in artificial respirators, or "iron lungs."

Holland and Coles interviewed 108 patients ranging in age from fifteen to seventy-eight. They came away from the study convinced of a role for psychiatry in the treatment and support of patients with this life-threatening illness. "Many patients enthusiastically welcomed our visits. Interviews offered them an opportunity to express their fears and anxieties. They were unable to express these feelings to their families or to a medical and nursing staff with little time to listen. A real need existed for a person with whom they could discuss the emotional impact of their illness ... It soon became clear that the majority of patients had substantial emotional problems related to the illness legitimately within the purview of a psychiatrist ... In addition, psychiatric consultation with the families, in some instances, helped them to adjust to the serious illness and long rehabilitation of their relatives."[81]

Jimmie Holland (with Coles, who never published anything further) was some twenty years ahead of the curve in recognizing the essential needs in patient support that psycho-oncology would address. She had also described a counselling role, a *listening* role. She was thinking exclusively in terms of support by professional psychiatrists, but it would have been possible to imagine patients who had been through the harrowing experience of polio providing peer support to current patients. Holland, however, had struck upon a need for a disease that was on the verge of being largely conquered. In April 1955, the Salk vaccine was declared safe and effective after a national field trial of 1.8 million schoolchildren. The major illness for which Holland identified such intriguing psychiatric components and opportunities for counselling support for patients and their families rapidly all but vanished in the Western world; there were fewer than one hundred cases in the United States in the 1960s, and fewer than ten in the 1970s.

The counselling response to polio was eminently transferable to cancer, which in the wake of vaccine successes with polio became the *cause célèbre* of health research. But with the essential disappearance of polio, Jimmie Holland's idea of psychiatric support for patients with a serious, life-threatening illness went unexploited. Coincidentally, she withdrew from active medical practice and research just as polio ceased to be a feared and terrible scourge. She married James Holland in 1956, and they settled in Buffalo. While Jim pursued a chemotherapeutic cure for childhood leukemia at Roswell Park, Jimmie mainly stayed home and raised their five children.

But it was impossible for Jimmie Holland not to be as intrigued by the psychiatric or psychological aspects of cancer care. "I would listen to Jim and his colleagues, who often came to dinner, discuss the new treatments for leukemia and the side effects patients had to tolerate to achieve the long-term goal of cure … Those long discussions over dinner of the troubling side effects would lead to my asking, 'But how do the patients feel about all this?' At that time, virtually no one queried the patients about how they were doing because the focus was on changing the dismal outlook all of them faced. Little was known about and little was done to help with the human side of cancer."[82]

She returned to work, as an associate clinical professor in the department of psychiatry at SUNY Buffalo and rose from an attending psychiatrist at a local teaching hospital to director of its department of psychiatry.[83] At Roswell Park, Jimmie began to collaborate with Jim, establishing what was called the Special Medical Clinic to provide psychiatric care to cancer patients. As Jimmie would recall, patients "didn't balk at being seen by a psychiatrist because it was, after all, *special*."[84] One patient remarked to her that doctors "have measured everything but my thoughts and mind. Somehow, my mental attitude, the stress, the anguish should be analyzed and studied the same as my physical condition." Jimmie Holland felt that this patient was onto something: doctors were missing the emotional component of cancer. "If we could measure what our patients were feeling psychologically, we would be able to add that information to the overall assessment of side effects and toxicity. This approach would give us much valuable information, not only about the physical but also about the human effect of a new treatment. That information could then be shared with patients contemplating taking the treatment."[85]

In this initial (and essential) conception of what the field of psycho-oncology could be, the patient's mental or emotional response to their illness and its treatment was to be gathered and used to improve patient responses to treatment—a valuable feedback loop for medical research and care. Through her many years chairing the Quality of Life Committee of James Holland's Cancer and Leukemia Group B (CALGB) trials, Jimmie Holland became a pioneer in including psychological and emotional well-being, through patient-reported outcomes using quality-of-life measures, as a component of the *clinical* outcomes of clinical trials.[86]

Yet what psycho-oncology would give rise to, foremost at Hope & Cope, was something that seemed rooted in Holland's experiences and insights as an intern in Boston, when she was interviewing polio patients, and in particular simply listening to those patients, and providing support not only to them but also to their families. Polio was not "just" a terrible disease. It was also a lived experience, with social and psychological dimensions that extended far beyond the specific behaviours of a virus that invades the spinal cord. Some work in the psychiatric dimension of the cancer experience, as we have seen, had been performed by Finesinger (and others) at Massachusetts General in the 1950s. As well, A.M. Sutherland and colleagues at Memorial Sloan Kettering Cancer Center in Manhattan at that time had published on the psychological impacts of cancer and cancer surgery. But Memorial Sloan Kettering closed its psychiatric department in 1961. Cancer was waiting for someone to recognize those same dimensions. Jimmie Holland, not surprisingly, became one of the most prominent members of that professional recognition, if not its leading figure.

In 1975, a small group gathered in San Antonio, Texas, for the first national research conference for the new field of psycho-oncology. The American Cancer Society began supporting research, and in 1977, Jimmie Holland was hired to revive the psychiatric group at Memorial Sloan Kettering. Sheila Kussner remembers this period, with James Holland encouraging his wife to press on with this aspect of cancer care. Jimmie Holland began to develop clinical services, a postgraduate training program for psychiatrists and psychologists, and a research initiative. Memorial Sloan Kettering became "a force for national and international development of psycho-oncology," as Jimmie Holland would write, but really, it was Holland who was that force. Jimmie Holland, as William Breitbart, her successor at Memorial Sloan Kettering, would remember, "created and nurtured the field of Psycho-oncology, established the clinical practice, advanced its clinical research agenda, and through her pioneering efforts, launched the careers of the leaders of a national and world-wide field."[87]

Jimmie Holland had scarcely started her work as this force for developing psycho-oncology as an international discipline when she came to know Montreal's own formidable force in the person of Sheila Kussner. With Jimmie's advice and encouragement, Sheila would radically change the trajectory of cancer patient care and support. In 1981, Sheila named her volunteer service for cancer patients Hope & Cope. That same year, Jimmie Holland published *The Human Side of Cancer: Living with Hope, Coping with Uncertainty.*

Jim Holland too recognized and supported Sheila's work. "When Fate willed against the leg bone connected to the thigh bone," he would write Sheila in a personal note, "it might have sensed your head bone was connected to your heart bone."

CHAPTER TEN

Landsmen and Landsladies

In the busy streets of immigrant Jewish Montreal in the late nineteenth and early twentieth centuries, one figure attracted more than their share of attention: the landsman. For a recent arrival, a landsman (from the Yiddish for a male "compatriot") was a fellow immigrant with shared roots in the Old Country—someone from the same city or shtetl, the same synagogue or school, or who spoke the same Yiddish dialect.[88] In Dufferin Square, Israel Medres would recall, Jews of the neighbourhood would gather on Saturday afternoons, to meet up with their fellow landsmen. The established and experienced landsmen dispensed advice on every imaginable subject—"finding a job, adapting generally to the new environment, and learning the manners and customs of the new homeland as quickly as possible."[89] Many decades later, Sheila Kussner would prove to be a different sort of landsman—a landslady, if you will—in drawing on her own experiences and expertise in whatever way she could to help the newcomers to another strange new land, that of cancer treatment and care.

That cancer represented a landscape was articulated by Susan Sontag in *Illness as Metaphor*, the American essayist's enormously influential book that was published in 1978, just as Sheila Kussner was on the cusp of launching Hope & Cope. Paradoxically, perhaps, Sontag insisted that "illness is *not* a metaphor, and that the most truthful way of regarding illness—and the healthiest way of being ill—is one most purified of, most resistant to, metaphoric thinking." She wanted to describe "the punitive or sentimental fantasies con-cocted about that situation: not real geography, but stereotypes of national character ... Yet it is hardly possible to take up one's resi-dence in the kingdom of the ill unprejudiced by the lurid metaphors with which it has been landscaped." Her goal, she said, was to eluci-date those metaphors, and seek a liberation from them.[90]

Sontag nevertheless wielded powerful metaphors of time and space, and especially of place. "Illness is the night-side of life, a more onerous citizenship. Everyone who is born holds dual citizenship, in the kingdom of the well and the kingdom of the sick." And even though she was not interested in describing (as someone who had experienced cancer) "what it is really like to emigrate to the kingdom of the ill and live there,"[91] we are left with an enduring conception of illness as an experience with its own geography, a place in which someone diagnosed arrives: often bewildered, confused, fright-ened, seeking answers, and unsure about the future. Today, Suzanne O'Brien of Hope & Cope routinely refers to someone's experience of cancer as being in "Cancer Land."

Cancer Land is a place of immigrants, but never a destination of choice. Hope might seem to be left behind in the kingdom of the well as the newcomers come ashore in the kingdom of the sick. And while for some there can be no returning to the kingdom of the well, sickness does not have to mean for them a banishment, or that hope itself remains out of reach.

Sheila Kussner's own experiences as a cancer survivor and amputee led to her engagement in related volunteerism, but it was Marvyn's illness that turbocharged her activities and gave them a fresh focus. Securing treatment for Marvyn introduced her to an emerging world of cancer care. More patients like Marvyn were procuring at times experimental but effective treatments in the 1970s. There was suddenly hope with many forms of cancer, where there had been little or none before. But at the same time, medicine as a practice and an institution was struggling to keep pace with the consequences of this dramatic and unfolding shift in the dynamics of patient care.

Several studies in the 1950s and 1960s, in the United States and Europe, had probed the way doctors communicated with their patients about cancer as they wrestled with the issue of whether they ought to deliver a frank prognosis, unencumbered by euphemisms for cancer such as "lesion," "mass," "growth," or "tumour." In a landmark study at one Chicago hospital published in 1961, ninety per cent of the staff members in internal medicine, obstetrics-gynecology, and surgery who filled out a questionnaire indicated they preferred not to tell patients that they had cancer. Such a diagnosis, they insisted, is "a death sentence," "a Buchenwald," or "torture." Telling the patient is "the crudest thing in the world," "awful," and "hitting the patient with a baseball bat." One respondent wrote, "no one can be told without giving up and losing all hope."[92]

While attitudes to revealing a diagnosis in the Chicago study varied widely across disciplines (ninety-four per cent of dermatologists favoured disclosure, compared to only twelve per cent of radiologists), most doctors (ninety-seven per cent of whom were male, and whose average age was fifty) were adhering to a paternalistic policy that they knew what was best for the emotional well-being of the patient. Doctors professed concerns about depression, even suicide, among patients who received full disclosure. But patients themselves appeared to feel very differently, even though, at the time, few cancers were curable. Two American studies in the 1950s had found that patients overwhelmingly favoured being told their diagnosis. Patients also resented being lied to and were capable of figuring out the truth about their condition (which was often terminal) themselves. As one woman in a 1960 Swedish study of inoperable cancer patients reported, "I could see from the doctor's face that I had cancer. Why did everyone's attitude to me change although they told me that the operation had not disclosed anything alarming?"[93]

The 1961 Chicago study found that "inconsistencies, opinion-atedness, and resistance to change and to research ... indicated emotion-laden *a priori* personal judgments" were the real reason for doctors' insistence on not disclosing a cancer diagnosis.[94] But despite evidence that most patients probably wanted to be told, even while most doctors surveyed didn't want to tell them, the study cautioned that full disclosure was not necessarily the answer. "Anxiety about death is ubiquitous ... To ignore wisdom based on insight into ourselves and to go about blithely telling patients they have cancer, obviously would be senseless."[95] And so, the widespread practice of not telling patients they had cancer persisted into the 1970s.

But change was occurring, rapidly, at least in North America. A 1970 questionnaire, for example, found that only nine per cent of responding doctors never shared the cancer diagnosis with their patients.[96] A 1977 study indicated that a general policy to inform the patient was adhered to by ninety-eight per cent of staff at Strong Memorial Hospital in Rochester, New York.[97] The study was far from scientific—it depended on staff returning a usable survey, of which only forty per cent did, and so there may have been some self-selecting by staff who advocated more openness. Nevertheless, the results were consistent with a trend toward greater frankness in how doctors communicated with cancer patients.

Jimmie Holland would argue that cancer emerged from a long-standing taboo of acknowledgment by physicians and patients because the public felt "a greater optimism about cancer," and that was mainly because in the 1970s the ranks of survivors were increasing through chemotherapeutic successes. Those survivors were being "vocal about their successful outcomes," which was a big change from the past, when people were more inclined to remain silent about the disease because of its stigma and fears about losing their jobs.[98] It was also a time when celebrities began coming forward, in particular Betty Ford, wife of US president Gerald Ford, who went public with the news of her radical mastectomy in 1974, and in speaking out, "broke through the existing taboos surrounding breast cancer."[99] Holland also saw at play "a surge of powerful social movements championing human rights that were the legacy of the Vietnam era, directing the nation's attention to previously underserved individuals: women, consumers, and patients."[100]

This shift in patient responses to their care confronted a medical system that might have been changing but was still wont to focus on the physician and the disease and sideline the patient, as the language of the profession tellingly revealed. The very idea that disease was something experienced by a person, as opposed to some biological process with which medical professionals battled, had long been poorly appreciated. Sheila's good friend Abraham Fuks has become renowned for his research in immunological aspects of type-1 diabetes and the molecular nature of tumours, but also for his explorations of the way medical practice has been defined or revealed through its choices of language, especially metaphor. He has probed the way medicine has for centuries resorted to the language of combat in describing the body's own responses to infection and disease, and in framing the role of medical science and physicians and surgeons in treating patients.

Cancer, when it was spoken of at all in the past (and to a fair extent still today), was framed in militaristic language, as in the case of Dr. Richards's 1946 address to the Jewish General Hospital's Women's Auxiliary on the "Fight against Cancer." Science declared "war on cancer," among other scourges. Well into the period in which major advances were being achieved in diagnosing and treating cancer, the military metaphor endured. A *New York Times* profile of James Holland in 1986 described him in his office at Mount Sinai Hospital "standing over his charts and graphs like a commander in chief preparing for battle."

The idea that a patient's individual experience with cancer constitutes a "fight" is common, as it is with any disease, or any sort of personal challenge. There is no harm, and even value for many, in framing their cancer experience as a form of personal combat against a defined adversary. But the analogy of combat on a military scale for the medical community, in confronting this disease, is still worth probing. "The physician in charge is the commander responsible for overall strategy" in addressing a patient's illness, Fuks explains in *The Language of Medicine*. He tends to be male and commands an "intelligence and spy corps" that includes radiologists, imaging specialists, clinical pathologists, microbiologists, and, increasingly, computer scientists. "The surgeon or physician-general is also the tactical commander of the war to conquer the disease, a fighter whose allies are the quartermaster in charge of the blood bank, the anesthesiologist providing sedation, and the radiation oncologist marshaling the radiotherapy machine."

Fuks asks: "In this bilateral militarized relationship between the doctor and the disease, what then is the role assigned to the person who is suffering?" The ill person, he says, "is the battleground on which the war is fought." The patient on (or within) whom this war is waged is secondary, if even acknowledged as being a party to the conflict. In this metaphoric model, the doctor is the protagonist, and the traditional, paternalistic model of medical practice "does not provide space for consultations with the patient as an ally in the fight and renders that person as a passive, perhaps anaesthetized, field of war." Fuks's analysis adds another dimension to the landscape metaphor offered by Susan Sontag. Cancer Land was not only the patient's experience of cancer—for the physician (and cancer), Cancer Land was also the terrain being fought over: the patient.

Jimmie Holland recognized a consumerist element to the shift in the relationship between cancer patients and the care they receive. Medicine is concerned with treatment, and a seemingly simple question like "how is a patient treated?" invites a wide range of responses. Cancer care had developed (to resort to the usual militarized language) an arsenal of weapons: surgery, chemotherapy, irradiation, adjuvant therapy, and ever-expanding clinical trials, all under the new disciplinary umbrella of oncology. This arsenal was the essential, and indispensable, response to a patient's condition. But "treatment" includes the manner in which patients are treated as human beings, and ranges from simple bedside manner to informed consent to treatment options to support services, and beyond. This aspect of treatment is patient- rather than disease-focused. It recognizes that beneath the white blood cell counts and regimens of radiation and drug cocktails there is a living, breathing individual with unique characteristics that are social, psychological, and circumstantial.

Medical care in cancer was racing ahead, by any historical measure, and that was creating new realities in patient numbers and needs, through the sheer size of survival ranks and the consequences of treatment regimens. But this changing scene also exposed or exacerbated existing problems and shortcomings in how patients were treated.

If you were to ask a cancer patient, "how are you being treated?" when Sheila was seeking care for Marvyn, they might reply by recounting their treatment regimen. But if you asked instead, "how is the medical system treating you, as a person?" you might get a very different answer. That system still might not even be willing to utter the word "cancer" in your presence. And even if it did, your answer to how you were being treated as a person still might be "badly." You might say: *I'm anxious. I'm terrified. I don't know if I'll live. I don't know if this is going to come back. I don't know if I can hold onto my job. I don't know what's going to happen to my kids, or my spouse. I don't know how to tell friends, family, co-workers, what is happening to me. I don't have anybody to talk to about any of this.* This list was (and is) endless.

This element of treatment, in a broad, non-superficial way, was a consumer-driven concern. The patient was a recipient of services, but the scope of those services largely was dictated to them by the medical system. A patient might, if they were fortunate, have some choices in the sorts of services they received—options in treatment, opportunities to participate in trials—but there was an array of needs for which there were no choices at all, because the medical system had nothing to offer. There was a vast, dynamic dimension to being a cancer patient for which the existing model of patient care had no answers. The medical system was too busy waging war on an enemy to notice the lived experience of the patients.

Something had to give. More to the point, someone had to give. Patients themselves began to demand not only better service but also participation in the delivery of those services.

At the Jewish General Hospital in Montreal, Richard Margolese developed a reputation for forthrightness, for not accepting the status quo. After attending Roswell Park for his fellowship in cancer surgery in 1967–68, he returned to the Jewish General, to chafe against the persistent social taboos of cancer that had become institutionalized within the hospital.

As a junior surgeon, Margolese recalls discussing with the chief surgeon the practice of "isolating" the patient from the reality of their cancer diagnosis. The hospital had a follow-up clinic for cancer patients. The sign on the door said SPECIAL CLINIC. Margolese thought the clinic ought to be labelled what it was: CANCER CLINIC. The chief surgeon told him, "You can't tell people they have cancer." Margolese replied, "I spent a year where everyone I treated knew they had cancer, and they did very well with it."

"I tried to get the sign on the clinic changed," Margolese recalls, "and they fought me. People more senior to me said, 'Be careful. You cannot speak to patients this way. You cannot take away hope.' People like me were saying, 'Wait a minute. You can't tell me that with an adult, thinking person who's just had disfiguring surgery, you're going to tell them that they don't have cancer and there's nothing to worry about. This is foolish.' We had to settle for a compromise. It was called the [Surgery and] Tumour Clinic, because "tumour" was not a word like "cancer." Eventually, we got it called the Cancer Centre."

In early 1969, Margolese also wrote an impassioned letter to the hospital's board, imploring them to cease the sale of tobacco products on the hospital premises. The first report of the Surgeon General of the US Public Health Service, five years earlier in January 1964, had reviewed the extant medical literature and concluded that cigarette smoking was a cause of lung cancer and laryngeal cancer in men, a probable cause of lung cancer in women, and the most important cause of chronic bronchitis. Margolese argued that the hospital "has both a professional responsibility, as well as a moral obligation" to end on-site tobacco sales, and in March 1969, the board agreed.

Margolese was especially concerned professionally with breast cancer, and the reluctance of physicians to openly address cancer with patients was likely compounded by the patronizing chauvinism of a largely conservative profession. "We didn't have biopsies in those days," Margolese explains. "If you had a lump, the doctor took you to the operating room and put you to sleep, and excised the lump and sent it to pathology, and waited around twenty minutes for the report. If it was cancer, they went ahead and did a mastectomy. So when a patient went to sleep, she did not know her diagnosis and did not know what treatment she would get. Then the patient wakes up, and the doctor comes in and says, 'Well, we found something we didn't like, but you're all right now.' One of my doctors, when I was a resident in New York City, used to say to the patient, 'You're really a lucky girl. You had something but we caught it in time.' And she looks down, and there's no breast, there's no muscles connecting the chest to the arm. That's all gone, and she doesn't understand what's lucky about this. But that was the attitude."

For Sheila Kussner and Hope & Cope, breast cancer would become the single largest area of activity. About half of the patients that Hope & Cope would support were women with breast cancer, and many of its volunteers were (and are) breast cancer survivors. There are several reasons for that. One is that, overall, breast cancer has long been one of the most common forms of cancer. Today, in the United States and Canada, it is the single most common form across both sexes and is experienced by about one in eight women in their lifetime.

And while it is important to keep in mind that Hope & Cope has never been a service exclusively for the Jewish community—about half of its clients today are from outside the community—Ashkenazi women face an elevated risk of breast cancer. Although the basis of the risk was not understood at the time Hope & Cope was founded, we now know that mutations of the BRCA1 and BRCA2 genes increase the lifetime risk of developing breast cancer from about twelve per cent to fifty to sixty per cent. These mutations occur in about one in four hundred women in the general population, but in about one in forty women of Ashkenazi ancestry. The BRCA mutations are also associated with elevated risks for ovarian cancer in women, breast cancer and prostate cancer in men, melanoma, and pancreatic cancer. (Two mutations linked to colon cancer, GREM1 and APC, also are more common among people of Ashkenazi descent.[101])

Breast cancer was also critical to Hope & Cope's mission because it was a focal point of excellence at the Jewish General, where Margolese became involved in an important series of clinical trials that challenged the prevailing wisdom of how breast cancer was treated. Breast cancer long had been one of the few curable (or at least treatable) forms of cancer because it was a solid tumour that could be surgically removed without fatal consequences for the patient. Breast cancer thus was a rare example of a cancer that created a large population of at least ten-year survivors, before the additional use of radiation, chemotherapy, and adjuvant therapy—treatments that follow the initial therapy to minimize the possibility of cancer recurring.

Until chemotherapy began to deliver on its controversial promises, surgery, augmented by radiation—two cancer-fighting tools that were known darkly as cutting and burning—was the solution to breast cancer, as it was for any form of cancer that could yield in some way to the knife. Abraham Fuks refers to what he calls "heroic surgery," epitomized by the career of William S. Halsted and practiced by those who were fearless in their willingness to carve away more and more of other peoples' bodies in pursuit of eliminating cancer. Halsted in late-nineteenth-century New York had been a pioneer in what he called the radical mastectomy, removing not only the breast and the pectoralis minor, a small muscle on the chest well that among other things helps stabilize the shoulder complex, but also the pectoralis major, the significant overlying muscle that allows you to move your shoulder and hand. From there, he went after the local lymph nodes as well. Halsted (who all the while was addicted to cocaine) performed so many of these invasive surgeries that he was able to amass a database purporting to show their effectiveness. Halsted's disciples continued this "macabre marathon" of cutting away more and more of the hapless, helpless patient.[102]

"All through the 1930s, 1940s and 1950s," says Margolese, "well-meaning surgeons increased the scope of radical surgery, but didn't really understand that they weren't doing any better. They had arguments like, 'Well *my* lymph node operations took out thirty-eight lymph nodes, and you only got twenty-four, so I'm doing better.' Without regard to the fact that it didn't matter how many you took out. We discovered that cancer grows as a cell, then two, then four, then eight, and so on … and at some time it develops the ability to spread to other organs. Some people can have a cancer in place for twenty years, and it will never proceed to learn how to metastasize. Others will metastasize when the tumour is so small, two millimetres, that it could not be discovered in those days by clinical means, because we didn't have imaging techniques that we have now. That's why taking out the tumour cured seventy-five per cent of the people, and when they weren't all cured, the surgeons went to take out the whole breast and then more than the breast in terms of muscles and lymph nodes. They failed to realize that either the patient was cured by the simple operation, or was not cured by *any* operation, because the cancer cells were beyond what surgery could accomplish. They were in the liver, the lungs, the bones, and surgery of any kind wasn't going to cure that."

In the first decade following the Second World War, according to a study of patient records at University of Texas MD Anderson

Cancer Center, about fifty-five per cent of women whose cancer had not spread beyond the breast (local breast cancer) were still alive ten years after diagnosis. If the cancer had spread to nearby skin or lymph nodes (regional breast cancer), the rate fell to about sixteen per cent. And if it had metastasized and spread elsewhere, ten-year survivorship was only about three per cent.[103]

In 1971, Richard Margolese and the hospital became involved in a significant trial of breast cancer care options that would challenge the prevailing practice of disfiguring radical mastectomies. The National Surgical Adjuvant Breast and Bowel Project (NSABP), led by Bernard Fisher of the University of Pittsburgh, initiated a long-term study, called B-04, involving 1,665 women who were enrolled between 1971 and 1974 at thirty-four NSABP institutions; the Jewish General was the only Canadian institution to participate. The study compared outcomes for patients who underwent a radical mastectomy versus patients who underwent a total (simple) mastectomy, with or without radiation therapy. Five years into the trial, results indicated there was no advantage in survivorship from radical mastectomies. In 1976, the NSABP launched a second study, called B-06. Through Margolese and the Jewish General, about one-quarter of the patients involved were from Montreal. Again, radical mastectomies were shown to provide no advantage in survivorship.[104]

By 1995–2004, according to the MD Anderson Cancer Center study, ten-year-survivorship for local breast cancer had reached eight-six per cent. Regional recurrence breast cancer survival had soared to seventy-four percent. With survivorship came women who had experienced the trauma of diagnosis, surgery, recovery, living with the disfiguring consequences, and hoping the cancer had not metastasized. Radiation and chemotherapy, and the reliance by surgeons on radical mastectomies in pursuit of higher rates of survivorship, multiplied the issues for women undergoing treatments that had consequences beyond clinical measures of physical health. The loss of one or both breasts impacted patients' sense of self as mothers, and as feminine and sexual beings. The disfigurement of surgery went beyond the loss of breast tissue: the removal of the pectoralis major changed posture; the removal of lymph nodes sometimes caused the arm to swell to twice its normal size.

Women were the subjects of the most aggressive surgeries in the treatment of cancer, and it may not have been a coincidence that they were being treated by surgeons who overwhelmingly were men and by inclination and process were generally not given to communicating frankly with the patient. Surgeons may have felt that they had done everything possible and justifiable to treat a patient, but the process created survivors who were emotionally as well as physically scarred.

It should not be surprising, then, that the form of cancer that gave rise to a peer-support movement was breast cancer. The real surprise, perhaps, was that it took so long for one to emerge. As Francine E. Timothy wrote in 1980, "a program dedicated to helping the woman who had just had breast surgery, is so logical that it should have existed since the very first mastectomy was performed." Nevertheless, it wasn't until 1953 that a support organization, Reach to Recovery, existed.

Reach to Recovery's founder was a New Yorker, Terese "Ted" Lasser, the spouse of Jacob Kay Lasser, author of a best-selling annual guide to the US tax code. In 1952, the forty-eight-year-old Lasser went into the hospital for a quick section biopsy of a breast lump, under general anesthesia. Her doctor had assured her that such lumps were usually benign. When she came-to in recovery, she found herself "bound like a mummy in gauze." She had undergone a radical mastectomy, just as Richard Margolese has described a typical experience.

The psychological and physical traumas of the surgery were compounded by the absence of support services. Neither her doctor nor the hospital staff could tell her where she could get a breast prosthesis, and they could not recommend any sort of rehab to help her recuperate. The lack of support was all the more shocking, considering the fact that breast cancer then was one of the most common forms of cancer, and would only increase in prevalence. Surgeons were performing radical surgery, and after the patients were discharged from recovery, they were on their own.

The year after her radical mastectomy, Terese Lasser founded Reach to Recovery. Lasser "ardently believed that peer support could help other women with coping, adjustment, quality of life, and survivorship issues. She also believed that women could work together to overcome the stigma of breast cancer."[105] That stigma had been part of her own experience: for the first seven months after she returned home from hospital, her husband would hide in the bathroom, to further ensure her privacy, while she undressed in a closet.[106] Her husband helped her found Reach to Recovery but died only a year later. Now widowed, Lasser at least had the financial support of her husband's tax guide, which outlived him as a publishing product (and remains a best-seller). With the book's proceeds, she was able to make Reach to Recovery her life work.

By 1969, she had built the organization into three hundred local chapters in the United States and beyond, including Canada. That year, Reach to Recovery was absorbed by the American Cancer

Society, which gave the program an enormous boost; Lasser continued to serve as national coordinator until 1977, two years before she died. In 1974, Reach to Recovery was becoming established in Europe, with programs in individual countries working with various partners ranging from the Red Cross in Sweden to the Lions Club in Luxembourg to deal with local points of resistance or bureaucratic impediments. At the time of Lasser's death, in 1979, over ten thousand volunteers in the United States alone were visiting with some fifty-seven thousand mastectomy patients annually.

As Timothy (who spearheaded Reach to Recovery's European expansion) has explained, "Terese Lasser's premise was that a woman after this operation would be more easily convinced of the possibility of a complete return to normal life by the example of another woman who had been through the same difficult experience and who had successfully adapted to the loss of a breast. Not only could the patient identify with this healthy, well-balanced woman, but she could ask her non-medical questions, some of which might be so intimate that only someone who had been through the same experience could understand and answer. Unasked questions take on an importance out of all proportion, so this possible dialogue could prevent serious misunderstanding and bleak speculations."

Sheila Kussner began fomenting the creation of Hope & Cope in 1979, around the time of Terese Lasser's death. She was aware of Reach to Recovery—"they did good work," she says. While Hope & Cope would be a much different sort of organization, it would negotiate the same challenges that Reach to Recovery had, and the strategies chosen and experiences of Lasser's organization remain instructive.

Foremost among obstacles faced by Reach to Recovery was the territoriality of medicine. Medical professionals were wary of intrusions by outsiders—and in the case of breast cancer, by outsiders who were unpaid women. Volunteers in a hospital setting were usually members of a women's auxiliary, a quasi-social entity whose proper contributions to hospital affairs were thought to be holding fundraisers, serving beverages, selling flowers, and staffing the gift shop. The auxiliary at the Jewish General Hospital was already showing itself at the end of the Second World War to be a much more dynamic organization than the stereotypical auxiliary, but it was true nevertheless that volunteers were thought to belong on the opposite side of an invisible wall that shielded the medical professionals from amateur meddling.

Richard Margolese can recall an unsuccessful attempt to establish Reach to Recovery counselling at the Jewish General in the early 1960s, when he was an intern. The chief surgeon at the time wanted nothing to do with them. "He said, '*I'll* manage my cancer patients.'" Margolese and his fellow interns "used to go around him and call the patients ourselves and set up Reach to Recovery to see them after they got out of the hospital." In 1971, Ellen Cohen, who had undergone a mastectomy, was able to establish a Reach to Recovery chapter at the Jewish General, the first Montreal hospital to accept one. The initiative, however, was short-lived. It was no longer active when Sheila came to found Hope & Cope.

In England, a breast cancer support group founded in the mid-1970s was stymied by the fact that no hospital would allow its volunteers on the premises. Reach to Recovery's solution in negotiating the delicate relationship between women volunteers and a largely male medical profession was to agree that no volunteer would visit with a patient in the hospital without the permission of the attending surgeon. As described in the early 1970s, a volunteer would visit a patient in hospital, about four days after surgery, "when the patient needs consolation and comforting words."[107] The volunteer brought along a kit containing a ball on a plastic string and some rope, for arm exercises, a temporary breast prosthesis for the patient to wear home from hospital, a Reach for Recovery manual that covered common questions ("How should I act around family and friends? How do I do the arm exercises? How should I dress?"), a list of manufacturers of artificial breasts (augmentation surgery had not yet become a common option), and a "Letter to Husbands," written by Lasser. If the patient was willing, a volunteer visited again, six weeks later, when it was time to be fitted for a prosthetic breast. No further contact would occur unless the patient desired it.

From a perspective some fifty years removed, Reach to Recovery's program as described in the early 1970s was strikingly simple. There was no pre-surgical role for the organization. It was focused on a woman's post-surgical experience of a mastectomy and was designed to help her cope with the physical effects and the psychological and social consequences, including their possible rejection by partners in a breast-obsessed, male-dominated culture. The counselling program presumed that women would want to replace the missing breast with a prosthetic device, to make themselves at least externally whole again and acceptable to society, above all to the male gaze. Nevertheless, Reach to Recovery was a bellwether of what was to come, and was essentially alone in striving to bring support to cancer patients that the medical system was failing to deliver. Its absorption by the American Cancer Society greatly aided its legitimacy, at least in the United States, but it still had to reach patients through the blessing of individual surgeons.

Sheila Kussner, by 1979, had a much different sort of volunteer program in mind, one that would service patients with all forms of adult cancer and be embedded within a hospital, working alongside medical professionals.

CHAPTER ELEVEN

The Cancer Concierge

Eden Polansky describes the sensation of coping with a loved one's cancer diagnosis, as she did with both of her parents. The news "hits you out of left field." Then every day brings something different. You get pulled in one direction, and then another. You have to gather information, and deal with waiting for results or referrals. "You're so confused, and you hear about things, and you have to do the listening for your father or your mother, or whoever. I just remember sitting and feeling numb. You've got a cold feeling. You don't function properly. You wake up, and for those first three seconds in the morning, you feel fine, and then you go, 'Oh—'"

You need help: someone to guide you and support you through the ordeal. For Polansky, Sheila Kussner, who was close to both her parents, "was this built-in"—the definition comes to her with a laugh—"cancer concierge!"

It sounds at once so superficial, in the life-and-death context of cancer, and yet so perfect. When you stay at a hotel and want recommendations on where to eat or what shows to take in, someone to act as an ad hoc secretary or personal assistant, delivering or accepting packages and mail, running errands, and arranging transportation, you turn to the concierge. They know things, and they can do things for you, especially when you are in an unfamiliar place. Sheila, the landslady of the world of cancer that frightened newcomers find themselves in, is also its most esteemed concierge in Montreal. And unlike an actual concierge, it is impossible to tip her. "You can't do for her one iota of what she does for others," says Polanksy, "and that, to me, is the fascinating part about her."

As Sheila negotiated her way through Marvyn's treatment for non-Hodgkin's lymphoma, she blazed an exploratory trail through Cancer Land, a new world of chemotherapy, radiation, and adjuvant therapies. She amassed knowledge and experience—and connections. She could see how and where things were being accomplished, and where the gaps were in accommodating a patient's experience, not as the embodiment of a battlefield in a war between physician and disease but as an individual caught up in a medical system that had an extremely limited sense of the scope of its role in patient care.

As treatments evolved, sensitivity to the patient experience badly lagged behind the science. The medical system might understand how many cc's of a particular drug should be administered, but it had precious little awareness or concern about how a patient was coping and responding emotionally. Medicine was focused on curing and mending physical ailments. It was largely oblivious to the patient experience of Cancer Land, let alone acknowledging that there was such a thing or that medical practice was largely responsible for the topography of Cancer Land, and that the terrain was changing radically, with every advance in treatment. And at the same time, the patients were changing. A younger generation of patients would transform the way cancer, in particular breast cancer, was confronted and experienced. A culture of "survivorship" was emerging. Referring to someone as a "victim" of cancer was falling out of favour, in part because survival rates were increasing for many cancers, in part because cancer patients refused to be seen as hapless victims. That said, many people who survived cancer rejected the "survivor" label. Nevertheless, many cancer patients were losing their fear of the word "cancer." They wanted it to be spoken aloud, by the people treating them, by friends and family. "Cancer came out of the closet," Jimmie Holland would write, "and the door opened for exploration of the psychological dimension of cancer."[108]

Sheryl Miller Adessky was eighteen, in her second year of CEGEP in Montreal, when she was diagnosed with Hodgkin's lymphoma in 1980. Her experience was emblematic of the time. On the one hand, she had a cancer that a little more than a decade earlier had been a fatal prognosis. Thanks to advances in treatment, hers was curable (in her case with radiation therapy). On the other hand, the cancer experience was still confounded by old taboos and hampered by the enormous lack of support.

Adessky had an older brother, at college in Boston, and she recalls how he returned home after her diagnosis. "He came into the house and said, 'I've been doing a little research, and I can't believe that Sheryl has cancer.' And my mom looked at him and said, 'Well, she has Hodgkin's disease.' And my brother says, 'It's cancer.'" Their mother, Jessica, knew that, as did their father, but Adessky's parents would not say *cancer*. "My mom was a librarian, and my father was an attorney. We're not talking about uneducated people. But it seems crazy now that, even then, people were almost hesitant or scared to use the word. I can tell you, with me, my brother saying that was almost like a lightning bolt. Going forward, my mom said, 'We're going to call it what it is, and we're going to discuss it.' My family is very open, and my mom said, 'This is what it is, and we're not going to shy away from it.' And she didn't shy away from telling anybody, nor did I."

But being forthright about cancer in 1980 in Montreal only got you so far. "There was certainly no Hope & Cope," Adessky says. "There was nothing. It was hard to even find people to talk to. Cancer was so hush-hush." Her parents found families for her to speak to in Boston and Toronto; in the Toronto case, one with a child who had been diagnosed with Hodgkin's the previous year. "We needed to talk," Adessky says simply. "And remember, this was before the Internet. To get information, you were going to the library. My father bought all kinds of books on cancer. Hope & Cope started right after that, with Sheila and about ten volunteers." Her mother would be among the first wave of volunteers.

"My sense is that Hope & Cope is a pioneering organization that could not have been started for other diseases, like heart disease," says Abraham Fuks. Tuberculosis, the great health scourge that preceded cancer in the public imagination and the priorities of medicine, "was a disease of the Romantic poets. They had pale cheeks, with little red spots. Cancer was very dark, literally and figuratively. It was a dirty disease. When you walked into a cancer patient's room, the shades were drawn. Sheila walks in, and kind of lets in the light, if you want. She says, 'Here's how we're going to help you, and you're allowed to talk about it. You're not jinxing yourself by discussing it.' Suddenly, there's an openness for the patient. 'Someone is going to talk to me about it, acknowledge that I'm not stupid, and let me get help from sympathetic figures.'" Despite all the progress made over the past forty years, Fuks says, "it's still a stigmatized disease, in a way that heart disease is not."

Hope & Cope is an organization with a complex history that now spans more than forty years. In many ways, its story and Sheila's story seem inseparable. Certainly, without Sheila, there is no Hope & Cope, and without Hope & Cope, a massive dimension of Sheila's life goes unrecognized. But we are here to appreciate Sheila foremost, not compose a corporate history of an institution. So we will view Hope & Cope through the lens of what Sheila accomplished, how she accomplished it, and how her presence made a difference for individuals, the overall success of an organization, and the larger phenomenon of support in the world of cancer care.

Sheila's support for cancer patients began with things as basic as where a chemo patient could find a wig. (For men, Hope & Cope would discover that the best source was New York City, because the acting community demanded high-quality wigs for various roles.) Today, people who turned to Hope & Cope for support have a distinct first memory of the little office space inside the oncology department at the Jewish General and its assortment of wigs. Wigs are not about personal, superficial vanity: they are about coping with the side effects of chemotherapy, about its impact on self-image and loved ones. But Sheila's vision of how cancer patients should be supported was much broader and deeper than a selection of wigs. Her support was going to be peer-based: volunteers, the landsmen and landsladies who had already been to Cancer Land, would help newcomers negotiate their journeys. And those volunteers would operate within the heart of Cancer Land, the hospital, in close coordination with medical staff. In other words, support services would not be a patch or salve applied to a patient once they were outside the system's gated walls. They were to be delivered within and as part of the system. In short order, support would expand into circles or groups—in some cases into what would be labelled clubs—of people who had arrived in Cancer Land, whether as patients or people supporting friends and family with cancer, who wanted to meet and share their experiences and gain from each other's trials and wisdom.

It was only natural, given her long-standing activities within the Jewish community and Marvyn's recent care, that Sheila would choose the Jewish General Hospital as the basis for her initiative in 1979. It also was no coincidence that the hospital founded its oncology department that year under Richard Margolese.

Beyond Reach to Recovery, efforts to create peer-based cancer support services were few and far between in the world. There was nothing like it in Montreal. The only model that was readily at hand was at Memorial Sloan Kettering in New York, where Jimmie Holland's psychiatry department was host to a volunteer initiative led by Robert (Bob) Fisher.

Fisher was a vice-president of the family-owned Fisher Brothers Steel Company in Englewood, New Jersey, when he was diagnosed with leukemia in 1974. He was about forty-six—not much older than Marvyn Kussner was when he was diagnosed with non-Hodgkin's lymphoma around the same time.

"Before I learned about my disease, I was a real mess," Fisher said in 1979. "I was a plastic, programmed, shirt-tie-suit kind of person. I had even tried to commit suicide. Now, I am living and enjoying my life as I never have before."[109] Wrestling his leukemia into remission, Fisher sold his interest in the family steel company, resigned his vice-presidency, and in 1978 launched the counselling program within Jimmie Holland's department, building up a team of about twenty-five volunteers. In 1979, he rode his ten-speed bicycle from California to the front steps of Memorial Sloan Kettering, "slimmer, trimmer and sporting a new beard." He gave lectures along the way, and otherwise celebrated a kind of personal rebirth before resuming his oversight of the Memorial Sloan Kettering's counselling program.

As Fisher told a journalist, one of his reasons for making the cross-country trip "was to dispel the notion that cancer is a constant, debilitating problem." He planned next to go hang-gliding, and to tour the country by motorcycle. But Fisher's remission proved to be short-lived: When Jimmie Holland introduced him to Sheila, Holland let her know that he was dying, but he was continuing with his volunteer work. As well as providing some guidance and inspiration for Sheila and the early volunteers at Hope & Cope, he was also helping establish a volunteer program at Baylor College of Medicine, Jimmie Holland's alma mater. He would die at Memorial Sloan Kettering in 1983. "Bob was very well liked, and he did a good job," Sheila says. "Jimmie really needed him. When he died, they lost momentum."

By the time Fisher connected with Hope & Cope, Sheila's initiative was already underway. "We were doing more than he was at the time," Sheila says. "We really were. He saw patients, but we were more in-depth. There was more to our organization, even then, and they knew it. Jimmie got a kick out of the way we were working."

When Sheila had the idea for Hope & Cope, she approached Archie Deskin, executive director of the Jewish General, who told her to approach the JGH Women's Auxiliary. Essie Rudy was president of the auxiliary, and vice-president Phyllis Waxman was about to begin a term as president. Sheila recalls saying, "Phyllis, we have to talk." Deskin told them that the hospital could provide space, supplies, and maintenance, but with the country in a deep recession and the hospital strapped for cash, it could not offer financial support. They agreed to the conditions, and Hope & Cope was launched in the spring of 1981, under the aegis of the Women's Auxiliary, with an initial six volunteers that quickly grew to ten.

As for the name, Sheila would say it came to her after speaking with a young woman with cancer who asked her, "How can I cope when there is no hope?" Sheila said she would help her with both. (The long-standing idea of "hope" in cancer care had received an enormous boost of recognition from Terry Fox's Marathon of Hope in the summer of 1980. Fox, like Sheila, had lost a leg to osteosarcoma.) The icon chosen for Hope & Cope was a butterfly. It symbolized rebirth, renewal, transformation, a fresh chapter in life. But it was also apt in that a butterfly does not emerge from its chrysalis until it is ready. You cannot make a butterfly emerge. Only the butterfly knows when the time is right. That fact became fundamental to Hope & Cope's peer-based counselling. Only the patient can know when they need support. They have to seek it out willingly, on their own terms, something Sheila already knew from her work with amputees.

If Hope & Cope was going to happen, never mind succeed, it needed the approval of Richard Margolese, head of oncology at JGH, as Hope & Cope would occupy a space in his ward and have access to his patients and staff. He readily admits he was skeptical. Although he had been supportive of Reach to Recovery's counselling to breast cancer patients, Sheila was proposing to have volunteers embedded within oncology and interacting with adult patients with all forms of cancer, throughout the hospital. "I remember saying, 'Sheila, I'm not so sure this is going to get you where you want to go, but I'm going to go along with you, because it could be a good idea.'" Sheila and Margolese remain good friends, but Sheila suspected at the time that Margolese thought her program would collapse in about six months. "Richard felt that Hope & Cope wasn't going to work out, that we were going to be a bunch of do-gooders and serve coffee and juice to our patients. And I said, 'Give them a chance, because you're wrong, and you'll see.'"

They crucially agreed that Hope & Cope needed to be supervised by a professional, a social worker. Sheila says that Jimmie Holland had impressed upon her the importance of that hiring (today, peer volunteers in cancer care at Memorial Sloan Kettering operate under the auspices of the hospital's department of social work). Although psycho-oncology in its formative years was dominated by the participation and perspective of psychiatrists, Jimmie Holland would note in 2002 that "social workers were the first, alongside nurses, to attend to the psychological and social problems of cancer patients and their families. They have continued as the 'front line' in clinical care and as important researchers in psycho-oncology." [110]

With an initial infusion of twenty-five thousand dollars from the Jewish Community Foundation of Greater Montreal, Sheila was able to hire part-time a social worker as coordinator. Megan McLeod was recently married and had just moved to the city. A Manitoban, she was thirty years old when she joined Hope & Cope in the spring of 1981. She had spent about ten years working in health care within the hospital system in Manitoba, and after securing a bachelor's degree in social work when she was twenty-two, she had gone back to school to earn a master's degree. She recalls being interviewed by Sheila and Phyllis Waxman, although Sheila says it was Huguette Batshaw, supervisor in the hospital's department of social services, who drove the recruitment process by placing an advertisement and then recommending to Sheila and Waxman that they interview McLeod. The job was structured so that McLeod would oversee the volunteers, and report to Batshaw even though McLeod was not employed by the hospital.

"I was a pretty young, pretty innocent woman from the prairies," McLeod recalls, "and I'm not Jewish. There I was, bumping into the Jewish community and the francophone community, and learning as fast as I could." She had just completed a French-language course when she accepted the job. "Sheila was totally welcoming and enthusiastic. I don't know how she got everything done, but she moved with the speed of lightning and at the same time she could stop and pay attention enough so that the young woman I just described could learn from her. She's always been an astonishing, wonderful force to work with."

"I don't know why they had faith in that young woman who was me," McLeod adds. "I wouldn't be surprised if there were not many applicants, because it was a job that was outside the system. A number of times, people said to me when I was there, 'Why don't you apply to the Jewish General social work department and get a real job?'"

McLeod was "lovely, sweet, down-to-earth," says Sheila. "Getting her was instrumental. She worked out well. We were lucky." Margolese says Megan McLeod was "wonderful" as Hope & Cope's first coordinator. "She helped steer the development, from something that was amorphous, sort of structureless, into what we could and would do."

McLeod would stay until 1985 with Hope & Cope and spend the rest of her career in the cancer field, ultimately retiring as a supportive care coordinator at CancerCare Manitoba. She well remembers how pioneering Hope & Cope was, and that Sheila launched it at a transitional period in cancer treatment. Before Hope & Cope, looking back into the 1950s, she says, "you got cancer and you lived or you died, and most of us died. And then in the period that Hope & Cope was developing, treatments were allowing people to live longer. They achieved remissions, or they were cured. And so you knew patients longer. You knew the psychosocial implications of their illness." She also recalls the stigma that still clung to the disease, and the lack of communication around it. "I remember some of our clients referring to cancer with a whisper as 'the big C.'"

A key element of Hope & Cope's success, McLeod says, was the support it received from Margolese, Waxman, and others to be integrated into the hospital. "That was an entirely different kind of access for patients, and of course for the volunteers." Those who were on hand for Hope & Cope's first years remember it occupying a "broom closet"–sized space, which quickly expanded to what amounted to two broom closets with the addition of a resource library coordinated by Jessica Miller. "We were located where people entered the oncology ward," says McLeod. "People got off the elevators, passed the pharmacy, and the two right-hand doors were our reception and library, and my office. People received treatment and saw their doctors for follow-up at the far end." Richard Margolese and fellow oncologist Lawrence Panasci had their offices on the ward.

On-site access to patients was critical but having properly trained and supervised volunteers was even more so. Margolese says McLeod "got the volunteers and trained them, and as a professional, she was a guide through all of this, so that we didn't have just well-meaning people not knowing what to do. We were teaching them what to do. And it grew from there."

Training and screening were especially important in that Hope & Cope was starting when the mind-body movement was in full efflorescence and was capable of doing considerable harm to cancer patients. Wilhelm Reich's early ideas about patients being responsible for their cancer through repressed emotions had found fertile ground in the 1970s among proponents of positivity as a healing mechanism. Empowering the patient's mental attitude also meant blaming the patient for not having the correct attitude if cancer claimed them.

By the late 1970s, popular literature was confidently espousing the ability of mental attitude to not only cure but also cause physical diseases. Reich's books were reissued several times in the 1970s by leading publishers.[111] In 1977, *New York* magazine published an article provocatively titled "Can Your Personality Kill You?" in which cancer was linked to certain personality traits. The article approvingly cited the recently published *You Can Fight*

For Your Life, by Dr. Lawrence LeShan, a local psychologist and psychotherapist who traced cancer back to feelings of isolation in childhood. O. Carl Simonton, a radiologist who operated the Cancer Counseling and Research Centre in Dallas with his wife Stephanie (who was in charge of counselling), published in 1978 the best-selling *Getting Well Again* (which remains in print). "Patients who continued to do well, for one reason or another, had a stronger 'will to live,'" he asserted of his experience with cancer patients while completing his residency.[112] Simonton claimed that "the difference between the patient who regains his health and the one who does not is in part a matter of attitude toward the disease and [a] belief that he could somehow influence it."[113] Simonton and his co-authors stated: "We believe that emotional and mental states play a significant role both in *susceptibility* to disease, including cancer, and in *recovery* from all disease."[114]

The claims of the mind-body movement so alarmed the oncological profession that in September 1981, Simonton's assertions were dismissed in an American Cancer Society evaluation by members of the departments of psychiatry at Memorial Sloan Kettering Cancer Center and Mount Sinai Hospital in New York, including Jimmie Holland. While they found good things about his positivity approach, such as decreasing anxiety and counteracting a psychological sense of helplessness, they found no evidence of a scientific basis for Simonton's claims, or that "psychological and psychosomatic factors will alter the course of the disease," and warned: "Potential hazards for patients are associated with induction of guilt feelings, over-reliance on the Simonton technique, and abandonment of generally accepted treatments, in spite of Dr. Simonton's advice to continue them."[115]

The precarious duality within the mind-body movement—of mental attitude causing as well as curing disease—nevertheless became a persistent dilemma for wellness advocates and movements. In 1997, Christoffer Johansen (now the head of a research department at the Center for Surgery and Cancer in Copenhagen) began publishing the first of a series of papers rejecting a psychological precursor to cancer, finding "no support for the hypothesis of an association between psychological stress and the incidence of cancer or mortality from non-malignant diseases. We conclude that the human organism is highly adaptable, even to extreme psychological stress."[116] Peer counselling in the meantime (and, in fact, still today) was vulnerable to well-meaning but unqualified volunteers espousing to patients fringe ideas about mental positivity that only placed further burdens on patients if they thought that their psychological profile had caused their cancer, or that their lack of positivity was to blame for a failure to be cured.

Richard Margolese for one would be rigorous in his demands that whatever programming Hope & Cope offered had to be scientifically valid, or at least not be making unsupportable scientific claims, and he would also press Hope & Cope to initiate, present, and publish research on the impacts of its peer-support model. The program, after all, was operating within a teaching hospital associated with McGill University. Nothing could be called "therapeutic," for example, if there was not some demonstrable medical benefit. That did not mean that all offerings in the ever-expanding programs and activities offered through Hope & Cope had to have some measurable benefit in the treatment of cancer, only that they remain within the bounds of improving a patient's quality of life, whatever the disease outcome.

As Hope & Cope moved into the realm of research, in particular through the work of Linda Edgar, the value of psychosocial
patient support was being judged not according to its ability to
change outcomes in cancer diagnoses, but in its effectiveness in
helping patients deal with the distress of the diagnosis and everything associated with treatment. "Distress" became recognized as
a "sixth vital sign" in cancer care; screening for and managing a
patient's stress became a central tenet of psycho-oncology. Illness
was the realm of the oncologist; wellness—a focus on thriving and
on quality of life—whatever the diagnosis or prognosis, became a
principal goal of peer-centred support.

Mike Flinker, who with his wife Marcia Gilman became a generous supporter of cancer research in Montreal, was deeply involved
in Hope & Cope's young-adult initiative and served on the board
of Marvyn Kussner's prostate-cancer research charity, PROCURE.
He has been through two different, unrelated cancer bouts—a rare
sinus tumour called esthesioneuroblastoma and prostate cancer—
and describes well the role of mental or emotional support afforded
by Hope & Cope.

After being diagnosed with the sinus tumour in 2004, Flinker was
referred to the old radiation department at the Jewish General and
found himself seated in a crowded waiting area. He decided he
would "look down at the floor and pretend I'm despondent, which
I was anyway," and not engage in conversation. But after only a few
seconds, the man on his left, who had an eye patch, asked why he was
there. Flinker told him about the sinus tumour, and his neighbour
explained he had lost his eye to a tumour. "I said, 'That's horrible.
He said, 'Not really.'"

His neighbour then asked him to look around the room and to tell him what he saw. "I literally looked for like a minute, just gazing around the room. I turned to him and said, 'All I see are a bunch of tired, sick-looking people.' He said, 'Look again.'" Flinker did, and couldn't come up with anything different. His neighbour said, "I see winners and losers. You walked in like you had already lost the battle. Ultimately, nobody knows who is going to win this battle, but to fight this battle successfully, and win this battle, you need the support of your family and your friends. If you take on an attitude of total depression and an attitude that you've lost the battle, your family won't want to deal with you, and your friends will just avoid you. I can tell you from experience, that's what happens. But if you look at the glass half full, they'll rally around you. Ultimately, does it mean you will win? No. But at least you won't be alone. And the last thing you want to do is be alone."

It was a random encounter, and the ocular cancer patient had nothing to do with Hope & Cope. But through his trucking business, Flinker had a connection to a vice-president of foreign exchange at the TD Bank, Bill Vrentas, who happened to be a Hope & Cope volunteer. Vrentas had testicular cancer, and although it was a different cancer than the ones Flinker experienced, he was still invaluable.

"What I found with doctors is they couldn't coach you through the mental aspect of cancer," says Flinker. "They could tell you that when you have this treatment, you're going to feel lousy; that when you have surgery, this is the kind of pain you'll experience. The mental aspect of cancer is far more difficult than the physical to deal with. I would have sleepless nights, looking at the ceiling and trying to figure out what's going on with my life. Bill was an incredible resource, having gone through it. Even though it's a different kind of cancer, it's the same mental process. I felt really comfortable talking to him. I'd call him sometimes early in the morning and say, 'Bill, I dreamt I was dying. Did you ever have those dreams?' 'Of course.' You don't feel like a pariah, and you don't feel like an idiot, knowing that other people have gone through the same issues."

The most important thing Hope & Cope provides, Flinker stresses, "is the mental support when you're going through this journey. I don't know of too many people that just walk through it. It takes tremendous resilience and I think everyone needs to lean on someone. They do an extraordinary job in that regard, and without them, I don't know where I would have been."

"There was training, and an element of screening," says Megan McLeod of the recruitment of Hope & Cope's first volunteers. "We interviewed everybody, individually. At the beginning, I think it was just me there, to do the interviews. We were looking for people who had empathy for others and had some cancer experience. As time went on, we looked more and more for people who were real peer supporters." Hope & Cope also developed something of a rule. It wasn't a hard-and-fast one, but "it was so close to being accurate. People had to be at least a year through their treatment, through their own cancer experience, before they could volunteer." It proved to be a reliable guide to knowing whether people "were emotionally ready to see and experience a cancer case other than their own." (Sheila agrees but remembers an effective distancing of nine months to one year.)

To be close enough to empathize and advise, and yet distant enough not to burden another patient with their own unresolved issues or to be too burdened by taking on other people's struggles, would always be a tricky balancing act in volunteers. Gerald Batist recalls how, after his mother, Gertrude, underwent a mastectomy, a volunteer from Reach to Recovery visited her. The volunteer broke down, and his mother ended up being the one doing the counselling; Gertrude would become one of Hope & Cope's early volunteers. Other volunteers found the experience of revisiting Cancer Land too much, after their own time there. But many others met the challenge and continued to support and counsel, even as their own cancer experience (what many have called their "cancer journey") continued to unfold.

"Volunteers had to have a certain amount of courage," says McLeod of the original group. "They were going for a variety of reasons, but they were all going into uncharted territory, and they were mapping what this support would look like."

One of the early volunteers was Jeannette Valmont, who joined Hope & Cope around 1983. "My daughter had left to go to university, and I wanted to do volunteer work," she says. "It didn't matter what." A neighbour told her about a new cancer support program at the Jewish General, started by a well-known woman named Sheila Kussner. Valmont is Jewish, but both she and her husband René were immigrants; she had come from Colombia, and he from France. "I wasn't an integral part of the Jewish community here, and believe it or not, I did not know who Sheila was. Thinking back today, I don't know how that was possible." (In 1983, some fifteen hundred people gathered in the Queen Elizabeth Hotel to see Sheila receive the State of Israel Bonds Eleanor Roosevelt Humanities Award. Sharing the head table with her were Pierre Trudeau, prime minister of Canada, and Yitzhak Rabin, former prime minister of Israel.)

Valmont had no personal experience with cancer, but a neighbour had just been through a traumatic experience with breast cancer, and she felt she could help. "I applied, was interviewed, and went through the training, and that was the first time I ever met Sheila. I told my husband, 'I've just met a hurricane.'"

Initially, Valmont performed what she calls a "welcoming" role, greeting patients and taking them from the waiting room to wherever they were being treated. "Sometimes we sat with them when they were having their treatment and spoke with them, just to alleviate their anxiety." As the program grew, Sheila and the coordinator prioritized "matching," finding volunteers with specific cancer experiences and calling upon them to provide peer support to a patient with the same diagnosis. "The philosophy is the value of the lived experience," says Valmont. She would come to manage the volunteer database. "Today, we have a database that would astound you. People that have a pimple of cancer on the tongue, we'll find somebody that had it to match with them. There was less of that at the beginning, but if someone had breast cancer, they wanted to speak to someone who also had it. Most of the founding volunteers were cancer survivors, and could take these on. Someone would call the volunteer and say, 'I'm about to start chemo and I'm so scared. What was it like for you? What drug did you get?'"

"Montreal was and is a small Jewish community, and so everybody seems to be connected to everybody," Marvin Rosenbloom explains. His life had been entwined with Sheila's since childhood. When he attended Camp Hiawatha, Sheila's brother Ronnie was his counsellor, and Sheila was also close to his own brother, and his sister-in-law. As well, Rosenbloom's father, Jack, ran Rosenbloom Paper Supply, which was a business of a kind though not in direct competition with the cardboard-box business launched by Marvyn Kussner's father and expanded by Marvyn into Biltwell.

Rosenbloom remembers Sheila taking him to lunch at Ruby Foo's in the 1970s when she was fundraising for the Montreal chapter of the Combined Jewish Appeal. She also got him involved in the Israel Cancer Research Fund (where he would rise to vice-president), all before Hope & Cope existed. Their relationship became much more personal in early 1980, when his wife, Rhoda, was diagnosed with cervical cancer. "It probably didn't take more than twenty-four or forty-eight hours and Sheila was ringing my phone, saying she had connections." Among the connections she mentioned were James and Jimmie Holland in New York. In short order, he was drawn into helping Sheila start Hope & Cope, as he strove to care for his terminally ill spouse. "I will always remember meeting Sheila in the Jewish General. There was just Sheila, Marvyn, myself, and Megan McLeod. An old friend of mine in the office equipment business gave her a desk and a cabinet." Rosenbloom would end up serving for about twenty years on the board of Hope & Cope.

Susan Polisuk was another early volunteer who, like Jeannette Valmont, was not a cancer survivor herself but had two friends who were cancer patients. One was Rhoda Rosenbloom, who she accompanied to treatments and otherwise supported in the early years of Hope & Cope, before the disease claimed her. Transitioning to a volunteer role with Hope & Cope was a logical next step for Polisuk, and she was already close to Sheila. Her husband, Teddy, had been married to a close friend of Sheila's, who had been involved with

Sheila in charitable work. After cancer claimed his first wife, Teddy met Susan, and they married.

Hope & Cope was a transformative experience for cancer patients, but one should not overlook the fact that Sheila's initiative was also transformative for those who volunteered.

"I should have been a nurse," Polisuk says. "That really was my calling. I became involved with Hope & Cope because there was no continuity for patients in the way of help." She could see the place for volunteers in the system. Sheila approached her while establishing Hope & Cope and asked if she wanted to be a part of it. "I said yes. For sure."

"We were very hands-on as a group," Polisuk says. After spending a shift on the floor, volunteers would meet with the coordinator, Megan McLeod, and later Jean Remmer or Suzanne O'Brien, her successors. "You would unwind and relate to them a lot of what went on in the shift, so they were always on top of it. If you ever had a problem, you went to them. There was always someone we could go to, talk to, and be able to feel that we weren't alone on the floor. We did a lot of educational group meetings, where we would inform volunteers of the different types of cancer." Experts were brought in to coach the volunteers. Bob Fisher came to speak in the earliest days of Hope & Cope, and Sheila took McLeod and some volunteers to New York, to meet Jimmie Holland and Fisher and attend one of Holland's early psycho-oncology conferences. Susan Polisuk remembers having dinner with Fisher, who shared with them what he was trying to accomplish at Memorial Sloan Kettering under Holland and encouraged them to do the same in Montreal.

Polisuk was aware that Sheila's initiative at the Jewish General was considered an experiment. "Richard Margolese sort of was testing the waters with us. We had to prove ourselves, which we did, *beyond* beyond. He became so grateful for what we did." In 1986, he would write to Sheila: "Hope & Cope brought a new dimension of personal concern and understanding into our area of the hospital, and we deeply appreciate the encouragement and the brightened outlook your volunteers offered to those who are under our care." On the floor, Polisuk cannot recall any friction with the medical staff. "They were fantastic, for me. There was really nothing like Hope & Cope at the time, and we just engrained ourselves into the whole system." She worked closely with the oncology department's assistant, Halima. "She would do the paperwork, and I would check in the patients. We were like a team." When she first started volunteering, Polisuk says, there was nothing that she did not do, but "my love was working on the floor, with patients." Her focus became the urology clinic, where cancer patients might come in weekly. Other volunteers would accompany patients to radiology. For patients, the continuity of seeing and speaking with the same volunteer on every visit was treasured.

The idea of peer support was for a volunteer to respond to questions from patients, drawing on first-hand experience of treatment. But patients also wanted to talk about their own experience, the impact on their lives, or simply about their lives. Medical staff were there to provide specific therapies; their questions were focused on symptoms and responses to treatment. Patients needed a listener, an empathetic ear. "They wanted to unload their stories," Polisuk sums up.

Over time, some of the patients needed much more than that. Polisuk recalls a patient at the urology clinic who had lost his wife to cancer and had five children. "He called me on a Sunday and said, 'Susan, I need help.'" She was at his home in half an hour. He needed to be cleaned and dressed. "He was so grateful that he could have someone to relate to, that knew him and liked him and cared for him, for the two years he was in treatment."

With another patient, her involvement went much deeper. She was a difficult cancer patient, with a husband who drank, and she happened to be a neighbour as well. Her behaviour when at the Jewish General was so demanding that Polisuk didn't know how the hospital resisted having her removed. "I told her, 'It's inappropriate. I'm not going to be here for you if you're going to act like this.'"

The woman's behaviour changed, but her cancer was terminal and her marriage failed. The couple truly loved each other, but the relationship collapsed under the weight of alcohol and her terminal illness. She was originally from the United States and wanted to visit there for two weeks, and asked Polisuk if she would mind her son, who was about twelve years old. Polisuk and her husband agreed. As death approached, the woman asked Polisuk to be executrix of her will and to take care of her son when she was gone. Again, she agreed, but she worked to ensure the boy had a good relationship with his father, with whom he lived, while she oversaw his finances and ensured he was able to complete an education. "We kept in touch for many years," she says of the son, until he moved to Europe.

The relationships and responsibilities were far beyond what anyone could have predicted or trained someone for when Sheila launched Hope & Cope, and they were more than what anyone could expect of a volunteer in every peer support case. But they testified to the sheer scale of unquantifiable need for support among cancer patients that Sheila was determined to address.

CHAPTER TWELVE

No Limits

Jean Remmer remembers seeing a notice in the newspaper about a special event when Hope & Cope was launched. Bob Fisher and Jimmie Holland from Memorial Sloan Kettering were coming to town to speak on cancer care, and the event was open to all. She decided to attend with her husband. It was a difficult time. Jean had earned a bachelor's degree in social work from McMaster University in 1973 (and later a master's degree from McGill) and had worked in the field of juvenile delinquency, but at the time Hope & Cope was launched, she had stopped working. In addition to being a new mother, her husband was dying of cancer, and she needed to take care of both infant and husband. Her husband died in 1982, and the loss, as she puts it, was "still fresh and raw" when Hope & Cope offered her the position of coordinator, after Megan McLeod chose to move on in 1985. (Years later, she and Marvin Rosenbloom would marry, after meeting through their Hope & Cope duties.) She was interviewed by Sheila, Richard Margolese, and Phyllis Waxman. "At that time, I had no idea of the momentum that Sheila creates, just by being who she is. Everybody catches on to it. It's quite infectious."

When Remmer joined Hope & Cope, the organization was experiencing rapid growth. In 1982, Sheila secured more than one million dollars from Marjorie and Gerald Bronfman, creating an endowment that provided long-term funding stability and made possible a full-time coordinator's position. Marjorie Bronfman (who had married into the Bronfman family) was a social worker by training and understood intrinsically what Sheila was striving to accomplish.

Hope & Cope began to expand in all directions. As already noted, Jessica Miller established the resource library in the broom closet next to the broom closet that housed the coordinator's office within the Jewish General Hospital oncology department. The number of volunteers grew, to about forty by 1984, and they expanded into such activities as transportation, delivering clients to and from their medical appointments. (Because of liability issues, Hope & Cope today still provides transportation services, but through taxi chits.) And with the Bronfman donation providing a secure financial floor for basic operations, Hope & Cope in 1984 created a dedicated circle of women, Chaverot (Friends) of Hope & Cope, to raise additional funds. Through the increasingly ambitious fundraising events, including galas and fashion shows, the Chaverot (and Sheila) ensured that Hope & Cope routinely ran a surplus, which allowed the organization to become a net contributor to the hospital by funding an assortment of positions and renovation projects over the ensuing years. By the time Hope & Cope held a twenty-fifth anniversary gala at the Queen Elizabeth Hotel, it could raise several million dollars in a single event. Throughout, Sheila's eye was on ensuring that Hope

& Cope could operate indefinitely. "Sheila wanted to feel and know that Hope & Cope would continue until there was no need, until cancer had been cured in all fields," says Marvin Rosenbloom.

Asked today about what Sheila's ambitions were for Hope & Cope, Susan Polisuk says, "There were no limits." As Jean Remmer recalls, when she arrived as the new coordinator in 1985, "we went through a big burst of growth. Sheila's vision was to have volunteers on the front line, and to get fully launched as a comprehensive program. That included volunteers doing fundraising, governance types of things, and serving on administrative and executive committees. We just moved into adding service after service." A key initiative in program offerings, underway by 1984, was to expand from peer-based support to patient self-help groups. An essential extension of services was into group sessions for caregivers. "Caregivers are thrust into a new role," Rosenbloom explains. "How do I cope? How do I even help myself? Without a caregiver being reasonably healthy, they'll not be of much value to their partner or child or friend."

"I always like to say that we didn't have a firm blueprint, because we thought it was really important to be responsive to the environment," Remmer notes. "Whatever we developed, it was because somebody said, for example, 'I need to be talking to people that have had metastatic disease.' So you would say to a couple other people, 'Would you be brave enough to come to a group?' I think the key to programming is not saying, 'Hey, we're here, and we do this.' It's saying, 'What would you like us to do?'"

"Sheila gave you the freedom and the flexibility to do that," says Remmer. "She had a vision that Hope & Cope could do anything and everything, but she didn't tell you what or how. And she trusted me enormously, and Megan, my predecessor, totally. And with all the other staff that came along, she has said, 'You guys are the experts. You know what you're going to do, and how you should do it.' There would be times that she would disagree, and all of us would hear about it. So while she gave us trust and freedom, she was also paying attention to everything that was done."

Sheila became famous for her phone calls to staff and volunteers, so much so that at a roast held in her honour, Jean Remmer and two other Hope & Cope staff members, Helen Rossiter and Irena Razanas, presented a Sheila Kussner survival kit, which consisted of a cassette tape that could be played in response to any call from Sheila. "It was the three of us," says Remmer, "and it went, "Hello, Sheila? Yeah, it's Jean … I've got that … yeah … I'll take care of that. I'll make sure … I'll make sure it happens. Okay. Bye.' Then Irena came on. 'Oh, yes, Sheila, hi. How are you today? … We've got this covered … Okay … Thank you very much. I'm glad to know that. Bye.' Then Helen did the very same thing. We played this tape on a loop, and it exemplified how we all knew we'd be getting a call from Sheila at some point, but we also knew that it was because she wanted to make sure things were happening. She gave us total freedom and trust, and I think trust was a very big thing with her."

Remmer would remain in her position as coordinator until the late 1990s, when she decided to step back and serve for a time as co-coordinator with Suzanne O'Brien, who arrived in 1997, and focus on research. She offers a fine snapshot of the sort of person Sheila was like to work with, but really to be with. "She had taken me out for supper, to talk Hope & Cope stuff." As they sat in the restaurant, Sheila suddenly said, "Would you like to meet Leonard Cohen? He's right over there, in the corner. Let's go over. We're going to say hello." The renowned poet and songwriter was dining with a woman that

Sheila had grown up with. (Sheila does not recall this episode but thinks the woman might have been one of Cohen's cousins.) Sheila knew Leonard Cohen the way she had come to know so many prominent Montrealers—almost organically, as a consequence of being Sheila. What was most interesting about Jean Remmer meeting Leonard Cohen was that Sheila did not introduce her to him first. Instead, Sheila approached his dinner companion, engaged with her, and only then, said, "Oh, by the way, this is Leonard Cohen. How are you, Leonard? This is Jean, my coordinator."

Sheila has long enjoyed a special touch with celebrity. She will preface a memory with, "Now, I am not dropping names," because she is aware of how many well-known people she has interacted with over the years. She was truly close to Pierre Trudeau. "I think he really respected her, and would enjoy being with her," Remmer reflects. Sheila was selective in how she shared that connection. Remmer recalls how Hope & Cope had a volunteer, Simone Paradis, who worked on the newsletter with Jean. Her husband was a francophone as well, from France. "Sheila really admired Simone. She was a beautiful writer. Sheila was going to dinner with Pierre, and she said, 'Simone, would you and your husband like to come with us?' And because they were very intellectual, it worked really well in providing conversation for Pierre." Sheila by then was renowned as a fundraiser for knowing what people could give, but she also was highly attuned to knowing what others needed to receive.

Hope & Cope was central to Sheila Kussner's activities in the cancer field, but her peripheral undertakings were hardly trivial. Hope &

Cope delivers support to patients and caregivers, including family and friends. That left two fundamental areas of cancer still to be addressed: research and medical treatment. A third area, as we will see in chapter 13, was struggling to find a proper place under the medical umbrella: palliative care.

In the 1980s, Sheila was drawn into the "refusenik" issue of Jews in Russia, who were trapped behind the Iron Curtain of the crumbling Soviet system but refused permission to emigrate. Gerald Batist became involved in the refusenik cause while still in the United States. Around 1985, his mother and aunt came to Washington, to attend an international conference of organizations supporting the refusenik cause. Batist went along to one of the meetings and could see both the justness of the cause and the unproductive discord between different organizations as to what should be done. After returning to Montreal in 1986 to serve as an oncologist at Montreal General Hospital, he launched a Canadian action committee.

He travelled to the Soviet Union to meet with individual cases in April 1987. By then, the refusenik cause had gained considerable political momentum. "I visited a bunch of refuseniks, in particular people who had cancer. I brought a lot of oral medications, hormones for breast cancer patients. I wrote an article in the *Washington Post*, describing a robe that I brought from Dianne Feinstein, now Senator Feinstein, then the mayor of San Francisco, to one of the refuseniks that she had met. Teddy Kennedy had been in the same apartment, a few days before me. It was an interesting time, in the midst of perestroika."

Once back in Montreal, he created the International Cancer Patients Solidarity Committee with other Montreal physicians, including Phil Gold, physician-in-chief at the Montreal General.

"We went on *CBS Morning News* and had press conferences around the world, but it all started with a press conference at the Montreal General Hospital, with Phil Gold and Sheila Kussner."

"I needed a big name, and I was a nobody on the scene," Batist says, "and Sheila was a top name. These two very gracious people, Phil and Sheila, gathered with me in a hospital conference room. The press came because of them. She said to me, 'What do I say?' I told her a couple stories of these cancer patients who were not only suffering from cancer but were separated from their families in the West. I talked about the right, the human right to be with your family and to access treatments ... I had a whole bunch of hospitals in North America that offered to treat them for free, and some of them eventually came. She said, 'Okay. Got it.' With her empathy, she understood right away. That was just the way she was. If she could help someone, there was very little questioning."

The refusenik issue came to the fore at the same time as Sheila's major initiative beyond Hope & Cope: the creation of a department of oncology at McGill University. The origins of the department are murky in people's memories, but Sheila is always at the centre of recollections. Phil Gold remembers Sheila's involvement percolating out of her interest in the McGill Cancer Centre. A graduate of medicine at McGill in 1961, Gold had pursued a PhD under supervisor Samuel Freedman, chief of the division of allergy and clinical immunology. Together, they made the groundbreaking discovery of the carcinoembryonic antigen (CEA), the first useful biomarker for colon cancer.[117] Their results were published in the *Journal*

of Experimental Medicine in 1965 to international acclaim. In 1977, Freedman became the dean of medicine and Gold the head of the allergy and clinical immunology division. The following year, Freedman spearheaded the creation of the McGill Cancer Centre, with Gold as director. Gold then became physician-in-chief as well at the Montreal General in 1980. As part of a major overhaul of the hospital's department of medicine, Gold hired Michael Thirwell to head up a medical oncology unit in 1981. Gold began thinking about an oncology department for McGill medicine, which could tackle an ambition of the Cancer Centre to better coordinate research across McGill's teaching hospitals.

Gold thinks he met Sheila for the first time around 1982, when he was completing his first term as director of the McGill Cancer Centre. "This woman walked into my office and handed me an envelope. I knew Sheila's name pretty well, because she was well known in the community, but we had never really met. She said, 'Take this, or my husband will kill me.' Marvyn was a sweetheart, a lovely man. He wouldn't have killed a fly. But I took the envelope, not wanting her husband to kill her." Inside was a sizable personal cheque to the centre. "My husband doesn't like it when I play the market, and I did, and I won," she explained.

"We chatted for a while," Gold recalls. "She said, 'You've been here now for five years. What do you want to do with this place?' I told her what my objectives, my ambitions were for the centre. She said, 'You don't have enough money to do that, do you?' No, not now. She said, 'So why don't we raise some?' I took her downstairs one floor, to Dick Cruess's office. They hit it off pretty well." It was the start of a long friendship between Gold and Sheila and their spouses, and of millions raised in support for cancer at McGill.

Richard Cruess was Samuel Freedman's successor as dean of medicine at McGill in 1981, and he remembers being approached by a determined trio: Sheila; Richard Margolese, who was head of oncology at the Jewish General; and Carolyn Freeman, who was chair of the department of radiation oncology at McGill (both Margolese and Freeman were elevated to those positions in 1979). The pitch, as Cruess recalls it, was not specifically for an oncology department at McGill: "It was that the cancer field was not flourishing, that we needed to better integrate the activities that were happening within the wider McGill community, and we needed to expand those activities. The particular issue was that we were not participating in groundbreaking clinical trials at a very exciting time."

Cruess credits Carolyn Freeman with directing the discussion toward the creation of a department of oncology that could unite the disparate resources and efforts of McGill's various teaching hospitals, which included the Jewish General. Freeman agrees with Cruess that she had been exposed to a multidisciplinary approach in training, at Westminster Medical School and Hospital at London University, a long-standing centre of cancer treatment. "I came from a background where oncology was not a program in the sense of today, but people worked together. There was a ward where we weren't only giving patients treatment with radiation. We were also giving them treatment with chemotherapy. It was very much a multidisciplinary field."

"There were some great scientists there, and there still are," says Freeman of the McGill Cancer Centre. "As clinicians, we used to meet at that centre, in the McIntyre Building, in the evenings, and talk about clinical trials. But there was no real cohesion between services in the hospitals, except at the level of chemo boards. Clinically, there were meetings of various disciplines on a very regular basis, to discuss patient care. So people got together, but there was no structure. I think the idea was that we should try to formalize the structure, so that we would be more productive." So disparate were the cancer initiatives under the McGill umbrella that when Brian Leyland-Jones left his position as head of the developmental chemotherapy section at the National Cancer Institute (NCI) in the United States to become the first chair of the new oncology department (appointed in June 1989, he moved to Montreal in 1990), he found the same clinical trial being conducted, independent of each other, at two McGill-affiliated hospitals.

The one field that had a coherent presence in McGill's teaching hospitals was radiotherapy, Freeman's discipline, thanks to John H. Webster, who had trained at Queen's University and was chief of therapeutic radiology at Roswell Park when he was named chair of the department of radiation oncology at McGill in 1974. Webster only stayed until 1979, but he created one of the world's largest centralized radiotherapy facilities, which incorporated the departments in the major Montreal hospitals, including the Jewish. During Webster's term, Freeman had performed radiotherapy work at the Jewish, and Sheila thinks she may have been involved in some way in Marvyn's treatment. Freeman in any event was well aware of who Sheila was by the time the idea of a McGill department of oncology began to coalesce. Freeman was around when Hope & Cope was established. "It was special," she says. And Sheila, she recalls, was "very present" in all the discussions about the future of cancer research and care under the McGill umbrella. "She was always there, in the background. She wasn't pushing anything, but she was supporting it, all the way."

"I was taken by the idea of a department of oncology," Richard Cruess says. "The feeling was that the McGill Cancer Centre was not integrating clinical activities within our network, and that we were competing with each other. We needed to do something to have a McGill presence, rather than a Royal Victoria Hospital presence, a Montreal General presence, a Jewish General presence. The idea of a department of oncology appealed to me because integration, along with increased activity, would come out of it. And it didn't take a very bright person to figure that cancer not only was a hot field, but that if you were trying to expand you could probably raise money for it."

A key first move was the creation of a chair in oncology. In 1985, (Aileen) Minda de Gunzburg, the wife of Baron Alain de Gunzburg, died of cancer. According to Cruess, her siblings Charles and Phyllis Bronfman wanted to create something in the cancer field in Minda's memory and sought proposals, including one from McGill. "I proposed that we establish the Minda de Gunzburg Chair in Oncology as the lead-in to setting up a department of oncology. That gave profile, financial leverage, and credibility to this idea, because to my knowledge there weren't any university departments of oncology in North America. This was a British phenomenon."

It became Cruess's job to navigate the oncology-department proposal through the various administrative and institutional shoals. "It took some internal convincing, and starting a new department in a university requires approval of the planning process, the university senate, and the board of governors. It actually didn't take long, in part because both David Johnston and Sam Freedman"—who had moved from dean of medicine to vice-principal of McGill— "were strong backers, and they were the university administration.

And once Sheila becomes interested in something, she's not quiet, which helped."

David Johnston had begun a fifteen-year run as principal and vice-chancellor of McGill in 1979; after several years teaching law full-time at McGill, he would serve as president and vice-chancellor of the University of Waterloo from 1999 until 2000, when he was appointed Canada's governor-general. He says that when Cruess brought the idea of an oncology department to the university administration, "I was marvellously enthusiastic, and when I met Sheila, I was even more so. She was the chief fundraiser, chief cheerleader, chief promoter, and she just led it brilliantly. She's enthusiastic. She has such a broad vision and is a real master at bringing different parties together in common cause. Her efforts on the fundraising front reflected that, but it also translated into an intellectual front, a strategic front, in terms of doing an even better job in teaching, research, and patient care in cancer, at McGill and across the country."

Gerald Batist had just arrived back in Montreal, working in oncology at the Montreal General with a junior academic position at McGill, when the drive to create the university's oncology department was unfolding. "It was a difficult period for a lot of people," he recalls, owing to a generational turnover in staff and institutional rivalries. "The unifying feature was the vision of Sheila Kussner. We were all forced to find a way to work together."

Cruess remembers the time as one of tough budget cuts, which made the prospect of creating a new university department especially challenging, regardless of the administrative buy-in. "If you're going to start something new, and you've got budget cuts, either you're going to take the money from somewhere, or you need new money. We all realized that we were going to have to find extra money. And this was where Sheila was absolutely rock-star stuff."

Sheila recalls people discussing a fundraising target of perhaps five million dollars, which she didn't think would come close to what the oncology initiative needed. She led a charge to raise funds not only for a new physical department but also a set of related endowed chairs, building on the Minda de Gunzburg Chair in Oncology. The fundraising drive was the patented version of the Sheila Kussner full-court press. "Sheila was the sparkplug," says Cruess. "She set up the contacts and managed the social side, because people give money to people. People were giving money to Sheila and to David, and to a lesser degree to me. She was kind of the general manager of this wonderful, wonderful exercise. And when you're on a roll, it's fun. We all just had a ball."

Sheila, Cruess, and Johnston formed "a troika that was unbeatable," says Marc Weinstein, McGill's vice-principal, university advancement. "They raised a ton of money for McGill. Sheila had a golden age at McGill, from 1985 to about 2005. Then she devoted her focus to the Hope & Cope initiative."

"We were the two boys, Dick Cruess and myself," Johnston recalls. "She would organize a lavish lunch at the Ritz Carleton, and we'd be there with our script and a potential benefactor or couple. Sheila of course would have taken over from the beginning to organize it, right on through to the follow-up. Dick and I would come in with our rehearsed lines from time to time, but we were there as the applauding spectators to Sheila's show. Dick and I were trying to provide some expertise, mainly Dick of course. Whatever expectation that potential benefactor had coming in, that was multiplied three or four times by the time he or she came out. Sheila was a great magnifier.

And we had a *lot* of fun. Being in Sheila's world was different. There was always a surprise, and you'd end up laughing."

"Sheila didn't just put time in," Cruess stresses. "She put resources in. When we raised money, we raised money at the Ritz, at lunch or dinner, and the maître d's were very well taken care of before we got there so that we had a choice table, and a fuss was made about us." Sheila was the one dispensing the generous tips, out of her own pocket, without recompense. The Ritz Carleton pitches, Cruess says, "were a virtuoso performance. They were Sheila at her creative best."

Cruess, Johnston, and Sheila formed an advisory committee that included Marjorie Bronfman, who with her husband Gerald agreed to contribute the millions necessary to create a department head-quarters. "Sheila was involved in the planning, and the celebrating," Cruess recalls. "We'd have the advisory committee meetings in my office, at the end of the day. Sheila would arrive with a caterer, with smoked salmon and some champagne. We were all sitting around at the end of one meeting, and she said, 'Dean, serve more champagne.'" As dean of medicine, Cruess immediately leapt to his feet and started refilling glasses. "The caterer started to laugh, because his first name was Dean." That episode became an exemplary story of how Sheila's lead was instinctually and unquestioningly followed by the esteemed men around her.

By the time the oncology department officially opened in 1990, Sheila's fundraising efforts had created the Herbert Black Chair in Surgical Oncology (1989), the Mike Rosenbloom Chair in Radiation Oncology (1989), and the Louis Lowenstein Chair in Hematology-Oncology (1990). Later came the Evelyn Steinberg Alexander & Rita Steinberg Goldfarb Chair in Medical Oncology (1997) and the Diane & Sal Guerrera Chair in Cancer Genetics (1999). Sheila raised more than twenty-seven million dollars, an endowment whose value has more than doubled. "The kind of money that was raised would have been like two hundred fifty million dollars to Harvard, Princeton, or Stanford," says Johnston, "partly because our costs of operation are so much lower, and partly because we didn't have the huge endowments that those institutions do. So it was a blockbuster. It led McGill into higher echelons of achievement in cancer. We were already pretty respected worldwide, but what Sheila led was a breakthrough that brought us into the really competitive ranks of the top centres in the world."

"This initiative to really dramatically expand cancer as a focus of excellence at McGill," Johnston explains, "helped us very significantly in bringing the teaching hospitals together under one umbrella, and to continue that process of working as a collective, and not as different fiefdoms of teaching hospitals—to develop strength in the Montreal General, for example, in one aspect of cancer and in the Jewish in another and in the Royal Victoria in another. It was a catalyst that not only brought more money but also brought a synergy that permitted us to function collectively much better and take one more step in what is today the McGill University Health Centre, which is the super-hospital. Also, it permitted us to play an even greater role on the national scene, in training health care professionals, in cancer, and in spurring research on a collaborative basis right across the country. It's a role that McGill has played over the decades, but in this particular area, it gave new impetus to that kind of collaborative, networked approach."

Sheila's involvement in the oncology department initiative led to a deserved honorary doctorate of laws from McGill in 1990. She also participated in the McGill Fund Council and held a seat on the university's board of governors from 1992 to 2001. Sheila was "a scintillating character that attracted people in common causes, and brought her enthusiasm into it," says Johnston. "When she joined the board of governors of the university, she was a sparkling influence. Always a lot of fun, and always quite able to ask the frank questions. She was very pragmatic: 'Okay, that's our problem. How do we solve it?' She brought that can-do attitude, not only to raising a whole lot of money for cancer but also to the governance and the strategic vision of the institution, with passionate support for that institution and what it stood for."

Sheila adored Johnston and was deeply upset to hear of his plan not to continue as principal and vice-chancellor of McGill in 1994 and to return to teaching law. If Johnston left, she threatened, she would join a convent. When Johnston made good on his intentions and chaired his last meeting of the board of governors, Sheila turned up in a full nun's habit. Few of Sheila's entrances have been more memorable. She and David Johnston remain dear friends.

CHAPTER THIRTEEN

The Lived Experience Broadens

By 1995, when Sheila Kussner made a presentation, "Innovative Approaches to Improving a Patient's Quality of Life: A Canadian Model Volunteer Program," as a panelist at the Fifth International Congress on Anti-Cancer Chemotherapy in Paris, France, Hope & Cope had achieved international renown. The previous five years had seen a fifty per cent increase in the number of clients the foundation served, surpassing six hundred at that time. More than one hundred volunteers were now active, and Hope & Cope had opened a satellite office in the Jewish General's radiation oncology department.

As Hope & Cope expanded its services, deciding on which directions to move by listening to those who needed support, and evolved, the layers of experience and identity within cancer care were likewise multiplying. As a volunteer organization rooted in peer counselling, it emerged in an environment of cancer care that was rapidly leaving behind the conditions and presumptions that prevailed a decade earlier when Reach to Recovery expanded as an adjunct of the

American Cancer Society. By the 1980s, all forms of cancer were beginning to experience a pronounced change through the survivorship movement: a process of empowerment in the way cancer patients responded to their illnesses, not only in terms of treatment but also in mutual support and advocacy, and in their expectations of the medical profession and its institutions, government funding of research and care, and challenges to societal attitudes and hoary myths. By the mid-1980s, the National Coalition for Cancer Survivorship (NCCS) had begun to take shape in the United States; cancer survivorship was being recognized as "a distinct phase of the cancer trajectory."[118] As well, a younger generation, some of its members inspired by AIDS activism in the 1980s, was altering the way cancer was confronted and experienced. As taboos about even speaking about cancer fell away, patients emboldened by hope began to demand more research and better service—clearer options and improved communication and bedside manner. They were also open to activities that may not have been part of an oncology regimen of treatment but could improve their lives, whatever the trajectory of their illness.

As Hope & Cope built up its list of peer volunteers, finding people with experiences of specific cancers was a priority, but it also became apparent that within those cancers there was a generational distinction or divide. Younger cancer patients had a much different perspective on the lived experience of cancer. In addition to coming of age when "cancer" was no longer an unspoken word, they had unique priorities. Sheryl Miller Adessky was in the lead when Hope & Cope founded its first young-adult support group in 1985, but it took well into the 1990s for the foundation's support, education, and fundraising efforts among young adults to blossom.

The young-adult element of Hope & Cope happened foremost because of those young adults, but Suzanne O'Brien feels that of all the initiatives the organization embraced, Sheila supported and intuitively understood the young-adult one the most. It resonated with her, foremost because of her own experiences as a teenager who had survived a dire prognosis and then had to find her way forward into adulthood as an amputee without an iota of support, whether professional or peer. Sheila became that support for others, without having ever received support herself. And even the experience of Marvyn's initial cancer, non-Hodgkin's lymphoma, had come in his early forties, in the prime of life.

"She invested in the young-adult division hugely, because she was the original young adult," says O'Brien. "She understood that trauma. She understood the challenges of a young person at university, and although her challenge at that time was dealing with her prosthesis and being accepted as normal as anybody, she absolutely transferred that empathy to these young adults struggling to get a start in life, to feel good about themselves, to get a career, to get a partner."

The incidence of new cancer cases in Canada peak in men and women between the ages of sixty-five and sixty-nine, and the rates peak between ages eighty-five and eighty-nine, but a young(er) person's experience of cancer had always been there, as Sheila herself represented.[119] Breast cancer, for example, typically had been viewed as a disease of post-menopausal women, but with more awareness and better screening—and better chances of long-term survival—breast cancer began to be acknowledged as a young women's issue as well. Recent projections for breast cancer alone in women in Canada expect that about five per cent of new cases annually will occur in women under the age of thirty-nine.[120] While that fraction may seem small, it amounts to almost thirteen hundred Canadian women a year. And, as noted, the BRCA mutations make breast cancer a higher risk among Ashkenazi women, who continue to form a significant portion of Hope & Cope's clientele.

Deborah Bridgman was just turning thirty when she was referred to the Jewish General in 1994 for a biopsy. She spotted the Hope & Cope office as she waited, with her mother, for the procedure that would reveal her breast cancer. Afterwards, she had a look inside. It was "full of wigs and books and scarves, a tiny little room, and two little busy bees in there." She had just left an abusive marriage, had two daughters aged eight and three, and was living in her parents' basement as she regrouped. Yet she was energized with optimism, having put an unhappy relationship behind her, and was starting an exciting new job. When the cancer diagnosis hit, she somehow absorbed the trauma and uncertainty into that energized optimism and ran with it. Almost thirty years later, with her cancer having metastasized, Bridgman has gone through numerous treatments yet has remained one of the most dynamic presences within Hope & Cope in supporting young adults and advancing their agenda.

"I was excited," she says, looking back on the time of her initial diagnosis, "because I was starting a new journey in my life—not a cancer journey, but a single journey, away from where I had been. I was friendly with everybody, talking with all the nurses in radiation. I had to go for five weeks straight, twenty-five sessions, and I made so many friends with people in that hospital. I was happy, and I was really gung-ho to talk about what was going on with me."

As she underwent chemotherapy and lost her hair after the initial diagnosis, Bridgman (who had a gorgeous head of reddish-blonde hair) chose to wear scarves and hats rather than wigs. Hope & Cope asked her to contribute to what would become known as the Look Good, Feel Better program. "It was a session where you would receive a huge box of free makeup and creams and bath and shower gels, all from different companies that donated." A volunteer would teach such skills as how to deal with eyebrows that had fallen out, and how to apply makeup on skin ravaged by chemo. "They asked me to give a demonstration on how to wear scarves and hats, which was really cool." Hope & Cope began turning to her more and more. "They were drawing off me. They were like, 'Oh my god, we could use this girl,' but not in a bad way."

Her first experience with Sheila was at a Christmas/Hannukah Party at Hope & Cope. "Most of the people that were part of Hope & Cope back then were Jewish, and I'm not Jewish, but it didn't matter. They always had a Santa Claus at their Hannukah party, and they told me, 'Bring your kids.'" She picked them up after karate class. "They were geared up and full of beans." She arrived to find the room full of big balloons, shaped like people. Her girls, with ample energy to burn, beat the tar out of them. "I was never so embarrassed. I was thinking, 'God, somebody paid a *lot* of money for these balloons.'" But they were all laughing, Sheila included, and saying not to worry. "She's just the type of woman that you love to death."

What stuck out about that party, other than Sheila's welcoming nature and the great balloon massacre, was that Bridgman was the only person there with children. It underscored how far Hope & Cope still had to go in catering to young adults. That young adults needed tailored programming became clear when she began attending a Hope & Cope breast cancer support group. The others in the group "were just incredible women, but they were Sheila's generation, all in their fifties and sixties. They were retired. A lot of them were mothers of grown children, with grandchildren, and they were all happily married. Here I am, thirty years old, a single mom with two young children. As much as I still do love these women, I didn't relate on so many levels. I wanted to talk about what happens when I want to start dating again. How do I go back to work and be normal again? There were just so many different things I wanted to talk about that I couldn't."

Very quickly, change began to happen. Bridgman was invited to a barbecue at Sheryl Miller Adessky's house. "I was in a backyard full of people who were like me: they were young, and they had cancer." She met Rita Fargnoli, a young married mother, who also had been diagnosed with cancer in 1994. "We became super close, and we started running the young-adult monthly meetings."

The meetings had been pioneered by Adessky. "It's almost hard to imagine that you could get sick and have nobody to speak to," Adessky says of her experience at eighteen with Hodgkin's in 1980. "It sounds crazy, because Hope & Cope today is such a huge part of our community, and it's so well-known and crucial in Montreal. But there just wasn't anything. I would have loved, when I was sick, to have had Hope & Cope. By the time we started the self-help group, I was already post-treatment, and I was kind of the caregiver. But to have had it at the time would have been huge."

"There was nobody to talk to," she emphasizes. "The whole idea behind the group was that young adults who had been diagnosed with cancer had different issues. We were single. We were dating. We had issues about whether we would be able to have children, and there was a different perspective for girls and guys. We just felt it was crucial to discuss issues you couldn't discuss with anybody but other like-minded young adults." After the initial shock of the diagnosis, and receiving a prognosis that at least put the live-or-die concern on a back burner, Adessky says, "my biggest fear was, 'Is my treatment going to stop me from having children?' And there was the fear of, when I started dating, at what point do I tell someone that I had cancer? 'So what's new in your life?' 'Well, I had cancer last year.'"

"Back then," says Bridgman, the group meetings were "nothing like today." The young adults gathered in an ugly room in a building next to the Jewish General, "a Kleenex box in the middle of the table. We'd sit, and we'd talk. It was much more awkward then, I guess because it was new to all these young people." There was no protocol to follow, as there is now. "We just knew to get together and try to talk to each other. As time went on, it became less about the cancer, and more about connecting with each other and understanding what we were dealing with, at our age."

"The first day I attended a young-adult patients' group," Fargnoli would share in a Hope & Cope publication in 2001, "an immediate bond was created. I walked into the room and there was an almost eerie silence knowing that we all understood how each other felt without having to say a single word. Being a newlywed, I was worried about my relationship with my husband and my future. Those who were single worried about dating and how their sexual relationships might be affected by these illnesses. Some of us were concerned about holding on to our jobs, others worried about whether they could continue with school. Cancer is devastating at any age, but when you are young, the first thing it robs you of is your innocence in believing that you are healthy and invulnerable and that only 'old people' get sick."

Bridgman also began doing educational outreach with fellow young adults, including Fargnoli, setting up kiosks at local CEGEPS and universities on information days, to spread the word that cancer was not a disease limited to students' parents or grandparents. And when Hope & Cope started En Famille, a support program for families in which a parent has cancer, she spoke at the inaugural event and enrolled her younger daughter, to help her better understand what her mother was going through as her cancer persisted.

The young adults with cancer were no more uniform in experiences and attitudes than young adults in general, but they embodied a generational shift in how cancer was addressed within their lives. They were franker, bolder, more irreverent than their parents (and grandparents). They could embrace speakers like Brian Lobel of Chicago's Steppenwolf Theatre Company, who delivered a thirteen-piece monologue on his experiences with testicular cancer called *BALL*. They reached out to other young cancer patients across the country, building networks of collaboration (for example, with RealTime Cancer, a website founded by a two-time cancer survivor, Geoff Eaton, in Newfoundland) that helped to make Hope & Cope a locus of this movement. Sheila supported the young-adult movement enthusiastically and saw that it became a core feature of the organization's activities. Working with the young adults became a priority activity of Suzanne O'Brien when she became executive director at the end of her co-coordinator phase with Jeanne Remmer. Hope & Cope arranged to send Bridgman to British Columbia in 2004 for a conference of young women with breast cancer called "The Young and the Breastless," and O'Brien remembers Bridgman returning, almost transformed by the experience and full of enthusiasm for what could happen next.

A crucial moment was a fundraising event for the new Young Adult Division of Hope & Cope at Montreal's The Globe restaurant in

May 2001, co-chaired by Pam Salzman, Sheryl Miller Adessky, and Stacey Sobol Kape. Sheila spoke that night. So did Sal Guerrera, who had come into Sheila's circle of philanthropy and support after his wife Diane (who became the first francophone peer-support volunteer with Hope & Cope) was diagnosed with breast cancer. Deborah Bridgman was also asked to address the packed restaurant. By then she was serving on Hope & Cope's administrative committee and would be asked to attend board meetings as a young-adult voice. She had nothing prepared. "I just told my story," holding nothing back, relating her experience with chemo and nausea along the way.

The night was such a success that it spawned Denim and Diamonds. Adessky, who spent years as its co-chair, says she was motivated to move into the fundraising side of the Young Adult Division because as she entered her forties, she no longer felt she could relate on an intrinsic emotional level to what young adults with cancer needed in peer support. She had also known Sheila essentially her whole life, and understood how important fundraising was to her in keeping Hope & Cope moving forward. She asked Bridgman to serve on the Denim and Diamonds committee, and the annual gala ran for ten years.

Signature events like the galas for Hope & Cope's twenty-fifth and thirtieth anniversaries made splashes in the society pages, but Denim and Diamonds achieved a renown seldom seen in Montreal as individual galas raised hundreds of thousands of dollars. The organizers developed a knack for sussing out A-list celebrities who happened to be in town and persuading them to turn up, gratis, in support: among them were Robert Downey Jr. in 2003 and, in 2005 alone, David Duchovny, Eva Pigford (Eva Marcille Sterling), and Missy Elliott. In 2008, the Spice Girls' Melanie C was in town on a tour in support of a solo album. She not only agreed to come and perform with a guitarist for thirty minutes but also confessed to being so unaware that cancer was a young-adult issue that she asked to have a tour of Hope & Cope's Wellness Centre, which had opened in 2006, to better educate herself.

The Wellness Centre had come about through a timely opportunity. The idea of having a stand-alone centre, still affiliated with the Jewish General, Sheila says, had been on Hope & Cope's mind when the travails of a local chapter of Gilda's Club opened the door. Started in 1995 in memory of *Saturday Night Live* star Gilda Radner, who had died of ovarian cancer in 1989, Gilda's Club was an innovative part of the wellness movement. A location opened in Montreal in 1998 on boulevard de Maisonneuve, on a property donated by Joel King and Max Haberkorn, but the concept struggled, in part because it was unaffiliated with any local hospital, in part because the model was prescriptive and managed out of New York. (In 2009, Gilda's Club merged with The Wellness Community to form the Cancer Support Community, with many local Gilda's Club branches retaining their identity.)

The wellness movement also had seen the rise of Wellspring in Canada, but Hope & Cope continued to stand out for its emphasis on peer-led support. "We have peer leaders in our support groups, our yoga classes, all kinds of things," Suzanne O'Brien explains. Other wellness models "are much more professionally led. They use volunteers in a very different way. Our model is quite distinctive from others, but we're all achieving the same general end." BC Cancer was particularly supportive of research into wellness, and O'Brien was invited to participate in a number of wellness-related research studies on behalf of Hope & Cope. "We became known for our wellness research, for testing out other people's ideas, not necessarily our own. Would this fit in a Montreal, a Quebec setting? We would translate some of it into French and try different formats that suited us, while B.C. was trying different formats that suited them, which were different to models in the Yukon, and so on. We were in a collaborative process together."

As Gilda's Club faltered in Montreal, King and Haberkorn sought proposals to assume its assets and goals. Hope & Cope proposed establishing a wellness centre on Côte-Sainte-Catherine Road, next door to the Jewish General, in a house much in need of renovation that happened to have been the childhood home of Bernard (Bernie) and Howard Stotland. Bernie grew up to serve as president of the JGH Foundation, and Howard sat on Hope & Cope's board. The proposal was accepted, and about half a million dollars in assets of the Gilda's Club location (along with a contact list for its existing clients) were transferred to Hope & Cope for the new Wellness Centre.

The key to making the centre happen was a generous donation by Joelle (Joey) Adler, whose husband Lou had died of cancer. Suzanne O'Brien recalls the pitch as an exemplary moment in Sheila's fundraising acumen. They took Adler to lunch at Milos, and O'Brien asked for fifty thousand dollars in support of the renovation. Joey readily agreed. Sheila then turned to Suzanne and asked, if she could wish for it, how much could she really use, to complete the project. O'Brien conceded that a million dollars was in order. A few months later, Adler let them know she could supply all of it. It was not the sort of donation that she was in the habit of making, to anyone. "What really enticed me was the vision, and I understood it right away," Joey Adler says. "I realized that the only way for someone to survive cancer is for them to really be supported physically, psychologically, and emotionally." Ron Kulisek, who had lost his wife to cancer, donated his services as the project's contractor and was the point person in bringing in subtrades and others, including architect Rhona Goldberg, as in-kind donors.

The Wellness Centre (also known as Lou's House) was up and running in 2006, with an official opening in 2007, and Hope & Cope retained a presence at the Jewish General in the new Segal Comprehensive Cancer Centre. There were now more than three hundred volunteers. The Wellness Centre's programming focussed on mind-body-spirit activities and included exercise, yoga, art, coping skills, nutrition, and support groups. The scope of programming was so wide and varied that Lillian Vinberg and her (late) husband Steven developed and funded I Thrive, a program with a guidebook that maps out the centre's many resources.

The Wellness Centre proved crucial in Hope & Cope's expansion into young-adult programming. Many of the initiatives adhered to a "club" model, with the Wellness Centre serving as the clubhouse. Because of the continued prevalence of breast cancer among cancers in the general population and its specialty at the Jewish General, Hope & Cope continues to be a female-dominated environment, but the Wellness Centre was part of a change to more programming for men, starting with a club that fundamentally arose from men with prostate cancer.

"We had people and volunteers who had done well with prostate cancer and were living well," O'Brien explains. They started the men's club, because, as she says with a knowing laugh, "men said, 'We don't want a support group.' Telling people, 'I'm going off to my club' had an entirely different connotation than 'I'm going to my support group.'" But some of the young men, who had entered Hope & Cope because of other cancers, told her that while they wanted to be with other men, the men's group, dominated by older men with prostate cancer, was not for them. Led by Rick Simoneau, they formed the Bro's Club, within the young-adult space of Hope & Cope. "They do interesting things like go to pool nights and galleries. They don't sit around in a circle, the way women do," O'Brien explains with a smile, because bros don't sit in circles and *share*. Both the men's club and Bro's Club dovetailed nicely with the Wellness Centre model, where the facility could serve as a clubhouse, allowing them to hold themed programs and educational sessions.

Hope & Cope was thriving, and for far longer than many had expected in 1981. Along the way, "survivorship" had become a dominant theme of activities, but not every cancer patient could expect to live, let alone be cured, no matter the recent advances in therapies. For many—because their particular cancer had no effective, long-term treatment; had been discovered at too late a stage; or had progressed or metastasized to the point that no further treatment was available to arrest the disease—Cancer Land was not a place they could expect to walk away from. Hope & Cope needed to pivot and confront this fact. It had a head start, because Sheila had been part of the larger struggle to confront end-of-life issues in cancer treatment and patient support for decades.

CHAPTER FOURTEEN

From Surviving to Thriving

The 1977 survey of attitudes to cancer among physicians at a Rochester hospital revealed that the profession's aversion to delivering news of a cancer diagnosis had changed in part because of a shift over the past decade in how death was confronted by physicians and the public alike. "Even when death is expected from the disease," the study (published in 1979) indicated, "physicians are nevertheless telling their patients the diagnosis. Perhaps improved therapy allows physicians to be overly optimistic with their patients. Perhaps some physicians feel more comfortable in relating to dying patients. At least, many understand better the dying process. This is certainly due, in part, to the recent upsurge of interest in death and dying."[121]

Medicine was undergoing an attitudinal revolution, parallel with its ability to treat once-fatal forms of cancers, in its approaches to death and dying. In the 1960s, psychiatrist Elisabeth Kübler-Ross, as Jimmie Holland would reflect, "challenged the taboo against talking to cancer patients about their impending death and challenged doctors and nurses to stop avoiding these patients and to listen to their concerns."[122] In 1969, Kübler-Ross published her seminal *On Death and Dying*, and as Holland put it, "galvanized both public and medical attention to recognize the isolation of dying patients and their need for dialogue about their situation. Her contributions were crucial to the beginning of the thanatology movement in this country, to fostering the concept of hospice care, and to humanizing end-of-life care."[123]

In the 1970s, Montreal became a global pioneer in palliative care, thanks to Balfour Mount of Royal Victoria Hospital. After visiting St. Christopher's Hospice in London, England, in 1973, and working under Cicely Saunders, Mount persuaded his hospital to launch an end-of-life pilot project in 1975. He was particularly inspired by Saunders's concept of "total pain."[124] As he would explain, the concept was "based on her observation that [while] suffering may be related to the pathophysiology of the disease, it is always modified by the psychosocial, existential and spiritual aspects of suffering. This was a major breakthrough. In terms of the control of pain, one needed to consider each of those domains, and if you did, you could almost always get total pain control. Also important was her observation that the patient and family need to be considered together as the unit of care."

For his Royal Victoria initiative, Mount came up with the term "palliative care," in part because francophone colleagues dissuaded him from using the term "hospice" because it had a negative connation in their culture as a dumping ground for the terminally ill. The term "palliative care" was adopted worldwide, and the early 1980s saw the formation of Palliative Care McGill, a consortium of programs at the university's teaching hospitals. But that did not mean palliative care was embraced readily in the local hospital system. A senior nephrologist, Michael Kaye, was able to set up a palliative care team at Montreal General in the early 1980s, but his initiative stalled because of lack of beds and human resources.[125]

There was also resistance at the Jewish General. Part of it was culturally rooted, but there was also a pragmatic aspect. As medicine achieved progress in cancer treatments, with further gains promised by additional research, some members of the medical community (and not just at the Jewish) balked at the idea of devoting funds to specialized care of patients they could not keep alive, when the money could be devoted to researching new treatments and cures. It didn't help that palliative care was widely understood only within a hospice model, as end-of-life treatment. "Palliative care," Mount would advise, "is relevant throughout life."

Sheila Kussner, for one, was adamant that palliative care belonged within the Jewish General. As she bluntly told one resistant senior member of the medical staff, "Jews die, too, you know." The issue came to a head just as she was beginning Hope & Cope. The hospital's chief of hematology, Arthur Rosenberg (who died in 2018), had a girlfriend, Shirley Berest, who was dying of breast cancer. Because of his medical expertise, Rosenberg was able to give her end-of-life care at home, almost to her final hours. The experience compelled him to advocate for palliative care within the hospital. Eden Polansky remembers her father, Hy, who was close to Sheila, hosting a cocktail party to raise the funds for a palliative-care initiative. "Arthur spoke, and they raised the money that was necessary *immediately*." Among the supporters was Joseph Ribkoff, a long-standing friend who had paid Arthur's way through medical school. They took the proposal to the hospital's executive, and as Eden relates, a senior figure rejected the proposal, declaring that the hospital was putting its money into the living, not the dying. "My father and Arthur, who had the money in hand, said, 'If you don't do it, we're taking it to the Montreal General, or to one of the other hospitals.'"

The Jewish General agreed to a limited palliative-care presence. In 1986, the monies raised, known as the Shirley Berest Fund, paid for a clinical nurse consultant in palliative care, a position filled first by Barbara Anderson and then Francine Venne. At the same time, an advisory committee was formed to develop the hospital's palliative-care approach. In 1993, eight palliative-care beds were opened. The following year, a long-time friend of Sheila, Kappy Flanders, established the Kappy and Eric M. Flanders Chair in Palliative Medicine at McGill, in honour of her late husband, Eric, who had died of cancer. Balfour Mount was named the first chair and held the position until 2009, when it passed to Bernard Lapointe.

Lapointe's hiring in September 2000 to serve as medical director of the Jewish General's palliative-care division was the culmination of several years of progress within the hospital. Through the Gertrude Vineberg Fund, a director of palliative-care services, Michael Dworkind, was hired in 1995. About six to ten beds were reserved for palliative care on 4 Main ward by 1997, and a task force was struck to set long-term goals for the program within the hospital. Serving on that task force was Balfour Mount, as well as Suzanne O'Brien, who had just joined Hope & Cope as a co-coordinator with Jean Remmer.

O'Brien was a social worker from Australia. Her husband Michael's career in civil aviation had seen them relocate to Hong Kong in 1981 and then to Montreal in 1987. She resumed her social work career in Montreal, but also volunteered in palliative care with the

Victorian Order of Nurses after the death of a friend. She reflects that loss had always been at the core of her work, whether it involved children in foster care who had lost parents and immigrants who had lost their homelands in Australia, or her work in Montreal in a veterans hospital and then with the Alzheimer Society of Montreal and Alzheimer Groupe Inc. (AGI), with clients who were losing their memories. "I've always done support groups, as a subtheme of my work, and I started them for people with dementia and for their caregivers." A social worker in geriatrics at the Jewish General asked to sit in on one of her AGI group sessions, as the hospital was considering doing more such work. Not long afterwards, the social worker suggested to O'Brien that she consider a position at Hope & Cope, which at first was co-coordinator with Jean Remmer, and then executive director. She also completed a masters in human systems interventions at Concordia University.

O'Brien could see that something was missing in Hope & Cope's ever-expanding services. "There was all this survivorship program-ming, and a bereavement group. What happens in the middle?" In the middle was the process everyone goes through at the end of life. In particular, in the area of young adults, which became a major focus of her energies, she says, "the penny dropped for everybody. Not every young adult does well. Some don't do well from the get-go, and some who we were very fond of, who were very much part of our place, started to have recurrences." They lost vital presences; among them would be Rita Fargnoli, who died at forty-eight in 2015. "We realized we needed to do more than just some of the 'fun stuff.'" Keeping with the popularity of the club model within Hope & Cope, Club Mets, for young people with metastatic cancer, was launched. The young adults came up with the Weed Team, for those who had entered a phase where pain management was the only treatment option.

The task force on palliative care at the Jewish General recommended the establishment of an academically strong program that integrated services at the hospital, and that it be led by a full-time medical director recruited on the hospital's behalf by McGill. In September 2000, the hospital hired Bernard Lapointe, a Montreal physician who had developed tremendous experience in palliative care through his treatment of clients at a Montreal clinic during the AIDS crisis. He settled into an office next door to O'Brien's. They were both raised as Catholics and were working in an institution that, despite a broadening clientele, was still fundamentally Jewish. Lapointe told her he needed her to serve as his interpreter for all things Jewish, and the two were close from the beginning.

Lapointe says he had heard about Sheila when he accepted the position but had never met her. When he did meet her, two things stood out: her energy and her welcome. "She really, really welcomed me, and I was welcomed to share my vision with her. She embraced the projects, and not only was supportive of what I and my team were trying to achieve, but she became a very dear friend, and that's very important."

Lapointe was aware of the historic struggle within the hospital to create a dedicated palliative-care division. "There was resistance, and it took a long time," he says. "In the 1990s, there was more and more acceptance of the concept. Sheila was really active in convincing not only the hospital administrators but also the clinicians, as well as the rabbis and the Jewish community, that palliative care was not 'counter culture,' and that respect for life was respect for quality of life as well." (Sheila benefited in her struggle from the support of Rabbi Myer Schecter, who died in 2005.) Lapointe continues: "Sheila always said, 'If we're there to hold the hand at the moment of diagnosis, we have the responsibility to care during the last hours or the last months of life.' That was a deep belief she had, and she really pushed the hospital to address this issue."

Palliative and supportive care, Lapointe stresses, "is not only about death. It's also about life. Palliative care is there to support people during their treatment, to make sure that pain and other symptoms are relieved, to put all the chances on their side to heal. For those who heal and have residual symptoms, we're there for them. And we're there for them if they have a recurrence. We were able to transform the vision of palliative care as a dying ward. We started seeing patients coming in, getting their symptoms under control and able to go back home, to the point that by mid-2010, about twenty-five per cent of patients were coming in and going back home. So it was not just end-of-life care."

When Lapointe arrived, a donation by Marjorie and Gerald Bronfman made possible the creation of a seventeen-bed palliative-care unit on 4 Main as well as the enhancement of the care program. But the unit's space was in desperate need of renovation. "I will always remember the little Dutch lady, coming with her dying husband," says Lapointe. "They were not rich, but she probably lived in an impeccable little home. When she came in the room and looked at the shades that were broken, the wall that was stained, she crumbled. She was crying. She looked at me and said, 'You're not telling me my husband will have to die here?' That broke my heart." Lapointe went to Sheila. "She said, 'Okay, what can we do?' And the first money to really patch up that unit, to repaint and redecorate, came from Hope and Cope."

The support from Hope & Cope did not end there. "We hired a music therapist, whose salary was supported by Hope & Cope," says Lapointe, "and we had a volunteer coordinator and a full team of dedicated volunteers who would offer all kinds of services, from cordial visits to tea or coffee during the day to 'happy hour' once in a while. There was a gift shop, for patients to give gifts for Christmas or Hannukah for their families. The volunteers would buy a gift, or collect a gift, and wrap it and give it to the patient, so the patient could give it to someone. These were all little examples of how Hope & Cope transformed a clinical environment into a vibrant and living environment. And that was very important."

Lapointe says it was critical that Hope & Cope volunteers were "professional volunteers. They were not paid, but they received training and supervision." Hope & Cope's reputation was such that it became involved in devising Canadian standards in volunteerism, including in oncology and palliative care. "A core belief of Sheila and Suzanne was that what we offer is high-quality care, and volunteers were part of the [palliative care] team. The volunteer coordinator always sat in the interdisciplinary meeting of the team, where we discussed the issues surrounding patients and their families. And volunteers were very often welcome to attend and bring their perspective." The vision of Hope & Cope's participation in palliative care was that they were "partners in care. It was not, 'Give me your money,' or 'Just come and distribute biscuits and tea.'"

With the rise of psychosocial oncology, the medical system came to far better grips with the needs that a pioneering service like Hope

& Cope could address. Encouraged by Richard Margolese, Hope & Cope became involved in research on the impact of volunteer and peer support, in particular the efficacy of different support regimens such as coping mechanisms, and launched its first research project in 1990. Led by Linda Edgar, who holds a PhD in nursing and who worked with Jean Remmer, Hope & Cope's efforts would result in numerous publications in peer-reviewed journals such as the *Journal of Psychosocial Oncology*. In 2010 Edgar would publish *Mastering the Art of Coping in Good Times and Bad*. As well, Suzanne O'Brien was a keynote speaker at the Sixth World Congress of Psycho-Oncology in 2003. In 2006, Montreal hosted the annual conference of the Canadian Association of Psychosocial Oncology, and Sheila and Jimmie Holland delivered the opening keynote address.

From 2008 to 2011, Tanya Fitzpatrick served as director for an ever-expanding Hope & Cope research program. Hope & Cope was becoming known for its rigour in evaluating patient support approaches. Oncology professionals from Canada, the United States, Israel, and Japan paid visits, to see what worked in Montreal and what might work in their own communities and cultures. In 2011, Hope & Cope's commitment to research took another step forward with the creation of the Christine and Herschel Victor/Hope and Cope Chair in Psychosocial Oncology at McGill. Carmen Loiselle, who holds a PhD in nursing, was named the first recipient, after a thorough assessment by Jimmie Holland. Loiselle at the same time became scientific director of Hope & Cope and a member of the organization's board.

Loiselle was not on hand for Hope & Cope's foundational years, but she wisely suspects that its success came about because of Sheila's vision "and yet her willingness to listen to all these scientists, oncologists mostly, and psychiatrists. And she's fierce when it comes to identifying the best, so that's why, yes, Jimmie Holland [was involved]."

Loiselle notes the migration of psychosocial oncology from its original "medicalized" perspective on the patient experience of cancer. (The term "psychosocial oncology" captures the social reality of the cancer experience in a way that "psycho-oncology" arguably does not.) The emerging discipline was dominated by psychiatrists "who saw people affected by cancer in terms of, 'Do they have anxiety? Do they have clinical depression? How do we treat them in a psychiatric way?' And it's only over time, when multidisciplinary people, like nurses, psychologists, and social workers, brought their own perspectives on psychosocial oncology, that it became de-medicalized and much more, 'What is the lived experience of people?'"

By "lived experience," Loiselle means the experience of caregivers, as well as cancer patients. "We have a big push to do person-centred care," she notes. "Some people say 'patient-centred' care, but it's really 'person-centred' care, because we're also dealing with caregivers, family members who don't have cancer but are deeply affected by it." The sort of questions researchers were asking changed. For example, instead of trying to quantify how stress is reduced through particular group therapies, researchers began to come to grips with stress as a lived experience, with the aim of improving patient care. "One of the papers we published asked: What does it mean for patients to be known by their health care team? What does it mean to feel known, versus to feel like a number and you're a diagnosis? Hospital people will say the colorectal patient in bed number six, rather than Mr. So-and-So."

"Patients have told us, over and over, that they're way more than their cancer," Loiselle says. "When someone is diagnosed with cancer, if you ask them what their priorities are, many might say, 'Well, I have this crisis going on. I'm getting a divorce, and that's really making me stop and think about my life and cancer.' Heath care providers often think that if someone is diagnosed with cancer, that becomes their main focus. Patients are much, much more than their cancers, and they don't like being called cancer patients. The literature is clear: people say, 'I'm a mother first,' or 'I'm a father first.' 'My cancer is just part of me. It's not me. It doesn't define who I am.'"

"There was a shift to wellness and 'thrivership,' rather than survivorship," says Suzanne O'Brien as she sits at Sheila's kitchen table, recalling with Sheila the changes in attitudes and service focus. "It used to be that the physician always knew best about your physical health, and the psychiatrist knew all about your mental health. It was doctor driven, and you just said, 'Yes sir, no ma'am.'" Medical expertise in the Hope & Cope model is not questioned in terms of diagnoses and treatments, but patient empowerment has changed the way the system functions. "We went from this domination of the medical model to what is now the delivery of care with patient preferences in mind. How patients prefer to receive information—that's been a real shift. Some like in-person, some like to read, some like the technology. We ask: how do we deliver care in a way that's most appropriate to a patient's preference and understanding? We're just constantly shifting to include patients and family members in whole-person care." Throughout, peer-based group support has remained a core approach. Hope & Cope likes to say that replacing "I" with "we" in "illness" gives you "wellness."

Sheila has been listening and occasionally commenting for much of this conversation, but then she disappears to her war room, to take one of her calls. The scope of services Hope & Cope has delivered has changed greatly since 1981, and so have its approaches, but Sheila remains steadfast, forty years on: still advocating, still listening, still finding answers.

CHAPTER FIFTEEN

Love, Reflected

On June 22, 2022, about fifty people gathered at Montreal's Jewish General Hospital for a special recognition and an unusual unveiling. There would have been many more in attendance, but COVID protocols had capped the maximum permitted number. The crowd was limited to what for Sheila Kussner was but a small sample of her greater circle: family, friends, staff members of Hope & Cope, people who had and still supported her causes, and among them more than a few people who had benefited from her concern and attention. It was an important day, not only for Sheila and the hospital but also volunteerism in general. Sheila's name and a butterfly image, rendered in stainless steel, had been affixed high on an exterior wall of the Jewish General. Below her name, a large metal plaque declared:

UN HOMMAGE À
A SPECIAL TRIBUTE TO

SHEILA KUSSNER, O.C., O.Q., C.O.M.

FONDATRICE ET FORCE VIVE DE L'ESPOIR. C'EST LA VIE
ET BÉNÉVOLE EXCEPTIONNELLE
FOUNDER AND DRIVING SPIRIT OF HOPE & COPE
AND OUTSTANDING VOLUNTEER

For the first time that anyone could recall at any hospital in any city, the name of a volunteer, not the name of a large-dollar donor, was being displayed, in perpetuity.

The tribute had been well over a year in the making and required the approval of the JGH Foundation, the charitable arm of the hospital, which controls the signage rights for the building. The foundation and Hope & Cope are somewhat intertwined. The foundation continues to process donations to Hope & Cope; Sheila holds an emeritus seat on the JGH board, and Bram Freedman, CEO of the foundation, sits on Hope & Cope's board. But the two organizations are hardly interchangeable, and persuading the foundation to agree to this highly public tribute to Sheila would require eloquent effort—not because Sheila was unworthy, but because nothing like it had been done before.

Honouring someone who was not a donor in such a way defied how signage and naming rights work in the philanthropic world. To put it bluntly, you give enough money, and you get a sign. You give more money than someone else, and you get an even bigger sign. You might get a wing, a department, or an entire building named for you. (Technically, the hospital is known as the Sir Mortimer B. Davis Jewish General Hospital.) There are ways to honour volunteers, but they take much different forms. For example, Sheila had received the hospital's distinguished service award.

Sal Guerrera, the longest-serving member of the Hope & Cope board and a close friend of Sheila, made a formal presentation to Freedman and several other key people in the foundation's and hospital's leadership on why Sheila deserved a permanent tribute. Freedman remembers the pitch as impressive and novel. Sheila deserved the recognition on her own merits—who, for example, had *raised* more money for the hospital?—but the recognition would also be a way to celebrate volunteerism.

As Freedman says, "the initial reaction to his presentation was, 'Well, that's nice, but we don't do that. What are we going to say to existing donors, who gave X amount of dollars and got this, and we like Sheila fine, but...' I have to say, because it was Sheila, that reaction dissipated relatively quickly."

The tribute resonated with the hospital's determination not to be bureaucratic and impersonal, to engender a feeling of family and community. "The people who this idea was being pitched to all recognized what she had done for this hospital, for Hope & Cope, for cancer patients," says Freedman. "So the mindset switched from, 'Oh, no. We don't do that,' to 'Oh, *interesting*. Is there a way we can do that?' to an enthusiastic, 'Yeah, we *should* do this.'"

"When we put names on walls," Freedman says, "yes, partially it's to thank them, to recognize them, but it's also to encourage other people to donate." In a similar vein, recognizing Sheila might encourage others to follow her example as a volunteer. "Every non-profit organization needs volunteers," Freedman explains. The non-profit sector is "having a tough time finding them. We all come up with reasons as to why that is. It's society today. It's the Internet. It's people's attention span. It's whatever it is. So the idea of trying to do something that, in Quebec we'd say, would *valorize*, would promote the value of volunteerism in such a significant way was appealing. There isn't going to be another Sheila, because she's such a unique person. But we could encourage other people to take on these big tasks and say, 'Well, if Sheila could do it, and I'll never be another Sheila, but I could be something. I could *do* something.'"

Bram Freedman served as emcee for the June 22 gathering, and the speakers that followed him underscored the dimensions of Sheila's impact. "I think the rabbinical declaration that whoever saves a life, it is as though they save the world, is of course true," said Gerald Batist, in a video address from New Jersey. "Every individual is important. But I think you managed to capture more than that. Not only do you save individuals and reach out to individual people, every day and every night, sometimes late at night, but you also built an organization that can have even greater impact and can reach out to tens of hundreds of thousands of people. And I've been in many other cities where people in cancer centres are modelling their patient outreach and volunteer services after Hope & Cope and Sheila Kussner. So in fact you reached hundreds of thousands of people. You not only focus on saving a life, but you're saving the lives and changing the life and saving the world of so many other people. I so much appreciate what you do."

"Sheila's contribution to the JGH not only has had a profound effect on our hospital, but has also cascaded throughout the province, the country, and beyond," noted Myer Bick (speaking on his own behalf as a past president of the JGH Foundation and on behalf of the hospital's board chair, Edward Wiltzer, unable to attend because of a bout of COVID). He referenced her "many good deeds," including her advocacy for palliative care within the hospital, Hope & Cope, her support of cancer research, medical education, and innovative treatments; and her "focus on the individual and [being] a helping hand and a comforting voice whether it's three in the afternoon or three in the morning." Those deeds were "not for her, but rather for people everywhere—for our community, for those in need, who are desperate for succor and need."

Sal Guerrera was the last to speak, before the microphone was turned over to Sheila. "How do we compare a volunteer to a donor, and what is a volunteer, and why is being a volunteer so important?" he asked. "Well, volunteers are people, or a person, who gives up their talent, their time, and their skills. A person who has empathy and reaches to all hearts in need. Only one person that I know who's been a volunteer for more than sixty years is sitting right here … To my dear Sheila and friends, you have exemplified the essence of life: surviving adversity, staying alive, and seeking health and security for others, pursuing liberty and justice, and, above all, building a purposeful existence through giving with heart and soul … She's always been a great community friend, a leader, a volunteer. She's inspired countless others to follow in the same footsteps, to build, expand, and enhance the network of loving support which enables patients and their families to hope and to cope. For these good reasons, she deserves sainthood. We love you."

"I am beyond grateful for your support of me personally and of Hope and Cope," Sheila said in her prepared remarks. "I am acutely aware of how rare it is for a hospital to honour volunteers in such a bold fashion, yet this boldness is typical of the Jewish General Hospital, an institution which since its founding has always led the way not by asking why, but rather why not. Why not showcase the importance of volunteerism with more than the usual accolades and heartfelt speeches? Why not express our hospital's deep and abiding respect for its volunteers in such an enduring and tangible way, visible for all to see? Why not dedicate precious real estate, usually reserved for the names of exceptional benefactors to a volunteer?

"Make no mistake, however, that while it is my name that is on the side of this building, the honour does not belong to me alone. It belongs to various doctors, the original pioneers, enthusiastic volunteers, and generous donors, who more than four decades ago, in an era when cancer was considered a shameful burden to be borne in silence, agreed wholeheartedly that the time had come to break that silence. The honour belongs to the hundreds of men and women, of all ages, who have profoundly worn the badge of hope and cope volunteer, who reached out to frightened patients and their loved ones, with heart and compassion and the wisdom of a lived experience. The honour belongs to Hope and Cope's creative, incredible staff who are here this evening, and here I must single out our executive director, Suzanne O'Brien, who's worth her weight in gold. It belongs to our visionary, exceptional donors and enthusiastic cheerleaders, who over the last forty years took my original idea, and ran with it. Together we have worked tirelessly towards a goal of living in a world where no one has to go through cancer alone."

Sheila then turned to recognizing her family. "The honour belongs to my daughters, Janice and Joanne, who have supported me at every twist and turn, my son-in-law, John, and my grandchildren, Justin and Carolyn, who flew from New York to be here this evening.

"Most of all," she began to add. There was a pause. She tried again, tearing up. "Most of all ... oh shoot—"she gathered herself, then pressed ahead—"*Most of all*, the honour belongs to my late husband Marvyn. If not for his unwavering support, his willingness to see less of me, and to spend less time with me, because the demands of helping those with cancer were too great to ignore, Hope and Cope would have remained a fanciful, unattainable pipe dream."

In September 2003, Marvyn Kussner's business partner exercised a right in their agreement, to sell Biltwell to A & R Belley of Sherbrooke, Quebec. Like Biltwell, A & R Belley was in the box business and acquiring Biltwell created the largest company of its kind in Quebec, with annual sales of about forty million dollars. Denis Lessard, then and now the head of A & R Belley, allows that the sale was not what Marvyn would have had in mind as a transition into retirement. While Marvyn at least retained ownership of Biltwell's building, there was no role planned for Marvyn in A & R Belley going forward. But when Lessard met Marvyn, as well as Sheila, he liked and appreciated them both. "We came to an understanding for him to stay with us."

When Marvyn's health struggles became dire, says Lessard, "I said to him, 'We can be of help to Sheila and her to us, if she wants to keep on going after you're gone.' And as he was dying, he welcomed me into their home and said, 'Can we consider this to be Team Kussner?' I said, 'Yes, I've always said yes.' I said to Marvyn that I would take care of Sheila.'"

After Marvyn died in 2013, Lessard was true to his word. Several large accounts that had come to A & R Belley from Biltwell and belonged to Marvyn were assigned to Sheila. The sales commissions were enough to ensure that Sheila could live comfortably (the sale of Marvyn's building also helped) while continuing to spend the way she long has in support of her causes, both official and unofficial. The accounts were with companies owned by people Sheila knew, and that she could service as only Sheila can. "She's very active and extremely personable in taking care of the accounts," says Lessard. "She will drive to Vermont and bring employees cookies. We take care of the business aspect. The relationship thing, we don't have to show her anything. She's a natural."

The accounts management hasn't always gone smoothly. Mike Flinker remembers getting a call from Sheila, who he had long known; he also had been close to Marvyn, serving on the board of his prostate cancer charity, PROCURE. "Sheila said, 'I've lost this big client of Marvyn's and I need your help.' I said, 'Sheila, I don't know anything about boxes. You're asking the wrong guy.' She said, 'You're smart. You'll figure it out. I need you to go see this guy with me.'" Flinker told her he had a very tight schedule but could spare half an hour. She should meet him at the business at one o'clock.

Flinker arrived early and asked to speak to the owner. "I'm a sales guy; that and finance were my functions in my organization. And when you lose a sale, regardless of the industry, you want to find out what the issue is. At least, if you don't get the business back, you won't make the same mistake."

The owner explained he was in a low-margin business, and that a competitor of Sheila's had offered a box that would save him about seventy-five hundred dollars a year. "I said, 'I don't know anything about boxes. I'm in trucking. I'm sure that's a fair bit of money.'" But Flinker asked him, a fellow Jew, if he believed in *tsedaka*, an ethical obligation of charity. "He said, 'Of course.' So I said, 'Do you realize that, other than the money she needs to live, this woman takes every penny that she makes and pumps it into Hope & Cope, which is a charity that supports cancer patients?' I told him, 'I've had cancer twice, so I know what this organization does. I hope that you never have to deal with cancer, but if you do, at least there's an organization out there that will help you. That money's not going to her. Don't look at it as an increase. Look at it as a donation.' He said, 'Now I feel terrible.'"

Sheila arrived, fifteen minutes late, and asked Flinker where things stood. "I said, 'I'm done, Sheila. He's giving you the business. I've gotta go.' She said, 'You're a better salesman than Marvyn!' She still has the account to this day. He's actually increased the business since then. And she's really appreciative.'"

In March 2016, Sheila decided she should be more proactive for A & E Belley, by drumming up new business. She asked Lessard to join her for a day of visits to prospects she had lined up. He agreed, and arrived at her house to pick her up in his car.

"She's very directive. She said, 'Can you take care of the wheelchair, put it in the back?' Yes, sure, of course. And we go to a very large business. It's the first time that she's been there. There's no wheelchair entrance at the front. She said, 'Keep on driving, and we'll go around the building.'"

Lessard asked her if she knew of another entrance. No, but she assured him they would find something. It was an industrial building, and they could see a loading bay. "She said, 'Go to the garage door. Honk. They'll open it up.'" He did as commanded. Staff appeared and opened the door. "'Go in,' she said. 'We don't know these guys,' I replied. 'Don't worry. Go ahead,' she told me."

Lessard pulled his car in and stopped. "'Get the wheelchair,' Sheila told me." By now, staff were milling, wondering who these people were and what was going on. Sheila seated herself in the wheelchair and took command of the staff. As she departed with her newly minted entourage, she instructed Lessard to "go park the car in front and meet us inside. I'll find you."

"And it went like this *all day long*," Lessard says, laughing at the memory. "It was an adventure. It was incredible."

During the day, they traded stories about public figures they knew. After he dropped Sheila off at home, he turned on the car radio and heard that one of the very people Sheila had been talking about, Jean Lapierre, who had been Paul Martin's Quebec lieutenant in the federal Liberal party, had just died in a plane crash in the Magdalen Islands. "I called her immediately and said, 'Sheila, your friend Jean Lapierre is dead.' And she said, without thinking twice, 'It's impossible. I have a meeting with him next week.'" When Lessard stops shaking his head, he says, "She's impossible. She's unstoppable."

Sheila's den is a small, comfortable space with the television she no longer has time to watch and a wall of framed accolades: magazine covers with her face on them, clipped articles, photos of Sheila with public figures. On the shelves of a wall unit are albums crammed with news items and magazine articles that itemize Sheila's activities and achievements across several decades. When you visit Sheila for the first time, and she ushers you into the den, she may point to a few framed family photos and tell you, "these are mine—I did these." The rest, she makes you understand—the framed magazine covers, the archival binders—were Marvyn's work.

Love has a way of refracting and reflecting. The framed items, the painstakingly curated albums—they form what seems to be a shrine to Sheila, amassed by a devoted husband. But with Marvyn gone, they are in truth a shrine to a departed husband's love for his wife, offering a daily reminder of how much Sheila meant to him. Sheila in return keeps the shiva candle in her front hall burning next to a photo of him, some nine years after Marvyn passed. "She still talks to him," her friend Jeannette Valmont says, and Sheila can be wickedly funny. "She will come in the door and say, 'You won't believe the meeting I just had, Marvyn. If you had been there, you would have had a heart attack, if you hadn't had one already.' She will also say, 'I had a good day, Marvyn. You would have been very proud of me.'"

"Marvyn was fiercely in love with her, her greatest supporter in every way, including her extravagant fundraising style, and the proudest spouse I have ever encountered," Myer Bick told the audience for the June 22 ceremony. "I am sure he is kvelling on high today." The ninth anniversary of his death had fallen seventeen days earlier. Sheila, as she does every year, placed a notice in the obituary section of the *Montreal Gazette*, with a poem: "We know you would be with us today / if heaven wasn't so far away."

Friends of the couple all attest that Marvyn was enormously proud of what his wife accomplished, and he constantly looked out for her. If a publication spelled her name wrong, he would correct them. If on some rare occasion Sheila did not receive the respect she deserved, the offending person would hear directly from Marvyn. When Joan Rivers was secured as a performer for a Hope & Cope fundraiser and stunned the largely Jewish audience by opening with an Anne Frank joke—and delivering a monologue that went downhill from there—it was Marvyn who called the star at her hotel and dressed her down.

Mike Flinker says that in June 2009 after he underwent prostate surgery in Florida that used a new robotic process, he literally flew home and delivered a talk before about one hundred prospective donors who were considering contributing to the system's purchase at Montreal General Hospital. In the audience was Marvyn. "He came over and said, 'Your talk was really compelling. We need you on our board at PROCURE.' I had no idea what PROCURE was. I just knew that Marvyn was Sheila's husband." Flinker would serve for about a decade on the PROCURE board and, with his wife Marcia Gilman, would make prostate and colorectal cancer (along with Hope & Cope) major focuses of their considerable philanthropy in the Montreal medical system.

After Marvyn's death, Sheila asked Flinker to speak about her husband at a Hope & Cope function, which he was honoured to do. "Two things about him were extraordinary," he says. "He was extremely low-key." Even though he was a successful businessman, "he was always known, at least to the Jewish community, as Sheila's husband. The other extraordinary thing was how he went about creating and funding PROCURE."

Marvyn was diagnosed with prostate cancer around 2000 and moved quickly into a leadership role in the realms of education and research. He wanted to raise awareness of a form of cancer that still flew under too many radars. Men were (and are) notoriously bad at speaking about the disease and getting themselves screened. But there were also great gaps that needed filling in medical understanding of the disease.

He began in 2001 with a new entity, the McGill Prostate Cancer Fund, which supported research at Montreal General Hospital by urologist Armen Aprikian (who today is head of the department of oncology and urologist-in-chief at McGill University Health Centre, professor in the department of surgery/urology at McGill, and director of Cancer Care Mission). Very quickly, the fund's board spun off a new entity, which was formally incorporated in 2003 as PROCURE, with Marvyn serving as the founding board chair.

Sheila was encouraging and advising Marvyn, but PROCURE was very much Marvyn's project and passion, pursued in Marvyn's low-key but determined way. "Marvyn was behind the scenes doing his own thing, making sure that he had people around him," says Laurent Proulx, who joined PROCURE in 2010 and became CEO a few months before Marvyn died. "He was someone that didn't want to be at the forefront, but he was present and active, making sure that everything happened."

Malvina Klag, who was completing a PhD in organizational behaviour, began working for the prototypic form of PROCURE in 2001 out of a small office in the Montreal General Hospital Foundation. "This was Marvyn's show, his dream and his vision, and it was beautiful to see," says Klag, who was a member of PROCURE's board and chair of the nominating and governance committee until 2011. "It was Marvyn who said, 'We need to do more in research, and in education,' because even today, we have big issues around education and awareness in prostate cancer and screening. At the time, prostate cancer was really taboo."

PROCURE built an educational website, in both French and English, and that was important, says Proulx. "It's a sickness that men don't want to talk about, and Marvyn gathered people around him who were willing to talk. Having influential francophones speak about the disease is another part of Marvyn's legacy."

The funding for projects within the Jewish community, Flinker notes, comes primarily from within that community. "Marvyn's funding base came from the francophone community. How an anglophone Jew from Montreal was able to tap into the francophone community with extraordinary success was a real lesson in fundraising. I remember, when first sitting on his board, that nobody spoke English. I'm fluent in French, but I thought, 'Where did he find these people?'"

"Marvyn said, 'We need to raise ten million dollars,'" Flinker explains. "He was in the box business, and had some tremendous customers and suppliers, and he got guys in no time flat to write million-dollar cheques." Many were the elites of Quebec's francophone business community.

A critical element of Marvyn's ability to reach beyond his own community was the unique proposition that francophone Quebec presented for prostate cancer research. The population is far less geographically mobile than much of the rest of North America, and while PROCURE's efforts have not been restricted to francophones, the cultural reality presented an unusual opportunity to conduct long-term research through a biobank at Quebec's four medical-school affiliated hospital groups. (Today, the biobank contains specimens from more than two thousand individuals whose data are available to researchers.)

PROCURE's biobank was truly groundbreaking. "Marvyn was spearheading this," Klag stresses. "The idea was, 'What can we do, research-wise, that hasn't been done by others, that is unlikely to be done by others?' Funding agencies didn't fund biological banks. *Nobody* did. But they're foundational to so much needed research. We created a biological bank unlike anything in the world." Laurent Proulx affirms the biobank's groundbreaking nature. "It was quite an innovative move, that many years ago. I think we're ahead in Canada, in cancer research, because of the biobank that Marvyn brought to the table."

Malvina Klag notes that organizations in the charitable and community sectors "for the most part fail in the first few years of life.
It takes a lot to get an organization to where it can be viable and
sustainable. It doesn't happen overnight. It can take decades, and
Marvyn stuck with it, all the way through to the end of his life.
He was incredibly persistent. He kept pushing and pushing, which
needed to be done, because we encountered many difficulties." With
PROCURE approaching its twentieth anniversary, Klag says it's
"a thriving and vibrant organization. Without Marvyn, we really
wouldn't have a PROCURE."

PROCURE vice-president Sal Guerrera, like Mike Flinker, found
himself swept into an intertwined world of philanthropy shaped by
Sheila and Marvyn. In 1977 Guerrera founded SAJO, a Montreal-
based, internationally renowned business in the field of design-build,
project management, procurement, and construction. In 1996, he
was involved in organizing a series of lectures by a Disney executive
at several Quebec companies on how enterprises can best interact
with staff and communicate their vision internally. Guerrera was driving the Disney executive to the headquarters of Jacob, the women's
apparel chain, when his phone rang. It was his wife, Diane Proulx-
Guerrera, telling him her breast biopsy had just come back positive.

Guerrera phoned Joey Basmaji, the head of Jacob, to tell him he
wouldn't be able to stay for the Disney executive's talk, because of
the news of Diane's breast cancer. "He said to me, 'Maybe you need
somebody to talk to. I'm going to call Marvin Corber.'" Corber, as
we have seen, had long known Sheila. When Basmaji called Corber,
none other than Marvyn Kussner was standing in his office when
the phone rang. Corber asked Marvyn if he could speak to Sheila, to
see if there was anything she could do for Diane. "Lo and behold,"

Guerrera says, "she called." He imitates her gravelly voice: "Hello, Sal. How are you? This is Sheila Kussner." How long did it take for her to act on the reference from Marvyn? "Instantly."

The first time the Guerreras met Sheila in person was an event at the Jewish General. "It was in the auditorium," Guerrera remembers. "I didn't know at the time she was an amputee. I was looking around, wondering if I am going to see her. Don't ask me why, but I said, 'Diane, I think *she* must be Sheila.'" After the event was concluded, Sheila approached. "Oh, you're Sal!" she gushed. "Good-looking boy! I like this!" (Suzanne O'Brien, who is listening to Sal recount this meeting, interjects: "She's a flirt extraordinaire.")

It was the start of a long, close association and friendship, "a good spiritual connection," Guerrera says, between Sal and Diane and Sheila and Marvyn. "They had an impact," Guerrera says, "because we were at a crossroads in our lives." As noted, Diane volunteered at Hope & Cope; Sal serves on the boards of both Hope & Cope and PROCURE. In 1997, the couple formed the CURE Foundation, a charity that funds services for breast cancer patients in early detection, prevention, treatment, and support. One project provides financial assistance to women in need so that they can access their treatment. Its National Denim Day fundraiser has been running since the foundation's inception and has attracted up to four hundred thousand participants.

Would Mike Flinker and Marcia Gilman, and Sal Guerrera and Diane Proulx-Guerrera, to name but a few people, have become so deeply involved in cancer initiatives without Sheila? Would they have found their way into so many aspects of cancer research, education, and support without her presence and inspiration? Would Marvyn have even founded PROCURE? (In Marvyn's case, at least, he would not have been around to form PROCURE had Sheila not advocated so strenuously for his treatment in the 1970s when he was diagnosed with non-Hodgkin's lymphoma.) Like many other people in Sheila's circle, they are good people; they would have done something. But Sheila's example has managed to be both inspiring and galvanizing. It is not enough that people admire what she has done and continues to do; they also feel empowered rather than obliged to act themselves. And her actions have changed the landscape of cancer research, treatment, and care: people see opportunities to contribute and build in an ecosystem of support and institutions that she has helped make possible.

It is also true that people feel they have not done, and cannot do, enough for her in return. Having Sheila's name fixed to the side of the Jewish General Hospital was a way to give back, to secure for her a legacy of acknowledgment. The sign was not a birthday present that she could regift to someone else. It was something that would outlive all of them. It was also something they knew that Marvyn would have dearly loved to see.

A few days after the unveiling ceremony, Sheila called one of the guests, to thank him for making the long drive to attend. She shared how she was told that some passersby saw her name on the hospital exterior. One said to the other, "I think I've heard of her. She must have died." Sheila finds this enormously funny. She rings off, the planning for her ninetieth birthday in August having moved up on her busy to-do list. Tomorrow, there will be bread to deliver.

Epilogue

Here is a story from Sheila's vast storehouse of experiences. She is walking down the street in Montreal, heading to Ogilvy's with a friend to buy a new pair of gloves. They come across a young man sitting on the sidewalk, cup outstretched. Major cities do not lack for panhandlers, but the sight of this young man compels her to stop.

Sheila looks in his cup. "There was a two-dollar bill and some pennies. I said, 'You're doing very badly today. I'll tell you what I'm going to do. I'm going to sit with you and see how I do.'" She tells her friend to go on to Ogilvy's without her. Sheila hides her Chanel purse beneath her coat and hitches up the left leg of her pantsuit so that passersby can see her prosthetic leg. She also thinks, *If anyone who knows me, sees me, they'll think I've lost my mind.*

It is a spectacularly profitable debut at panhandling. "I made eighty-seven dollars and twenty cents inside of twenty minutes." Rather than simply leave the money with the young man, she asks what brought him to this state. He explains he is schizophrenic, is using street drugs, and has been disowned by his wealthy family. "I told him, 'I can help you. You're bilingual. I envy you. I can take you to the Jewish. I promise you, give me a month or two, and you'll see—you'll be back to normal.' He said to me, 'I like this life.' I gave him my phone number. 'If you think maybe you want to change your life,' I said, 'I'll be happy to help you out.'"

The story ends there. What goes unspoken is that the sight of someone reduced to panhandling wasn't sufficiently impactful for her. Sheila wanted the actual experience of panhandling. Sheila's empathy brings to mind that of Samuel Plimsoll, the nineteenth-century British crusader for ship safety: "It was the intensity of Plimsoll's empathy that seems to have fuelled his fight through all the obstacles," Nicolette Jones has written. "He could not understand how anyone could know of suffering and be indifferent to it, and he could not detach himself from it any more than we can ignore our own. He even cultivated his empathy: he once related a story of how, hearing that the soldiers of the Crimea had to sleep on the ground, he tried it himself, 'to bring my sympathies into touch with them.'"[126]

Panhandling was something Sheila's disability never reduced her to, but in another time and place, very well could have. Sitting on a cold sidewalk beside that troubled man and offering a cup to strangers was an opportunity to experience what it would have been like to pass through a door that her own determination and circumstances had otherwise kept closed. It was a "there but for the grace of God" visit to an alternate path of her existence.

Empathy, we are reminded, is about more than imagining the circumstances and needs of the other: it is about imagining yourself as the other, and asking yourself if you would want to be treated the way they are. This element of empathy is captured in what broadly has become known as the Golden Rule. Hillel the Elder, the Babylonian Jewish religious figure of the first century BCE associated with the development of the Mishnah and the Torah, converted a gentile to Judaism who wanted to be taught the entire Torah by telling him: "That which is despicable to you, do not do to your fellow, this is the whole Torah, and the rest is commentary, go and learn it." Christians hear an echo of Rabbi Hillel's pronouncement in Matthew 7:12: "Therefore, whatever you want men to do to you, do also to them, for this is the Law and the Prophets," as well as in Luke 6:31: "And as you would that men should do unto you, do you also to them likewise." Versions of the rule are also found in Buddhist and Confucian thought, as well as in ancient Greek philosophy.

Sometimes, to "do" something to someone is to do nothing—to turn away from need. To turn away from the other that you imagine as yourself can be seen as turning away from yourself as well. Instead, if you strive to perfect or repair the world, so too do you perfect or repair yourself. We make ourselves whole by helping others complete themselves.

As it happens, something else goes unspoken in Sheila's determination to assist this young man. "I can help you," in her imprecations might as well have been "*Let me* help you." Sheila became someone not only responding to those who needed help but also seeking them out: learning what she could about strangers, seeing if there was some way she could repair whatever it was in their life that needed repairing. And in this proactive response to the world, Sheila's empathy has come to transcend what most of us would consider their social duty. It is not something that can be moderated or measured out, much less switched on or off whenever convenient. The need to repair is untiring, regardless of how tiring that constant searching for both solutions and the things that need solutions might be.

When people repeatedly tell you that, even at ninety, Sheila is unstoppable, there is part of you that wishes she could stop—that she has done much more than enough and that she deserves a graceful retirement without a schedule that revolves around counselling strangers, lobbying doctors, staying abreast of the latest medical literature, writing mountains of thank-you notes, and making her night rides with gifts and meals. But when people ask, "How does she do it?" they might be better served by considering that fundamental need within her and instead asking, "How can she not?" The need for support is all around her, as it is around all of us. Sheila astounds us by her relentless commitment to fulfilling the needs of so many—still working at hurricane strength, ever mindful about the lives of strangers and securing the future of a vital organization that has not only repaired the worlds of so many people but has changed the world of cancer care and support.

Acknowledgments

This book was made possible by the initiative and generosity of Salvatore Guerrera, and was guided from conception to completion by a committee comprised of Mr. Guerrera, Myer Bick, Abraham Fuks, Janice Kussner, and Suzanne O'Brien. The committee secured Douglas Hunter as the author, and while he was given free rein in shaping the story, the committee was invaluable in its support and advice.

The author formally interviewed the following individuals, and he is grateful for the time they spared and the memories and insights they shared: Sheryl Miller Adessky, Joey Basmaji, Gerald Batist, Rubin Becker, Myer Bick, Deborah Bridgman, Charlotte Colson, Marvin Corber, Richard Cruess, Michael Flinker, Bram Freedman, Carolyn Freeman, Abraham Fuks, Phil Gold, David Johnston, Malvina Klag, Janice Kussner, Bernard Lapointe, Joanne Kussner Leopold, Denis Lessard, Carmen Loiselle, Richard Margolese, Megan McLeod, Suzanne O'Brien, Eden Polansky, Susan Polisuk,

Laurent Proulx, Marvin Rosenbloom, Alison Silcoff, Jeannette Valmont, Lillian Vineberg, and Marc Weinstein.

Foremost, the author thanks Sheila Kussner for her generous co-operation in a project for which she entrusted her story without condition or oversight.

Bibliography

Anctil, Pierre. Transl. Judith Weisz Woodsworth. *History of the Jews in Quebec.* Ottawa: University of Ottawa Press, 2021.

Breitbart, William. "In Memoriam: Jimmie C. Holland MD 1928–2017." *Psychosomatics* (2018) 59, no. 2: 123–124. HHS Public Access author manuscript.

DeVita, Vincent T., Jr., and Edward Chu. "A History of Cancer Chemotherapy." *Cancer Research* (2008) 68, no. 21 (November 1, 2008): 8643–8653.

Fidler, Miranda M., Raoul C. Reulen, David L. Winter, et al. "Risk of Subsequent Bone Cancers among 69,460 Five-Year Survivors of Childhood and Adolescent Cancer in Europe." *Journal of the National Cancer Institute* (2018), first published online September 26, 2017. doi: 10.1093/jnci/djx165.

Fuks, Abraham. *The Language of Medicine.* New York: Oxford University Press, 2021.

Gerle, Bo, and Philip Sandblom. "The Patient with Inoperable Cancer from the Psychiatric and Social Standpoints: A Study of 101 Cases." *Cancer* 13, no. 6 (November–December 1960): 1206–1217.

Glass, Joseph B. "The Jewish Peddler on Prince Edward Island." *The Island Magazine*, Spring/Summer 2019. (Article proof provided by author.)

Government of Canada and Canadian Cancer Society. *Canadian Cancer Statistics*, 2021.

Gurd, Fraser N. *The Gurds, The Montreal General and McGill: A Family Saga.* Burnstown, ON: General Store Publishing, 1996.

Guttman, Frank Myron, and Alexander Wright. *The Sir Mortimer B. Davis Jewish General Hospital.* Montreal and Kingston: Published for the Jewish General Hospital Foundation by McGill-Queen's University Press, 2018.

Hanaway, Joseph, and John H. Burgess, eds. *The General: A History of the Montreal General Hospital.* Montreal and Kingston: Published for the Montreal General Hospital Foundation by McGill-Queen's University Press, 2016.

Hogan, R. (1969). "Development of an Empathy Scale." *Journal of Consulting and Clinical Psychology* (1969) 33, no. 3: 307–316. https://doi.org/10.1037/h0027580.

Holland, Jimmie. "History of Psycho-Oncology: Overcoming Attitudinal and Conceptual Barriers." *Psychosomatic Medicine* 64 (2002): 206–221.

Holland, Jimmie, and Sheldon Lewis. *The Human Side of Cancer: Living with Hope, Coping with Uncertainty.* New York: Quill, 2001.

Holland, Jimmie C.B., and Martin R. Coles. "Neuropsychiatric Aspects of Acute Poliomyelitis." *American Journal of Psychiatry* 114, no. 1 (July 1957): 54–63.

Incollingo, Beth Fand. "Jimmie Holland Never Stopped Working in the Field She Founded, Psychosocial Oncology." *Cure.* Published online January 8, 2018. www.curetoday.com/view/jimmie-holland-never-stopped-working-in-the-field-she-founded-psychosocial-oncology.

Jaffe, Norman, Ajay Puri, and Hans Gelderblom. "Osteosarcoma: Evolution of Treatment Paradigms." *Sarcoma* (2013). Published online May 27, 2013. doi: 10.1155/2013/203531.

Jamison, Leslie. "The Empathy Exams." In *The Empathy Exams: Essays.* Minneapolis: Graywolf Press, 2014.

Johansen, Christoffer, and J.H. Olsen. "Psychological Stress, Cancer Incidence and Mortality from Non-Malignant Diseases." *British Journal of Cancer* 75 (1997), no. 1: 144–48.

Johnson, John A., Robert Smither, and Jonathan M. Cheek. "The Structure of Empathy." *Journal of Personality and Social Psychology* (1983) 45, no. 6: 1299–1312.

Jones, Nicolette. *The Plimsoll Sensation: The Great Campaign to Save Lives at Sea.* 2006; London: Abacus, 2007.

Kleiman, Dena. "Cancer Care Where Even Pain Serves a Purpose." *The New York Times*, February 18, 1986, section B, page 1.

Klemesrud, Judy. "Those Who Have Been There Aid Breast Surgery Patients." *The New York Times*, February 8, 1971, section L, page 28.

Landau-Chark, Susan. "The Montreal Rebbetzin: Portraits in Time." *Canadian Jewish Studies* (2008–2009), 16–17, no. 1: 185–206. https://doi.org/10.25071/1916-0925.31325.

Levine, Allan. *Seeking the Fabled City: The Canadian Jewish Experience.* Toronto: McClelland & Stewart, 2018.

Medres, Israel. Transl. Vivian Felsen. *Montreal of Yesterday: Jewish Life in Montreal, 1900–1920.* Montreal: 1947; Véhicule, 2000.

Mukherjee, Siddhartha. *The Emperor of All Maladies: A Biography of Cancer.* New York: Scribner, 2010.

National Research Council [US]. *From Cancer Patient to Cancer Survivor: Lost in Transition.* Washington, DC: The National Academies Press, 2006. https://doi.org/10.17226/11468.

Novack, Dennis H., Robin Plummer, Raymond L. Smith, et al. "Changes in Physicians' Attitudes toward Telling the Cancer Patient." *JAMA* 241, no. 9 (March 2, 1979): 897–900.

Oken, Donald. "What to Tell Cancer Patients." *JAMA* 175, no. 13 (April 1, 1961): 1120–1128.

Phillips, Devon. "Balfour Mount." Palliative Care McGill. www.mcgill.ca/palliativecare/about-us/portraits/balfour-mount.

Reich, Wilhelm. Transl. Theodore P. Wolfe. *Character-Analysis*, 3rd enlarged edition. New York: Noonday Press, 1949.

Rome, David, comp. *The Immigration Story: The Jewish Times*, etc., Montreal: National Archives, Canadian Jewish Congress, 1986.

Roswell Park. "Cancer Risk in Ashkenazi Jews: What to Know, What to Do." www.roswellpark.org/cancertalk/202001/cancer-risk-ashkenazi-jews-what-know-what-do.

Simonton, O. Carl. *Getting Well Again: A Step-By-Step, Self-Help Guide to Overcoming Cancer for Patients and Their Families.* 1978; Toronto, New York: Bantam Books, 1980.

Sontag, Susan. *Illness as Metaphor* (1978). Republished as *Illness as Metaphor and AIDS as Metaphor*. New York: Doubleday (Anchor), n.d.

Stein, Justin J. "Osteogenic Sarcoma (Osteosarcoma): Results of Therapy." *American Journal of Roentgenology* 123, no. 3 (March 1975): 607–613.

Taschereau, Sylvie. "Les sociétés de prêt juives à Montréal, 1911–1945." *Urban History Review/Revue d'historie urbaine* 33, no. 2 (Spring 2005): 3–16. https://doi.org/10.7202/1016381ar

"Tribute to Terese Lasser (1904–1979)." *Bloom* 16 (May 2013): 13.

"Unproven Methods of Cancer Management: O. Carl Simonton, MD." CA, *A Cancer Journal for Physicians* 32, no. 1 (January–February 1982): 58–61.

Warrier, Varun, Roberto Toro, Bhismadev Chakrabarti, the iPSYCH-Broad autism group, et al. "Genome-wide Analyses of Self-reported Empathy: Correlations with Autism, Schizophrenia, and Anorexia Nervosa." *Translational Psychiatry* (2018) 8, no. 35. doi: 10.1038/s41398-017-0082-6.

Zakaria, Dianne, Amanda Shaw, and Lin Xie. "Risk of a Second Cancer in Canadians Diagnosed with a First Cancer in Childhood or Adolescence." *EClinicalMedicine* 16 (2019): 107–120.

Notes

1. Alan Richman, "Tough on Others, Tougher on Himself: The Perfectionist behind the Milos Restaurants." *The New York Times*, March 5, 2019. [Online version; published as "The Perfectionist," March 5, 2019, section D, page 1.]

2. Jamison, "Empathy Exams," 23.

3. Ibid., 6.

4. Ibid., 23.

5. Hogan, "Development," 307.

6. Warrier et al., "Genome-wide Analyses," 1.

7. Hogan, "Development," 312.

8. Cited in Johnson et al., "Structure of Empathy," 1301.

9. Johnson et al., "Structure of Empathy," 1306; Table 1.

10. Ibid., 1306.

11. Warrier et al., "Genome-wide Analyses," 8.

12. Ibid., 6.

13. Joseph Glass ("Jewish Peddler") unearthed a trove of details, including the names of Jewish peddlers that began appearing as early as the 1840s. I am

grateful for the assistance he has provided in unearthing the Golden family's involvement in the trade.

14. See Kevin Yarr, "From Peddlers to Doctors to Fox Farming: Hidden History of P.E.I.'s Jews Uncovered," November 20, 2018, www.cbc.ca/news/canada/prince-edward-island/pei-jewish-history-joseph-glass-1.4912847.

15. Anctil, *History*, 82–83. Anctil was discussing Eastern European Jews who began to arrive in large numbers after 1904, but the comments apply equally to those who arrived in the late nineteenth century.

16. The 1901 census of Canada gives an arrival for Myer Golden of 1898 from Austria, but because his father, Abraham Golden, was already in the Montreal directory of 1897, the family must have arrived sooner than that. (Abraham Golden never appears in a Canadian census, and he may have died around 1899–1900.) The 1911 census says Myer emigrated from Romania in 1892, which seems too soon, given that his father does not appear in the city directory until 1897. The 1921 census gives an impossible arrival date (from Austria) of 1903. The source of much erroneous information in the 1921 census may have been his mother-in-law, Chaie Schwartz, née Berman, who was the first member of the household listed (as Choine Golden).

17. See Glass, "Jewish Peddler," 3–4.

18. Glass, "Jewish Peddler," 7.

19. See Glass, "Jewish Peddler," 9–10. For the *Anne of Green Gables* quotes, see chapters 2 and 27.

20. Anctil, History, 63.

21. Noteworthy as well was the arrival of liberal or Reform Judaism, which had arisen in nineteenth-century Germany and become popular in New York City, home to a much larger immigrant Jewish population driven by the same forces in Eastern Europe, and which had tremendous influence on Jewish life in Montreal. The city's first Reform congregation, Temple Emanu-El, was founded in 1882, and moved into its own temple in 1892, on Stanley Street, south of Sainte-Catherine West.

22. Medres, *Montreal of Yesterday*, 21.

23. The Montreal city directory suggests a family connection behind this move. In 1894, we find a Marcus "Goldin," watchmaker, living at 24½ Leduc Lane. Abraham Golden appears at 3 Leduc Lane in 1898.

24. The records of notary Joseph-Alphonse Brunet note on April 20, 1898, a "contract and agreement" between Abraham Golden, Abraham Ford,

and William Bloom. I have been unable to learn anything about Abraham Ford, but the 1898 city directory lists a grocer, J.W. Bloom, at 74 Maurice, west of McGill and south of Notre Dame. For *klappers* and custom-peddlers, see Medres, *Montreal of Yesterday*, 24.

25. The marriage record for Myer Golden and Leah Schwartz states that she was the daughter of Judah Schwartz and Chaick [Chaie] Berman of "Doubref, Galicia, Austria." There is no direct evidence that either or Leah's parents had emigrated by this time, as Judah Schwartz does not appear in the city directory. Leah's mother, however, was living with her and Myer in Montreal in the 1921 census of Canada. To confuse matters, that census stated that her mother had emigrated from Romania in 1891. In 1898, when Myer Golden would have been living with his parents at 3 Leduc Lane, there was an Abraham Schwartz, who like Abraham Golden was a peddler, at 42 Leduc Lane. It is easy to imagine that Leah was living there as well, perhaps with a brother, and that their parents emigrated later. Leah's year of emigration is stated as 1896 in the 1901 and 1911 censuses.

26. I cannot find Abraham Golden in any census, or in the Montreal city directory after 1898. The 1899 peddler's licence in P.E.I. is my last confirmed sighting for him.

27. The 1901 census of Canada in Charlottetown indicates Myer was born in Quebec on October 26, 1899, and his sister Ida in Prince Edward Island on October 25, 1900. The 1911 census in Montreal adds another three births: Moses (Morris) in September 1903, Abraham in June 1906, and Gurtie in May 1909. All five children are erroneously recorded as having been born in Quebec. Gurtie must have died young, as she is the only child absent from the household in the 1921 census of Canada.

28. Anctil, *History*, 88, 89.

29. Levine, *Seeking the Fabled City*, 103.

30. Belkin, "Le Mouvement ouvrier juif," 86–87, quoted and translated by Anctil, *History*, 89.

31. Morris Golden had been recorded at the same address the previous year with a fellow tailor, Moses Golden. Moses at least was captured by the 1901 census as a twenty-one-year-old Jew, two years younger than Myra Golden, who had emigrated from Romania in 1894. As he would have been fourteen then, he probably was accompanied by an older family member. I suspect that Moses and Morris were brothers or cousins of Myra.

32. Myer Golden (and his spelling variants) is absent from the city directory in 1907 through 1909, 1912 through 1914, and 1916. It is not easy

to disentangle Myer Golden from other Goldens, especially Morris and Moses. The whereabouts of Morris and Moses are unclear after 1904. M. Golden appears as a peddler at 311 Cadieux in 1906 and 1907, and he must have been a different person than the Mayer Golden who is listed as an operator at 340 Cadieux in 1906. In 1908, M. "Goldin" is listed as a tailor at 177 Cadieux and is listed again in 1909 at 307 Cadieux. It's possible this was Myer, as he would appear as a tailor in the 1915 directory. The M. Golden, peddler, listed at 850a Henri Julian, not far from 1260 Cadieux, in 1912 could have been Myer.

33. "Mya Goldin" is recorded as a labourer at 1260 Cadieux in 1910 and 1911.

34. Medres, *Montreal of Yesterday*, 24–25.

35. Taschereau, "Les sociétés," 10.

36. Guttman and Wright, *Sir Mortimer B. Davis Jewish General Hospital*, 57.

37. Ibid.; Medres, *Montreal of Yesterday*, 40–44.

38. Rome, *Immigration Story*, 26.

39. Landau-Chark says Jacob Kaplan was the rabbi at Chevra Shaas ("Montreal Rebbetzin," 197). He appears nowhere in the database of rabbis of Quebec compiled by the Jewish Genealogical Society of Montreal, but there are evident gaps in its accounting of primary and signing rabbis during Kaplan's time in Montreal, from Kaplan's arrival in 1906 until his death in 1928.

40. Landau-Chark, "Montreal Rebbetzin," 189.

41. Guttman and Wright, *Sir Mortimer B. Davis Jewish General Hospital*, 61.

42. Ibid.

43. For Goodman's biography, see Archibald D. Campbell, "James Robert Goodall, 1877–1947," *Transactions of the American Association of Obstetricians and Gynecologists*, vol. 58 (1947): 281–282.

44. Guttman and Wright, *Sir Mortimer B. Davis Jewish General Hospital*, 63.

45. Myer Golden was recorded as a tailor at 81 Rivard in 1915, as a peddler at 123 Rivard in 1917 and 1918, and regularly as an operator at 119 Rivard, beginning in 1919.

46. Jacob and Taube Kaplan at the time were still in the old immigrant neighbourhood, living in a flat on Sanguinet, south of Ontario Street; the furthest north they would ever reach on Cadieux was number 539, also

south of Ontario Street. From 1918 onward, they seem to have lived at 500 Cadieux.

47. Medres, *Montreal of Yesterday*, 42.

48. Ibid., 43–44.

49. "Jack Golden Insurance Salesman Dies at 75," *Montreal Gazette*, July 6, 1977, 38.

50. I cannot find any record of the Saxe family in the Canadian censuses of 1911 and 1921. Nathan Saxe was buried December 15, 1955, in the Hebrew Sick Benefit Association section of Baron de Hirsch Cemetery, his age given as seventy-nine years. Sheila recalls her grandfather working for the *Montreal Star*, and Nathan Saxe appears in the 1936–37 Lovell's Montreal directory as a printer living at 4518 Esplanade. She recalls visiting him at home at 5296 Hutchison.

51. See Landau-Chark, "Montreal Rebbetzin, 197; Guttman and Wright, *Sir Mortimer B. Davis Jewish General Hospital*, 63–67.

52. Guttman and Wright, *Sir Mortimer B. Davis Jewish General Hospital*, 76.

53. Ibid., 77.

54. Anctil, *History*, 251.

55. Ibid., 250.

56. Guttman and Wright, *Sir Mortimer B. Davis Jewish General Hospital*, 113.

57. Associate Surgeon-in-Charge, S.E. Goldman, Sub-Department of Orthopaedics, 11th Annual Report of the Jewish General Hospital, 1944. Also 12th Annual, 1945; 13th annual, 1946.

58. Gurd, *The Gurds*, 229.

59. Quoted by Jaffe et al., "Osteosarcoma."

60. Jenkin et al. (1972), cited in Stein, "Osteogenic Sarcoma," 610.

61. Stein, "Osteogenic Sarcoma," 610.

62. See Abraham (Abram) Stilman's author profile at Goodreads, www. goodreads.com/author/show/6863628.Abram_Stilman. Shipping records indicate he arrived in Canada from Liverpool aboard S.S. Megantic on August 7, 1925, as a medical student, bound for Montreal to live with his uncle. He gave his place of birth as Uchitzza [Ushytsya], Russia, and erroneously lists his nationality as Romanian, recording next of kin as his father, Leib Stillman [sic], in "Taratino, Roumania." Library and Archives

Canada, RG76-C, Canada, Incoming Passenger Lists, 1865–1935, roll T-14718. The entry at Find a Grave for Abram Stilman's headstone, marked Abrasha Stilman, indicates his place of birth as Stara Ushytsya, Khmelnytska [Khmelnytski], Ukraine. www.findagrave.com/memorial/215116927/abram-stilman. The record of his marriage to Tania Miller at Montreal's Temple Solomon on October 3, 1926, can be found at Institut Généalogique Drouin; Montreal, Quebec, Canada; *Drouin Collection*; Author: *Gabriel Drouin, comp.*

63. See Mukherjee, *Emperor of All Maladies*, 32–36.

64. Guttman and Wright, *Sir Mortimer B. Davis Jewish General Hospital*, 58–60.

65. It appears as Jewish Hospital of Hope in Lovell's Montreal directory for 1943, page 1428.

66. Reich, *Character-Analysis*, 248–249.

67. Sontag, *Illness as Metaphor*, 23.

68. Fuks, *Language of Medicine*, 97.

69. Ibid., 42.

70. 13th Annual Report of the Jewish General Hospital, 1946, 12.

71. Patricia Lowe, "Amputee Dispenses Hope and Understanding," *Montreal Star*, September 10, 1975, D-2.

72. See Stein, "Osteogenic Sarcoma."

73. Fidler et al., "Risk," 185.

74. Zakaria et al., "Risk," 110.

75. Mukherjee, *Emperor of All Maladies*, 152.

76. DeVita and Chu, "History of Cancer Chemotherapy," 8647, 8648.

77. Ibid.," 8650.

78. Kleiman, "Cancer Care."

79. Holland and Lewis, *Human Side of Cancer*, 5. Incollingo, "Jimmie Holland."

80. Holland and Coles, "Neuropsychiatric Aspects," 54.

81. Ibid., 61.

82. Holland and Lewis, *Human Side of Cancer*, 6–7.

83. Incollingo, "Jimmie Holland."

84. Breitbart, "In Memoriam," 3.

85. Holland and Lewis, *Human Side of Cancer*, 7.

86. Breitbart, "In Memoriam," 3.

87. Ibid., 1.

88. Anctil, *History*, 90.

89. See Medres, *Montreal of Yesterday*, 22–25.

90. Sontag, *Illness as Metaphor*, 3–4.

91. Ibid., 3.

92. Oken, "What to Tell Cancer Patients," 1125.

93. Gerle and Sandblom, "Patient with Inoperable Cancer," 1210.

94. Oken, "What to Tell Cancer Patients," 1120.

95. Ibid., 1127.

96. Novack et al., "Changes in Physicians' Attitudes, 897.

97. Ibid.

98. Holland, "History of Psycho-Oncology," 213.

99. Corinna Wu, "A Leading Lady," *Cancer Today*, Fall 2012, www.cancertodaymag.org/Pages/Fall2012/betty-ford-yesterday -and-today.aspx.

100. Holland, "History of Psycho-Oncology," 213.

101. See Roswell Park, "Cancer Risk in Ashkenazi Jews."

102. See Mukherjee, *Emperor of All Maladies* 60–72, quote, 65.

103. "Breast Cancer Survival Triples in Last 60 Years," Breastcancer.org, February 22, 2022, www.breastcancer.org/research-news/20100930.

104. Patients were randomly assigned to three groups: one received a total mastectomy, another a partial mastectomy ("lumpectomy"), and a third a lumpectomy with breast irradiation. (All patients then underwent an axillary node dissection; those with positive nodes received two years of adjuvant chemotherapy.) Although the study found that radiation therapy prevented a substantial number of local recurrences, a five-year analysis found no difference in long-term survival or incidence of metastases for any of the three groups.

105. "Tribute to Terese Lasser (1904–1979)," 13.

106. Klemesrud, "Those Who Have Been There."

107. Ibid.

108. Holland, "History of Psycho-Oncology," 213.

109. Barbara Basler, "Leukemia Victim, 50, Ends Cross-Country Bicycle Trip," *The New York Times*, June 15, 1979, 95.

110. Holland, "History of Psycho-Oncology," 214.

111. To name but a few editions of Reich's works issued by leading New York houses in the 1970s, both Simon & Schuster and Farrar, Straus and Geroux released editions of *Character Analysis* in 1972; Farrar, Straus and Geroux issued *Discovery of the Orgone, Function of the Orgasm*, and *Cancer Biopathy* in 1973. As well, Farrar, Straus and Geroux published *Genitality in the Theory and Therapy of Neurosis* in 1980 and *Bioelectrical Investigation of Sexuality and Anxiety* in 1982.

112. Simonton, Getting Well Again, 5.

113. Ibid., 6.

114. Ibid., 10.

115. "Unproven Methods," 60.

116. Johansen and Olsen, "Psychological Stress," abstract.

117. See S.O. Freedman, "Research Institute," 517, in Hanaway and Burgess, eds., *The General*.

118. National Research Council [US], *From Cancer Patient to Cancer Survivor*, 3.

119. Government of Canada and Canadian Cancer Society, *Canadian Cancer Statistics*, 2021, 13.

120. Ibid., 26.

121. Novack et al., "Changes in Physicians' Attitudes," 899.

122. Holland, "History of Psycho-Oncology," 213.

123. Ibid.

124. See Phillips, "Balfour Mount."

125. Michael Thirwell, "Medical Oncology," 216–217, in Hanaway and Burgess, eds., *The General*.

126. Jones, Plimsoll Sensation, 44–45.

Index